NEVER QUIT UNTIL YOU WIN
A Journey of Faith and Medicine

by Louis West

PRESS

Table of Contents

෴

To God be the glory...

Foreword

M y purpose in writing this book is to educate you about the healthcare system and also to share with you the blessings and challenges of being a caregiver. One book will certainly not answer every question you may have. However, my prayer is that *Never Quit until You Win* will challenge you to never give up.

While writing this book, there were many days I wanted to quit. There were days while writing that I cried. Other times I laughed. I kept writing because God encouraged and assured me that I was not writing for myself. His purpose in my writing was for you.

Perhaps you, a family member, or a friend is facing insurmountable challenges where very little hope and faith remain. You want to "throw in the towel" and give up. If so, this book was written especially for you. I hope in these pages you will find the inspiration you need to continue. I could not have survived the past ten years without God's help. I want you to know that God is on your team. I hope you will experience His love and support as you Never Quit until You Win.

Acknowledgements

❦

O ver the past years many friends and family have encouraged and inspired me and made *Never Quit Until You Win* possible. Thank you for praying and encouraging me. However, there are a few people whose contributions are so significant I want to give them special recognition.

I especially want to express my love and admiration for the most significant person in my life, my wife, Betty Hurst West. God blessed me with forty years of a marvelous marriage with three children and five grandchildren. However, the last three years of our life together were even more blessed. I thank God every day for allowing me the privilege of expressing my love and also His love to Betty.

Second, I want to express my love and admiration for our son Mark, his sweet and encouraging wife, Cheryl, and our wonderful daughters, Dawn Buegeler and Jamie West. Thank you for the love and support you gave your Mom and me during a very difficult time and the continual love you show me even now.

To my precious grandchildren, Bryan, Caitlin, Lauren, Kristen and Colton God did exceedingly and above all I could think or ask when He gave you to "G:" and "G-Pa."

Third, I want to thank my editors, my daughter Jamie West and our dear friend Judie Gustafson. Their ability to keep me focused and encouraged was nothing short of a miracle. Without them this book would have died from suffocation in a cardboard box stuffed under my bed.

One who does not like to receive praise was and continues to be a "rock" in my life is my friend Richard (Sam) Schultz. God uses him so many times to encourage and pick me up when I fall. Thank you, Sam, for the candid words you have given and continue to give when I need them.

Praise for *Never Quit until You Win*

ℐℐℐ

Betty West was the kind of woman who kept you on your toes. Although often impervious to pain, she was inquisitive and was always looking to improve herself and those around her. As her doctor for a number of years, I learned to explain my plans to her knowing that she would give her opinion right back. I learned as well that she had a teammate in her battles, her husband Louis. When she took a turn for the worse, again and again Louis would be not only her eyes and ears, but also her common sense and practicality. Now, Louis has written a book for all of us to inspire the best in our human nature under the harshest of circumstances. He speaks of how to move from fear to faith and on to fight – a moving tribute to a partner, but also a lesson in humanity.

—Edward Fox, MD PhD

Louis West had worked in healthcare for almost fifty years when the unthinkable happened. His wife of over forty years developed an incurable disease and within a few years had a massive stroke that affected both sides of her brain. As doctors, we felt she could not survive. We watched over the next months as miracles happened. Louis and his wife refused to give up. Together, they displayed an unbreakable spirit as they dealt with their many ongoing challenges. This is a must-read book for those who want to have a life-changing experience. Louis's book also illustrates how to navigate the ups and downs of the medical system, including how to advocate for a family member with doctors, nurses, or therapists. Included are tips for caring for stroke patients, such as pet and music therapy to promote encouragement and healing.

—Jon F. Dietlein, MD

My uncle has written an inspiring story of faith, steadfast love, perseverance and healing. He provides a template for advocating for the patient who cannot advocate for herself from the perspective of someone who is part of the health care system, but is often placed in a role of needing to challenge the medical care response. Most of all, this book is a testimony of God's daily and ultimate triumphs. It will particularly bless those who are struggling to remain hopeful in the context of a seriously ill loved one. For us all, it is a poignant reminder of God's tender, personal love for us. Although we can expect to face difficult challenges, we are assured that joy will come in the morning.

—Diane Solomon, MD Neurology

Louis West glorifies the sovereign power of God by sharing a heartfelt story of him and his beloved spouse, Betty West. Louis and Betty West shared an exemplary life practicing steadfast Christian faith, praying for and serving friends and strangers alike, and nourishing loving, long-lasting relationships. As Betty's health slowly declined and spontaneously plummeted, their faith was encouraged to grow, their prayers were miraculously answered, and their friendships were strengthened. Louis and Betty inspire the reader to 'never quit until you win.' Through the strength of Christ and the support of family and friends, Louis fought for competent and compassionate care for Betty and change in clinical policies that benefit all. Louis's fight was purposed to support Betty in the continuance of her fight. In spite of her inability to talk or walk, Betty fought to encourage believers and win lost souls to Christ. Betty fought the good fight and WON!

—Lisa M. Jeffery, PT, DPT

Thank you, Louis, for this important reminder that a journey of medicine and a journey of faith are not parallel roads. They cross so often that, at times, they are one. The faith journey of moving from a God of accepting petitions for intervention to a God of grace, love and, finally, peace (even joy!) is available to all of us who travel the road of illness (in ourselves or in loved ones). This book is a must-read for all providers of healthcare, aides, housekeepers, lab technicians, social workers, therapists, nurses, physicians, and even administrators. Betty West was a once in a lifetime individual. The same can be said for her amazing husband.

—Bob Stern, MD

"Sympathy" is one of those great words lost on over usage and wrong application. It literally means, "to suffer with." Few in life can give real sympathy for few have really suffered. Louis's account of losing his love qualifies him to offer real sympathy to those who are hurting. Having watched him work his magic with people in the hospital or people in our church family, he understands the healing touch and the power of "Yes it's hard, but you can make it." I hope you are encouraged by this book as you encounter the life of a true sympathizer who tells his story of pain and hope.

—Matt Hudson, PhD, Senior Pastor, First Baptist Church, Taylor, Texas

From the very first paragraph Louis captures your attention and keeps you involved in his (and Betty's) journey of life and love. I had intended to just get started with this book over my lunch break, but couldn't put it down until I had completely finished it! In this wonderful first-hand account of his experience with faith and medicine Louis shares great honesty in his emotions and thoughts about illness and healing. He also gives us a manual in hospital advocacy, care, and etiquette. This could also be used as a Bible study/ discussion on healing – and how God uses all three means of healing: through the medical community, through miracles, and through His final and perfect healing. You'll laugh, you'll cry, your faith will be encouraged, and you will be inspired to *Never Quit until You Win!*"

—Rev. David Johnson, First Baptist Church, Midland, Texas

This book documents the trials and tribulations of a journey initiated by a massive stroke ending in the ultimate passing of Betty West, Louis's "soul mate" for over 40 years. In the very first paragraph, Louis begins his saga by noting that he was involved in the healthcare system for over 40 years at all levels concluding as a hospital administrator. He also was a devoted Christian. Finally, as Betty's husband for 40 plus years, he knew her better than any living soul. Louis called on all three of these vocations in the years following Betty's stroke. He found that even with his intimate knowledge of the medical system, he encountered roadblocks and resistance in getting Betty what she needed. Just like an average person on the street, he became impatient, even furious, with the bureaucracy in medical care as Betty was handed off from one provider to another, and as her care fell through the cracks. Likewise, knowing what Betty was thinking and what she would prefer/want, often left him with feelings of inadequacy and guilt at his helplessness in providing the very best care for her. Ultimately, Louis fell back on his Christian faith to power him through. This was the only thing that could not be influenced by external forces.

Very few people have traveled the road forced on Betty and Louis. It is hard to say how one would persevere under such extreme circumstances. Louis West provides us with a revealing, day-by-day journey that he and Betty walked together. To me, the central core of the book is that when faced with such overwhelming circumstances, each person must dig deep inside to find that immovable strength, be it faith or some other force, which helps us survive.

—Thomas E. Tenner, Jr., PhD

Chapter 1:

Get Me Out of Here

As a hospital administrator for over 40 years, I had routinely traveled the journey of medicine. As a lifetime Christian I had regularly traveled the journey of faith. As a husband of 41 years, one call put me at the intersection of both.

As I concluded a routine meeting with one of my managers in the hospital where I was working, the overhead paging system seemed to scream, "Medical alert! Emergency room! Medical alert! Emergency room!" Another page followed quickly, "Mr. West, please call the operator. Mr. West, please call the operator, stat!"

My telephone had rung a few minutes before but I ignored it. I could not imagine why I was being paged so urgently. Normally, I would have been paged by a code rather than my actual name. Surely the page for me was not related to the medical alert page. I picked up the phone and dialed the operator, who informed me, "Mr. West, I've been trying to contact you. They are taking your wife to the emergency room. They asked me to tell you that you should get there as quickly as possible."

As I rushed down the hall, thoughts raced through my mind: Why would they be taking Betty to the emergency room? She came to work with me this morning to have her monthly I.V. Gamma Globulin. She had been having this procedure every four weeks for over three years with no complications.

Just two hours earlier she was fine when I visited her in Ambulatory Care (ACC). She had told me she would like to go to

Rosie's Tamale House in Austin before we went home to Taylor. Rosie's was one of our favorite restaurants. We visited so often that all of the staff knew us and knew exactly what we would order.

As I got closer to the emergency room, I moved to one side of the hall so that the employees from radiology, laboratory, and the cardio-pulmonary departments could pass me and respond to the medical alert. I assumed Betty had blurred vision as this happened occasionally and the staff was being extra cautious by calling a medical alert. Normally, a medical alert would not have been called for blurred vision. I tried to remain calm as I entered the emergency area.

A familiar nurse greeted me as I entered the emergency department. "She isn't here yet." I immediately headed for ACC and met two nurses pushing Betty on a stretcher. Before I could greet them, one of the nurses spoke to me. "She has slurred speech and cannot move her left side." Emotions flooded over me. I wanted to cry and scream at the same time. I knew what those symptoms indicated.

Betty's beautiful, brown eyes fixated on me. "Take me home, Louis. There is nothing wrong with me. Just take me home." Although her speech was slurred I understood perfectly what she was saying. Her eyes told me far more than her voice. It was not difficult to see the fear that she was experiencing. I felt so helpless. I wanted nothing more than to wrap my arms around her, take her home, and protect her from everything that I assumed she was going to endure.

Trying to remain calm, I attempted to explain that she would need to be examined and tests run to determine what was wrong. Her response was, "No, just take me home." It was even more obvious that her speech was slurred.

When Betty was sixteen years old, she experienced the death of an older sister. She also had been a caregiver for her parents before their death. She knew the pains of death. I did not believe she was in denial but merely wanted to be at home when she died.

Betty was the one who took care of emergency situations when our children were still at home. She had a calm demeanor that could quickly diffuse a tense situation. However, she did have a few exceptions. If there was an accident and bleeding was involved, it was my turn to provide the care and advice that was needed.

If there was ever a perfect wife and mother, it was Betty West. She had many friends and relatives who felt as I did. Now, after almost forty-one years of marriage, she was the one having an emergency and I had never felt so inadequate.

The hospital had many drills for emergencies; therefore, I had complete confidence in the employees responding to Betty's needs. However, there are no drills that would have prepared me for this situation.

As we reached the emergency room, we were met by Dr. Mark Shepherd, the chief ER physician. He did a quick exam and ordered a CT scan and various blood tests to be done immediately.

I tried to pray and wait patiently while the procedures were being done. However, knowing Betty's health history certainly did not help me to be optimistic about the results.

Betty had been experiencing health challenges for several years. In 1989 after what seemed to be a simple fall in a supermarket parking lot, she began to experience severe pain in her back, arms, legs, and feet. The diagnosis at that time was fibromyalgia. She was treated with various medications and physical therapy with no significant improvement. The pain became so intense that she could not tolerate even minimal activity.

Prior to this condition, a normal week would consist of fulfilling her duties as a wife and mother. In addition she enjoyed doing other things such as mowing the lawn, washing the car, teaching a class of young girls at church, visiting a sick friend, taking a meal to a grieving family, and possibly a game of tennis with one of her many friends.

Our lifestyle changed drastically after we finally had the name of the disease that caused her pain and immobility. As the pain and disease progressed, we were no longer able to visit our children and grandchildren or attend family reunions. Church attendance was sporadic.

Pain medicines dulled her senses. She seemed to be literally consumed by the disease. Her main social life was going to see the doctors. Betty could not tolerate sitting for long periods and she was not comfortable in any bed except her own. Our main outing was to eat Mexican food about once each week at Rosie's Tamale House in

Austin. After eating we would immediately drive home. There was no sitting around the table sipping tea or visiting with friends.

Through all of this, Betty attempted to conceal the pain and discouragement. On one occasion, I asked, "Betty, just how badly do you hurt?" Her response was, "If it were you...you would be screaming."

She always exhibited faith and confidence that someday God would totally heal her. I must admit that at times I grumbled. "I can't understand why God hasn't healed you," I would complain.

She would respond with a smile and say, "He will in His time, not ours." I asked how she could bear the pain and the marked difference in her lifestyle. She would smile again and say, "There are so many people far worse off than I am." She always encouraged me to go out without her. How could I? We had been almost inseparable for over 40 years.

After many attempts to diagnose and treat her pain by a team of excellent doctors, in 1997 Betty was referred to a rheumatologist. He ordered more testing which included a muscle biopsy. The tissue was sent to a specialist at the Mayo Clinic in Rochester, Minnesota. After several days, the rheumatologist called her with the report. "You have polymyositis, which means 'many muscles inflamed.'"

Betty explained to me as best she could what the rheumatologist had told her. The cause is unknown. The disease has some of the characteristics as an autoimmune disorder. The immune system actually attacks the body. The doctor said that normally the immune system works to protect the healthy cells from attacks by foreign elements such as bacteria and viruses. When a person has polymyositis, something may act as a trigger for the immune system to begin producing autoimmune antibodies that attack the body's own tissues. The doctor also told her that the disease would worsen over time.

Usually, the disease affects the muscles in the hips, thighs, neck, upper arms and shoulders. The doctor also warned her that complications could develop such as difficulty in swallowing, which could lead to malnutrition and weight loss. If she developed problems with swallowing it could cause aspiration pneumonia.

To monitor the amount of muscle damage caused by the polymyositis, the rheumatologist periodically administered a test called creatine kinase (CK). Betty's CK level was usually as high 800 or more. The normal maximum level is 215.

Over the course of Betty's treatment, she acquired even more doctors through referrals from other physicians in an attempt to treat the causes and symptoms of the polymyositis. Her doctors tried many medications to slow the progress of the disease and to control the pain. Most of the medications were very upsetting to Betty's system. The first medication tried was an oral chemo, which Betty took for two months. Although the chemo brought the CK down, the side effects caused her to feel as if she had a terrible case of the flu with severe aching. She also became so weak she could hardly walk across the room.

In place of the chemo, she took a couple of medications, Prednisone and Plaquinil. Betty had an allergic reaction to the quinine in Plaquinil that caused her to lose her hearing and also affected her eyes. Thankfully, once the medicine was discontinued, those side effects went away. She continued taking the Prednisone for a period of time but it also began to cause side effects. Therefore, the doctor advised her to stop taking it.

It seemed any medicine she took would either affect her digestive system or her mental status. She shared with me that she could tolerate the pain better than the mental status change.

Because Betty had such a loving personality and a grateful heart for her doctors, it was apparent the doctors were even more diligent and caring. They increased their efforts to help her conquer this strange disease. We heard them say quite often, "I wish we could find something to help you." We appreciated their attentiveness and many times doctors at the hospital who knew of her illness would also inquire about her.

In 1999, a Physical Therapist told Betty that she believed Betty should be seeing a neurologist and recommended Dr. Edward Fox in Round Rock. Betty immediately made an appointment with him and told me that she was impressed with his knowledge and his caring attitude.

Dr. Fox began to treat her aggressively. He explained that if something was not done quickly, she would be in a wheelchair permanently. We were already using a wheelchair when we would go shopping or when it would be necessary for her to walk more than just a short distance.

Dr. Fox prescribed Imuran, a pill that Betty took on a daily basis, along with intravenous immunoglobulin (IVIG). IVIG is a purified blood product that contains healthy antibodies from thousands of blood donors. The healthy antibodies in the IVIG can block the damaging antibodies that attack the muscle. Fortunately, she responded to some degree. Her CK test results fluctuated but Dr. Fox was satisfied if her CK level remained below 350.

Every four weeks, Betty would go with me as I went to work at the hospital in Georgetown to receive her IVIG. This particular treatment began a journey that would bring us to this emergency room.

Dr. Mark Shepherd suddenly interrupted these memories. "We have the results of the CT scan, and Betty has had a massive stroke on the right side." I began crying. He put his arm around me and didn't say a word. I didn't need words at this time; I needed comforting. He did just that. Speaking softly, he continued, "I'm going to call Dr. Fox and Dr. Shallin and get their opinion." Dr. Shallin was the internist who had been treating Betty as well.

In a few minutes Dr. Shepherd returned. "Because we don't know exactly when she had the stroke, we feel it would be dangerous to give her TPA. It could cause hemorrhaging, which could be fatal." I knew that TPA (tissue plasminogen activator) was a powerful clot buster and must be given within three hours of the stroke to be successful.

Speaking softly and with concern, Dr. Shepherd said, "Dr. Shallin is on his way to the hospital and Dr. Fox has given orders for treating Betty and will be in later." As best I could, I explained to Betty that she had a stroke. She continued to insist that nothing was wrong. I tried again to explain that the doctors said she had a stroke.

She replied, "Well, I don't want the kids to know." I assured her that we had no choice but to notify them. She was adamant that she did not wish to upset them.

Amazingly, Betty was able to give me the names of the medications that she was taking and the medicines to which she was allergic. Although she was able to do this, I sincerely wished I had carried a list of her medications and allergies with me for such a time as this.

Betty appeared to sense she would not be able to communicate for very long. "Call Mary Baldwin," Betty urged and gave me Mary's telephone number. Mary was a close friend and Betty's prayer partner. I knew that I could not emotionally handle making calls at this time. I had no idea how I was going to call all those who needed to know about the stroke. The nurse told me they would be taking Betty to ICU immediately. I kissed Betty and told her how much I loved her. Somehow, I managed not to cry in her presence.

Immediately after I had spoken with Betty, a good friend and colleague, Jayne Pope, Director of Medical and Surgical Nursing, came to support me. She said that Ken Poteete, the hospital CEO, had asked her to come. We had recruited Jayne from Canada approximately two years before. She is a highly educated and intelligent young woman and very capable of handling any situation. We had worked together on several teams and she was a pleasure to be around. I asked her to make calls for me while I attempted to sort through all that had taken place. Hopefully, my thought patterns would be clear so I could make decisions. Because our children would not be familiar with Jayne, I decided to wait until our friends, June and Gene Prater, could contact them.

After Jayne called Mary Baldwin, she called the Praters who live in Georgetown. Betty and I had known them for over 16 years and loved them like family. Our children have said that they are our angels. They rescued us on many occasions and are very loving and supportive. I asked Jayne to call our pastor, Jeff Ripple, in Taylor. When she reached him, he told her he was walking out the door on his way to the hospital because another person had called him. Word had traveled fast through our Christian – or faith – community because of the efforts of Mary Baldwin and other friends whom she had called.

I went upstairs to the ICU and met Dr. Shallin in the hall. He looked very somber and told me that Betty was no longer able to communicate and apparently was in great pain. I went immediately to her bedside and she attempted to talk. Her speech was unintelligible. I was devastated. Terrifying thoughts came to me. *She may live through this and if she does, she may be a vegetable.* I knew that she would not want to live in that condition. Suddenly,

I realized I could not depend totally upon medical interventions. Betty's recovery would take a miracle from God.

Why did Betty have to suffer a stroke in addition to all the other problems she had? In addition to the polymyositis she had developed neuropathy in her hands and feet. There were times when she would be sitting in her recliner and scream as the pain shot into one or both of her feet. I was not angry with God; I just wanted to be assured He was with us.

Obviously, He knew my concerns because He reminded me about a particular time that He had performed a wonderful miracle for me.

In the summer of 1972 we planned a family vacation to the Grand Canyon. We finally set a date, after working around chicken pox, little league baseball and my job as the administrator of the hospital in Taylor. A few days before we were to leave, I was bending over to pull up my pants when pain shot through my lower back as if someone had hit me with a red-hot poker. I screamed and Betty came running. "I can't straighten up," I cried. With her assistance, I was able to get into the car and she drove me to the emergency room. I was in such pain that I could not lie on the x-ray table. I was immediately admitted to the hospital and given strong pain medications and placed in traction. At that time we did not have CTs, MRIs, or wonderful physical therapists who could help me.

I continued to insist that we would still go to the Grand Canyon on vacation. Betty had other thoughts. She let me know that she was not about to leave with three small children and an incapacitated husband for the Grand Canyon, which was over a thousand miles away.

After a couple of days in the hospital, a hospital bed was set up in our living room and I went home. I agreed that we would not leave for a few days. Betty kept insisting that we not go at all. I was stubborn. "No, we are going. You can drive and I will lie in the back seat with one of the kids." At the time, seat belts were not required although we used them in the front seat. We had no problem remembering the belts. Before we could even start the motor, all three kids would remind us in unison, "Fasten seat belts. Lock the doors."

Three days after I went home from the hospital, we left for the Grand Canyon. We drove to Ft. Stockton, Texas the first day and spent the night. I was in misery with excruciating pain. All I had to take for the pain was muscle relaxants. We drove to El Paso, Texas the next day and spent two days with Betty's sister and her family. I spent most of the time in bed or in a recliner with a heating pad to my back.

Our next stop was in Hatch, New Mexico, near Las Cruces, visiting our friends, Don and Jerean Archer, whom we had known for several years. Betty attempted once again to convince me that we should go home. I was even more stubborn. "No, we are going to the Grand Canyon."

After a few days we left Hatch and drove to Tucson, Arizona. We arrived there on Saturday afternoon and rented a motel room. We were exhausted and the kids were hungry, tired, and irritable. Betty took them to eat and told me she would bring something back to the motel for me.

While they were gone, I cried and prayed. The pain was worse and I realized I was being foolish in insisting that we continue the trip. I had never really prayed for God to heal me in the past because I did not have faith that He would. I really did not know anyone who had been divinely healed. Wasn't that why we had hospitals and doctors? However, I was ready to try anything. I submitted myself to God. "Heavenly Father, I am asking you to take away this horrible pain. If you will, I promise that I will always give you the praise. If you choose not to do so, in the morning I will have to take a plane home because I cannot tolerate a long trip. Betty will have to drive home alone with the children. I ask for this in the Name of Jesus." Nothing happened.

Betty and the children came back to the motel and night finally came. I did not tell them of my prayer. I dreaded the night. I hurt so badly and it was almost impossible to turn. Surprisingly, I quickly went to sleep. I slept until approximately 2:00 a.m. When I awakened, I knew I needed to turn. I dreaded doing this, as I was afraid I would cry out and awaken everyone. I very cautiously began to turn. No pain so far. I turned completely over on my other side and experienced no pain. I almost cried. Not from pain or disappointment but because of joy and thankfulness to God. However, I thought I had better try this one more time. I turned from side to side several times with no pain.

When everyone awakened, I shared the good news. I knew that God had touched me. We continued the trip with no reoccurrence of the problem. I was able to drive normally and lift the luggage with no discomfort. I never had that same problem again. I have been true to my word. I continue to tell anyone who will listen how God totally healed me. Some smile and say the muscle cramp probably just left. I realize that very few actually believe God intervened. I know without a doubt that He did.

Reality returned as I realized that Sam Schultz was standing next to me outside the entrance to the ICU. He was the hospital controller and although he is much younger than I am, we had been close friends since he joined the hospital two years before. His eyes reflected his concern. Usually he would have been smiling and teasing me, but now he was all seriousness. He gave me every conceivable way of contacting him and insisted that I do so if he could help me in any way. Sam is always quick to grasp a situation and get to the heart of the matter. His warmth and practical support were just what I needed. I thought of the many times I had helped others in similar situations. Now others were helping me.

When June and Gene Prater arrived, they immediately began making calls to our children. Our son, Mark, his wife, Cheryl, and their three children had just moved from Texas to Georgia the week before. Mark was an instructor at the Federal Law Enforcement Training Center there. Our daughter Jamie lived in Houston and was a lead writer for BMC Software. Our daughter Dawn was on her way back to Houston from Frisco, near Dallas, where she was in the process of buying a house because she planned to teach in the Frisco schools. Her two children, Bryan and Caitlin, were staying with Jamie. Bryan, age 12, was attending a camp that week at the Baylor College of Medicine in Houston. At that time he had a definite interest in going to medical school and eventually becoming a neurosurgeon. He had also attended this camp for a week the previous year.

When June called Jamie, she was in the kitchen with Bryan and Caitlin, age 9. Jamie put down the phone and turned to the kids, "Mom's had a stroke." She started crying. "I'm sorry," she said. "I don't mean to cry."

Bryan's blue eyes widened, "She's your *mother*," he said emphatically as he enveloped Jamie in a hug. Caitlin reached around them both and all three stood hugging each other and crying.

Although Dawn was traveling, Jamie knew that she would want to know about her Mom as soon as possible. She called Dawn by cell phone and told her. Like the rest of us, Dawn was devastated.

I was unaware of how the family was reacting as I waited for news of Betty. Barb Neid, the RN patient care evening supervisor, is a tall, slender lady who always speaks with authority, yet is compassionate. She kept the Praters and me posted on everything that was going on with Betty and also took care of the Praters. She informed me that she had a room set up for me to stay the night if I chose.

I could only leave Betty for short periods. It was so hard not to be able to communicate, although I felt that she understood what I was saying. Several friends visited that evening, including Pastor Ripple.

During that first evening, one of the nurses decided to get Betty a pad and pencil to see if she could write. As the nurse held the pad, Betty immediately took the pencil and wrote, "Louis, get me out of here." Although her writing was scribbled, I could read it. I felt helpless and hopeless.

Around 9:30 p.m., Dr. Fox arrived and examined Betty. When he concluded the exam, he looked at me and spoke, "I agree with the other doctors that Betty has had a massive stroke. Her left side appears to be totally paralyzed. She will definitely get worse before she gets better. If her brain continues to swell, we will have to consider taking other measures. She has very little room in her skull to accommodate additional swelling. Even if she lives, I do not believe she will be able to function because of the severity of the stroke. I'm sure you are concerned about her speech. I doubt she will be able to regain much. It is questionable her right leg will ever be strong enough to support her."

Dr. Fox continued, "After telling you all of this, I will tell you that if anyone can pull through this crisis, it is Betty. I have treated her for a long time and she is a fighter. Do you have any questions or concerns that we have not addressed?"

"Not at this time," I replied.

As he turned to leave he quietly spoke again, "I know you want to stay here tonight. You may do this. However, it will be better for you and Betty if you go home in the evenings. You are going to need your strength and you will need a good night's rest. It will also help to keep her oriented. She will come to realize that you come to see her in the mornings and go home at night." That advice was hard to follow, but I promised him I would.

After Dr. Fox left, I began to think about all that had happened since 3:00 p.m. It had been extremely stressful to me. It would have been worse had I not been familiar with hospital routine. I understood why all the questions were asked. Another person in this situation could have thought the questions weren't relevant. However, there was one question that I was asked more than once. Several hours later I began to think about it and my answer.

When a person is admitted to the hospital, the personnel are required to ask if there is an advance directive. An advance directive, also known as a living will, gives instructions that specify the actions to be taken for a patient's health in the event he or she becomes incapable of making decisions. The person making this directive also appoints a person to make decisions on his or her behalf. This is a very important document and can be furnished by attorneys. Forms can also be obtained at any healthcare facility or from the Internet.

The durable power of attorney is also very important. The durable power of attorney designates someone to make legal decisions on your behalf if you become physically or mentally unable to make those decisions for yourself. The durable power of attorney can be secured at the same as the advance directive. My purpose is to familiarize you with these forms, not to give legal advice.

Betty and I had discussed our wishes many years before and each of us had an advance directive, a will, and a durable power of attorney. That evening, I was asked on several occasions if Betty had an advance directive. Each time I answered, "Yes." Each time I was told to bring it the following morning to be placed on her chart. I was never asked what the directive stated or what Betty's wishes were. I realized later that because Betty could not speak, I should have explained her wishes to the hospital staff rather than waiting for them to ask.

As I continued to observe Betty, tears filled my eyes. It was difficult to believe this was the same young woman who had been so active and vibrant. It seemed impossible that I had known her for over forty years. Suddenly, my heart was filled with wonderful memories of the many years that she had enjoyed good health. I will always remember the first time I saw her.

We met in February 1961 in Hobbs, New Mexico. I had just moved to Hobbs and was working as a medical technologist in the hospital and was a member of a church there.

I had jokingly told my friends in Crosbyton, Texas that I was moving to Hobbs to find a wife. As I walked into church that Sunday morning, my eyes riveted towards a beautiful brunette. Being 24 and single, I was no fool. I immediately went over and sat next to her. She had white gloves on her slender hands. I wondered if she was married. She answered my unspoken question by removing the left glove. No rings. Did I have a chance?

How would I know who she was without appearing awkward? The associate pastor asked visitors to raise their hand. Her hand shot up. An usher came to her, handed her a visitor's card, and warmly greeted her, "Hi, Betty, we're glad to have you today." As she completed her card, my eyes almost twisted out of orbit as I attempted to get her name. Betty Hurst, Monument, New Mexico, telephone 7-1240. I had what I needed.

Some would wonder why I didn't speak to her. Actually, I was quite shy.

After church I went home. The woman whom I was renting from, Mrs. Eyre, was a 65-year-old who treated me like a son. As I entered the house I immediately began describing this beautiful young woman I had sat next to at church. "She lives in Monument."

"Do you know where Monument is?"

Grinning, Mrs. Eyre replied, "I believe you're just a little excited. It's about 12 miles west of Hobbs."

The next morning, one of the techs called across the lab to me, "I saw you sitting by Betty Hurst yesterday. How do you know her?"

"I don't. I certainly would like to know more about her. How do you know her?"

He answered, "Betty used to attend the church and sang in the choir but I believe she moved to Monument to live with her parents awhile ago."

I had every intention of calling Betty and asking for a date. However, a roadblock appeared. The next Sunday evening while doing the blood work for surgical patients scheduled for the next day, I suddenly became very tired and sick. I was in a patient's room of all places. After I drew her blood, I sat down and asked the patient to turn her call light on. The nurse answered right away and I explained that I did not feel well. The nurse came to the room and assisted me to the emergency room. One of the young doctors, whom I greatly admired, examined me and assured me that all I had was a minor sore throat. I was relieved.

Unfortunately, by the next morning I was very ill. After further testing, the diagnosis was infectious mononucleosis that had also affected my liver. I was in the hospital for over a week and was told to stay home for three weeks before going back to work.

Consequently, it was almost three months before I felt like going on a date. I summoned the courage one afternoon and called 7-1240. Betty answered. I explained who I was, and she said she remembered me. "Would you like to go to the rodeo in Hobbs?"

"Yes."

I could have shouted.

The hours dragged by on the day of our first date. I worked the early shift in the laboratory, 6:00 a.m.—2:00 p.m. My health had improved but I had lost several pounds that I really did not need to lose. I appeared to be skinny. My plan was for us to attend the rodeo and then eat dinner at a popular Mexican restaurant in Hobbs. Because Betty was a native, I decided if she did not like Mexican food she could suggest another place.

Because I did not have the "proper" clothes for a rodeo, I dressed as casually as possible. Fortunately, I had bought a pair of western boots a few years earlier. I tried to get to Betty's home at exactly 7:00 p.m. because the rodeo started at 8:00.

When I turned off the main highway to drive the two miles to Monument, I glanced to my right. It was hard to believe the sight. There was a small herd of buffalo grazing in the pasture. I must truly be in the "Land of Enchantment," I mused. Monument consisted of a general store, a couple of churches, a school building and a few homes. There was also a very tall statue of an Indian facing the west with his right hand shading his eyes as he looked into the sunset. I had no idea which house Betty lived in. I pulled my white 1960 Pontiac Catalina up in front of the store. Three men were sitting on a bench outside the store visiting and smoking cigarettes. All three spoke to me as I walked to the store. One stood immediately, "Need some help?"

"I'm looking for the Hurst house."

"Well, the old man lives up on the hill and the boy lives down there across the road."

I assumed Betty lived on the hill where the "old man" lived. I drove over a cattle guard, which is common in cattle country. It is similar to a small bridge except it is made of metal pipes with space between the pipes. Cows learn quickly that if they attempt to walk across the guard, their hoofs will hang between the metal pipes.

As I drove up to the house, a very large dog with his tail wagging came bounding off the porch to greet me. At least I was hoping that was his purpose. A tall, stately lady with streaks of gray in her dark hair came to the door and called, "Prince!" The dog stopped quickly and returned to the porch. The lady smiled and invited me into the house. She introduced herself as Stella Hurst, Betty's mother. "Betty will be right out."

Soon Betty came from one of the bedrooms. She was as beautiful as I had remembered. She was a brunette with olive skin and flashing, brown eyes. However, I did not like her attire. She had on black riding pants and a green and white checked blouse with buttons down the front. She also wore stylish, white moccasins adorned with a few colorful Indian designs. I don't know what I thought she would wear to a rodeo but I did not expect her to look like a tomboy. I really had no concern about how she felt about my attire.

We chatted briefly and said goodbye to her Mother and walked to the car. I opened the door for her and as I was getting seated I began trying to impress her by telling her I had been raised on a farm.

The conversation progressed rapidly. It was easy to converse with Betty. I began asking questions. "Were you born in New Mexico?"

"Actually I was born right here in Monument. At that time it was much larger than Hobbs."

"Do you work in Hobbs?"

"Yes, I began working for Tidewater Oil Company after graduating from business college in Lubbock. My dad worked for oil companies even before I was born. At the present time, he is working the midnight shift with Warren Petroleum Company and he was still asleep when you came."

"Do you have brothers and sisters?" She responded by telling me about her blended family.

I shared with her about my family, my education and my present employment as a medical technologist at the Lea General Hospital in Hobbs. I did not tell her that I came to Hobbs to find a wife. A few weeks later she laughingly commented, "When I saw Catalina on the dash of your car, I mistook it for Cadillac and thought, WOW! med techs must make a lot of money. I also thought you were about eighteen years old until you told me differently."

She was such a charming young woman that I soon forgot about her attire. I sensed very quickly that living a Christ-like life was important to her. It was definitely a prerequisite for me. We were both twenty-four and she was fifteen days older than me. I assumed she had never been married. I soon discovered that my assumption was correct.

I have absolutely no recollection of the rodeo. I was too busy conversing with Betty. I learned she loved to play golf and tennis and enjoyed competing in tournaments. She played the French horn in high school band and also loved to sing. I had never picked up a golf club or tennis racquet. The closest I had come to a club was using a hoe in the cotton or peanut patch and I was in the 4-H Club in high school. The only band instrument I ever played was when I was in the Rhythm Band in the second grade. I played the sticks. I did not feel these talents would impress Betty so I kept quiet and listened. As if these activities were not enough, she also enjoyed rabbit hunting. I had never hunted animals in my entire life.

At the present time I was "hunting" for a wife and I did not feel I was batting very well. Later in the evening I remembered to tell her that while in the military I had received a medal in recognition of my ability to shoot an M-1 rifle. She appeared to be impressed. Finally I remembered to tell her that I could play the piano. I could tell by the look in those beautiful, brown eyes that I had hit a home run. After the rodeo, I asked if she liked Mexican food. "I love it."

We ate and chatted in the restaurant until closing time. She reminded me there was a piano in their home and asked me to play for her another time because now it was very late. I agreed, although I had not played since moving to Hobbs.

When I took her home I walked her to the door. I wondered if she would allow me to kiss her goodnight. I did not have to wonder long because just as I reached to put my arms around her, a large animal jumped between us. Prince was protecting his dear friend. We both laughed and said goodnight after I asked if we could go out again the next night. Her answer was yes.

I smiled all the way back to Hobbs. I've never stopped smiling when I think of her, which is almost constantly.

When I arrived the next evening, I met her dad. He was a pleasant man with brilliant blue eyes. He enjoyed talking and told me he was retiring within the next two weeks. Instead of going out that evening, I played the piano and Betty sang. Occasionally, we sang a duet.

Betty's mom fixed sandwiches and made a delicious caramel cake. Betty and I dated almost every night for the next two weeks. I had planned a trip to my parents at Callisburg near Gainesville, Texas. I asked Betty if she would like to go. "Yes, I've never been in that part of Texas." I felt my batting average was increasing.

On the weekend that we visited my parents, all of my brothers and sisters and their children came to see me and meet Betty. I could tell they all liked her and I knew that my mom and dad did also. Betty seemed to like them as well. Betty told me later she could tell my family loved and respected me, and that influenced her opinion of me. Mom told me later she knew I was serious about Betty because I had never invited anyone home before.

Betty and I left for Hobbs on Sunday afternoon. About five miles from my parent's home, I stopped at a highway intersection. As I waited for traffic, I turned to Betty and asked if she would marry me. "Yes." I was ecstatic. On the way back to Hobbs we planned our wedding. Both of us wanted a simple wedding with few in attendance. We tentatively set the date for September 16. Later we changed that date to July 29. We didn't want to wait.

My thoughts were interrupted by Barb Neid, the evening supervisor. "Mr. West, I want to remind you that I have a room ready for you when you wish to lie down." I explained that Dr. Fox suggested I go home rather than stay in the hospital. She agreed and assured me that the nurse would call if there were any significant changes in Betty.

It was late when I pulled out of the parking garage that night. I turned to my faithful Source—God. On the way home I prayed. I don't remember most of my conversation with Him. I do remember asking why He did not intervene. I never once believed that God had brought this upon Betty. I remember also asking, "God where were you when I needed you the most?" Almost immediately, I remembered the words to a song called *God on the Mountain* that I had heard Lynda Randle sing. God on the mountain is the same God in the valley.

I knew I had my answer. God was there all along and I finally accepted the fact He had a better plan than I could even imagine. I needed to be patient and wait on Him. Even though I was faced with the possible death of the person who was closer to me than anyone, I made a definite decision to believe God was God in the bad times as well as the good. If He chose to never heal another person, He would still be God and I would continue to trust and love Him.

Before Betty had polymyositis, I criticized people who attended healing services and actually believed that God was still in the healing business. However, when the one you love most in your life suffers from excruciating pain, your thought patterns begin to change. We found ourselves going to healing services hoping to receive a miracle.

In one service Betty was greatly touched by God. After prayer she was able to run around the auditorium. Some might think it a sacrilege to run around in a church building. After all, isn't this God's "house?" I have no doubt that God was pleased to see Betty running. She improved markedly and was virtually pain free for several weeks until she decided to mow the grass. She apparently pulled a muscle in her back and the pain returned in greater force. What had been gained quickly was lost as quickly. Betty never lost faith that someday she would be totally healed of polymyositis.

Driving along the curving, country road with the moon shining on the cotton and cornfields between Georgetown and Taylor reminded me of the farms that we rented when I was a child. I never enjoyed farm life, so as soon as I graduated from high school I went to college. To pay my expenses, I got a job in a hospital and began training as a medical technologist and radiology technician.

Because it was a small hospital, I also had to learn to care for the male patients. This was not what I wanted to do the rest of my career. However, God had other plans. And so God dragged me kicking and screaming into a healthcare career that has lasted over fifty years. I have been an orderly, radiology technician, medical technologist, medical transcriptionist, Army medic, histology technician, and spent over forty years in hospital administration. These experiences gave me an excellent way to pay my way through college and led to a career that has provided me with employment I have learned to love.

I had no idea that my fledgling faith and my performance of the most menial medical tasks would prepare me for a time when my wife would need me the most. God knew all along what our needs would be.

Chapter 2:

God, I'm Disappointed

⌘

I slept well until the alarm awakened me. I went into the kitchen and made a cup of coffee. As I walked to my recliner, Pepper, our Sheltie, arose and sat close to me. She was obviously puzzled why Betty was not at home. I picked her up and cuddled her in my arms. Her soft fur was comforting and I realized she sensed something was wrong.

As I drank my coffee, I prayed the most candid prayer I had ever prayed. In the early seventies, I read a book, which was titled *Conversational Prayer* by Rosalind Rinker. It made such an impact on my life that I never forgot it. I taught it to a women's group in our church. The author taught that we should pray as if we are having a direct conversation with God. When we have a conversation with someone, we should stop and listen to what they have to say also. Most of my prayer life since that time has been merely talking with God and attempting to understand what He is telling me. Sometimes I realize I am doing all the talking and have to remember God wants to speak also.

I started our conversation by reminding Him how disappointed I was that He had not intervened for Betty. I should have begun the prayer by thanking Him for intervening and allowing her to survive the stroke. He responded by telling me I had not seen the big picture. I made a serious request. "If you are not going to heal her so she can be a whole person, please take her home quickly." He offered no response. I confessed He knew better than I that she would need many physical therapy and speech sessions. Due to the polymyositis, the physical therapy sessions would be impossible because of the pain.

I reminded Him that we had prayed for years for her to be healed and He had not done so. I should have thanked Him for allowing her to be able to continue to be at home and be able to do several things alone.

Apparently my hindsight is much better than my actual sight was at that time. I do not remember asking Him what His perfect will was for Betty and me. I remember quite well the things I told Him I wanted. In retrospect I realize I spoke as a spoiled brat. I also asked Him to make her better than before the stroke. I shared with Him that would be my prayer and I was going to instruct everyone who prayed for her to pray the same way so that our prayers would all be in agreement. Looking back I realize He knew exactly how I felt.

He is such a patient and loving Father. Even though it appeared that I was ungrateful for all He had done for us, He continued to pour His love out upon me. I felt as if He had His loving arms around me and with His hands He wiped away my tears. I knew He would never leave me or forsake me. The words came to me again: *Be patient.*

God impressed upon me I should get the tape player and the cassette with healing scriptures I had used several years ago and play the tapes continuously for Betty. I confessed, "I don't know where the cassette is. I have not used it in years." I immediately remembered exactly where the tape was located. I was so excited, I almost ran to the file cabinet, looked in an envelope and there was the tape. I realized this was going to be a life-changing adventure and I needed to hear every instruction from Him.

I admitted I did not know all the things I needed to be doing. He emphasized that He would tell me as the need arose and He would use individuals to tell me. He stressed that I must be very careful to whom I listened.

During this prayer time, God reminded me of several times He had provided for our needs. Although I had a good job in hospital administration, there was never enough extra money to do some of the projects we wanted to do for Him. Prior to our marriage, both of us felt that God wanted us to do something special for Him and others. Betty felt that He possibly wanted her to do mission work.

After months of prayer, Betty fulfilled a long-time ambition in 1980 when she opened a Christian book and gift store in the Taylor Plaza Shopping Center. We named it "Faith Bookstore." It was a beautiful store and Betty chose vibrant colors of green, blue and yellow for the interior. A wonderful friend, Darrell Gustafson, hand made one of the display units and donated it to Betty. To keep the little children occupied while the parents shopped, Betty had a large red barn in the back portion of the store. She had special books and toys available for the little ones to take into the barn for entertainment.

She felt that God had called her into this ministry. Our longtime friend, Mildred Fulfer whom Betty had known before our marriage called and volunteered to give us a large sum of money with no strings attached to help us open the store. This was totally unsolicited on our part. We accepted the gift but determined we would reimburse her as quickly as we could.

Betty ministered to many people who would not enter a church building but would visit with her in the store. She told me of a gentleman who came one day. As he entered, he greeted her and remarked, "I just want to read the walls." By this he meant he wanted to read the many plaques that were on the walls. This was not an unusual occurrence as she had other customers who enjoyed doing that as well. After several minutes, he made his way back to the counter. "Thank you for being here. When I came in here today, I had made up my mind to take my own life. I feel like that now I have regained my hope. I'm o.k."

She had other occasions that were very touching as well but not as memorable as that one. Betty felt the bookstore had fulfilled the desire for mission service. In 1984 she believed her time was finished there and sold the store to another couple who were customers.

Employees I encountered on my way to the ICU that Thursday morning had varying expressions and greetings. Some expressed concern while others looked away. Word had spread throughout the hospital that Betty was critically ill.

As I entered the ICU, I was greeted by nurses who were not present the evening before. Most looked familiar but I had to look at nametags to identify several of them. In the past, I had very little interaction with the ICU nurses. They were always behind the doors I did not want to enter. These nurses were to become good friends and supporters in the days to follow.

The curtains surrounding Betty's bed were open and I realized she didn't look any different than she did the previous night. Maybe the stroke was not as bad as the doctors had thought. She still had IV fluids going and the nasal tube was in place through which she received nourishment.

Her nurse was in the room almost constantly, which was very comforting to me. She gave permission for me to play the tape quietly. I immediately placed the tape with the healing scriptures into the small portable cassette player. I turned the volume low so it would not disturb other patients. I did not want to risk the nurses refusing to let me play the scriptures. After all, this was their turf and I had great respect for them. Although Betty was barely responsive, I knew she could hear the scripture and this was what God had told me to do.

Playing the scriptures reminded me of another miracle that I had experienced in the late 1970's. Since I was a small child, I had suffered from severe allergies. In the early 1960's, I worked in a clinic in Hobbs, New Mexico and a pediatric allergist insisted on skin-testing me. After the results of the skin test, I began taking injections three times each week. I did get some relief. Several years later, I was tested again by an allergist in Austin. He gave me the same diagnosis and prognosis. I resumed taking injections for approximately two years. Both specialists said I was a textbook case. The first allergist suggested I could live on a rock in the middle of the ocean and still experience allergies. I took antihistamines and had injections for many years, which left me feeling lethargic and drowsy a large part of the time.

Later, our good friend Mildred Fulfer introduced us to a new concept. At least it was new to us, although I had received miracles earlier. By using scriptures, she taught us that Jesus wanted us to be well and not sick. She gave me a list of scriptures to read and con-fess orally concerning divine healing. I did this for several months. During this time, I attended a Full Gospel Business Men's meeting in Austin. A businessman from Tulsa, Oklahoma prayed for me. I did not feel any differently but I continued to confess the scriptures at least once every day and believed I was being healed.

My health improved considerably. Several months later, on a subsequent visit to the allergist in Austin, he walked into the exam room and his words were, "What is so different about you? You don't look like the same person."

Grinning, I responded, "Do you believe in divine healing?"

"Yes, tell me about it." I did.

He examined me thoroughly and commented, "Without a doubt you are much improved." He explained how to taper off on the injections and medications. I followed his orders. For over thirty years I have been virtually free of all allergies and do not take any allergy medications.

Soon the nurse announced that we had visitors. June and Gene Prater had come early to pray with Betty. The therapy team arrived just as we finished praying. They began to work with Betty by sitting her on the side of the bed and attempting to get her to balance herself. I was fascinated and encouraged that they were assessing her abilities.

The Speech Pathologist, Occupational Therapist, and the Physical Therapist were all from the rehab department that reported to me. A few of the therapists knew Betty from having treated her mother previously and expressed their concerns to me. Betty could not communicate except by nodding her head. The Speech Pathologist brought an alphabet board and Betty was able to point to letters and spell a few words. They worked with her for some time with very little success and stated they would let her rest and would be back later. I cannot imagine how Betty must have felt. This woman who had been so active for most of her life was now totally helpless and unable to speak.

The radiology techs took Betty for another CT scan. The scan showed increased swelling of the brain. In spite of all the negative reports, I had peace that everything was going to be okay. I could tell by the expressions of the therapists, nurses, and doctors that they had different thoughts.

Close to noon, our daughter Jamie and one of her friends came from Houston. It was good to have family present. Because our grandson Bryan was attending the medical school camp, I asked Dawn not to come at this time. Betty would be upset if Bryan did not finish the camp. We also suggested that Mark not come at this time. Both Dawn and Mark told me later not to do that again. I eventually realized that I needed to let them make their own decisions after they had adequate information.

Jamie assured me she had notified my brothers and sisters. I knew all of them were committed Christians and would be praying for us. My oldest living brother, Weldon, and his wife, Emma Jo, also put Betty's name in their prayer room at church. We would later receive letters and cards from some of the people who prayed for us. It was very encouraging to know that even total strangers cared.

When the therapists returned, Betty was not responsive enough for them to continue with the assessment. The increased swelling of the brain caused her to be almost totally non-responsive. Her internist, Dr. Shallin, and also Dr. Fox, her neurologist, came to see her. Although they tried to be encouraging, they emphasized we would just have to wait and see what her brain would do. The scripture tape continued to play.

Employees from various departments of the hospital came to share their concerns. This was very comforting to me, even though the doctors were not encouraging. It was difficult not to think of the future. I could not imagine what it would be like not having Betty at home with me. However, I knew from what I heard others say that even if she lived they did not believe she would ever be able to go home. I knew her opinion about nursing homes. She would rather be dead. Her mother, daddy, and my mother had lived for years in a nursing home. I remembered my prayer. *God, either totally heal her or take her home quickly*. From what I saw at this time, He had chosen not to do either.

The Speech Pathologist warned the staff that it was not safe to give Betty anything by mouth because of her current lung status and her inability to swallow. Normally, the Speech Pathologist would have recommended a modified barium swallow; however, Betty was not physically capable of swallowing the barium. She answered simple yes or no questions by nodding or shaking her head. With maximum assistance, she used the alphabet board to spell out her needs.

Betty responded to voice and touch by "vocalizing." She made oral sounds but she did not have the ability to speak. She was able to move her right arm and it had to be restrained at times to keep her from pulling out her nasal tube.

It was a long day. Friends and family were calling to check on her. I continued to speak positively. Two of the nurses who had treated Betty in the Ambulatory Care Center when she got the Gamma Globulin came to see me. One of them, Brenda Johnson, asked if they could pray for Betty and me. The other nurse had just returned from a prayer retreat and was ready to pray. Brenda is a very sweet nurse and knows the authority that she has to use the name of Jesus. They took me into the family room and prayed for me. Their prayers lifted my spirits.

The next morning Betty did not respond to any voice except mine. Because of the pain from the polymyositis, she was placed on a special airbed. When the Speech Pathologist came, Betty was unresponsive. All therapy was put on hold.

Because Social Services knew that we were members of the Living Bank, they asked me to contact that organization. We would need to know which medical school would accept Betty's body if she died. We made plans several years ago to donate our bodies to medical science at our death. I knew that I needed to make that call but did not have the stamina to do so. I asked the Social Services employee to make the call for me. The Social Services director returned soon and told me that the Living Bank no longer made the arrangements and provided me with a list of medical schools that hopefully would accept Betty's body. After I made several contacts, I eventually made the arrangements with Texas A&M University for both of us.

By the afternoon Betty appeared to be more responsive. She would flail her right arm constantly. Jamie and I discussed that it appeared that she was directing a choir. It was possible she was remembering times when she had directed the junior choir at First Baptist Church in Taylor. She had also directed a choir when we lived in Hobbs, New Mexico. We speculated about what was going on in her mind or perhaps it was just an involuntary motion. Whatever the cause, we looked for every positive sign because she could not move her left side.

42

On Saturday following the stroke, Dawn, Bryan, and Caitlin arrived. They were somewhat apprehensive about seeing Betty. We were concerned that it would be frightening for Caitlin, at age 9, to see her "G" in this condition, so only Dawn and Bryan went in to see Betty. When I told Betty they were there, she immediately reached out to hug them with her right arm.

Years later, Caitlin told me, "People kept telling me that I couldn't see G because it would scare me too much and I wouldn't understand. They didn't realize that the only thing I needed was to see G. I wanted to be with her just like everyone else. I remember sitting in the waiting room with a lot of people that were family, but I did not know them. I just wanted to be with G and I didn't understand why I wasn't allowed. Finally, after what seemed like hours of sitting in the ICU waiting room feeling absolutely helpless, Mom walked me back to see G. Seeing my G was much better than anything I could have expected. I felt calm, secure, and safe knowing that she was in the hospital being cared for by many doctors and nurses. At long last I felt like there was a connection between what everyone was telling me and the truth."

In hindsight, I'm sorry we did not let Caitlin see Betty immediately. Children understand so much more than we give them credit for.

Shortly before noon, Betty's niece Diane Solomon, a neurologist from San Antonio, arrived with her husband, Dale, and their three boys. It was so comforting to have Diane present. She had visited us many times as a little girl and is now a brilliant physician as well as a beautiful lady with a sweet and caring personality. I gave the ICU nurses permission for Diane to review Betty's records.

After reviewing Betty's records, Diane and I went to radiology to view the CT scans. Before she looked at them she told me, "I told Dale this morning that I expect to see the brain of a 40 year-old instead of a 65 year-old." When Diane turned to look at the scans she commented, "I was right. Look at how large her brain is. It has not atrophied over time like most brains. She really has more brains than all of us put together. That is good in one aspect and bad in another. Because her brain has not atrophied, there is not a lot of space within her skull for it to swell." I commented that Dr. Fox said Betty would get worse before she would get better. Diane nodded in agreement.

I shared with Diane that I was praying God would make Betty better than she was before the stroke. Diane smiled and said that would be her prayer also. Diane has strong faith and I knew she loved her Aunt Betty very much. I appreciated her response and her comforting words.

Dr. Fox's associates visited Betty on Saturday and Sunday. They were equally as concerned as the doctors who had worked with Betty for years.

Late Saturday afternoon, Jamie and I were in Betty's room. The nurse informed us that the weekend hospital chaplain wished to see us. We went to the desk outside of the ICU and met Jeannie Stanley. She warmly greeted us and asked if she could do anything for us. We spoke together, "please pray for Betty." She consented. I explained how we were praying and she was in agreement with us. When we came into Betty's room, I asked Jeannie if she would like to anoint Betty with oil. I had a small vial of oil in my pocket and had anointed Betty several times as we prayed for her. Jeannie was delighted. She prayed a powerful prayer of faith. It reminded me of some of the prayers Catherine Marshall recorded in her books. Jamie and I emphasized to Jeannie she was welcome to come back at any time.

Betty's condition remained about the same through Sunday. Dr. Fox informed me he was going to be on vacation beginning the following Tuesday. He gave his assurance he would leave his number with his associates should we need him. He asked if I would mind another neurologist covering for his group while he was away. I assured him it would be okay. He shared with me the doctor would make rounds sometime Monday.

The following Monday, I could see very little change in Betty. Dr. Barbara Brightwell, a wonderful friend, member of the hospital board of directors, and director of the volunteers and chaplains for the hospital, visited with us. I mentioned to her how much Jeannie Stanley had encouraged us when she prayed with Betty. Dr. Brightwell asked if we would like to have a healing service for Betty and told us Jeannie had agreed to lead it that afternoon if we desired. I assured her that we would be very appreciative.

I contacted friends who had previously come to pray for Betty. All agreed to be present. We must have looked like a small army as we came into Betty's ICU room that afternoon. The group was completely inter-denominational. Representatives were from Catholic, Baptist, Methodist, Presbyterian and nondenominational churches. All were in one accord. All of us wanted Betty to be healed. Before I invited them to participate, I made certain they would agree to pray as I had been praying. Jeannie anointed Betty with oil and read several scriptures pertaining to healing. Several laid their hands on Betty and Jeanie led a prayer for healing. It was a wonderful, worshipful experience.

That evening about 6:00 p.m. the neurologist covering for Dr. Fox arrived. He introduced himself and went to check Betty. When he came out of her room, he told me he had grave concerns about her. He believed her brain was continuing to swell and indicated he did not believe she would live.

He asked, "What about the advance directive?" My voice trembling, I responded. "Neither Betty nor I want heroic procedures performed if there is no hope that she will have a good quality of life. We do not want her to be placed on a ventilator."

He frowned. "Well, we need to get a stat CT scan so that I can see what's going on. What *will* you let me do?"

"I will not agree to any procedure that will only prolong her life and I *will not* agree to any invasive procedure without your having consulted with Dr. Fox or one of his associates."

He turned to the nurse. "Call radiology immediately for a stat CT scan." I could sense the anger in his voice and see the anger and frustration in his eyes and facial expression. I had no understanding as to why he appeared to be angry and frustrated. I hoped there would not be another unpleasant encounter with him.

While waiting for the radiology techs to come get Betty, one of the ICU nurses came and put her arm around me. I began to cry. I asked, "Can you see a difference in Betty for the worse?"

"No, but I'm not the neurologist. Let's see what the scan shows." Her sincere concern for me was comforting and I was so thankful that we had nurses in the hospital that were not only excellent nurses but caring as well.

I went into Betty's room and held her as best I could. She did not appear any different than she had previously. I glanced toward the opening in the curtain of her cubicle and the doctor was there. He motioned to me.

"I have to know what procedures you will allow me to do." Our eyes met and I made sure my voice was firm. "We will talk about that when we get the results from the CT scan. I'm not going to discuss anything of that nature at this time."

Abruptly he turned and left the unit. I wondered if he was demanding with all families. He had been on our hospital staff for only a short period of time. I had not heard of any complaints but from admission reports I received, he rarely had a hospital patient.

Soon the radiology techs came for Betty. In less than an hour, they returned her to ICU.

Time passed and I received no report. I called radiology and they informed me the system that we use to transfer images to the radiologist after hours was inoperable for the entire Austin area. I asked, "Where is the neurologist?"

"I think he went home," was the reply.

I was extremely puzzled as to why the neurologist had not looked at the scan himself. Because he is a specialist he should have been able to see if there were any significant changes in the scans. I was even more surprised and disappointed that he had not informed me that he was leaving the hospital. Even though he told me that he felt Betty's condition was worsening, he never came nor called the nurse to inquire about Betty before leaving the building.

I called my niece Dr. Diane Solomon in San Antonio. I explained what was happening. "Oh, Uncle Louis, I am so sorry you are having to deal with this. Call him and ask him to call me when he looks at the scan." I paged him. He answered my page and obviously was irritated that I had contacted him. I asked where he was and he stated he was on his way home because the radiologist could not look at the scan at this time. When I asked him why he didn't look at it, he said that he was tired and was going home. I gave him Diane's number and asked that he call her. He said he would.

I hoped to resolve this situation without having to contact the medical Chief-of-Staff for the hospital. Had I not known the protocol in a situation such as this, I would have asked for the chief nursing officer on duty and filed a formal complaint against the doctor. The nursing officer would have contacted the chief of the medical staff. From my many years of experience, I knew the doctor should not have left the hospital and, as a courtesy, should have visited with the family. He could have checked the scans and told us what he saw and as soon as he got the radiology report he could let us know. He should have informed the family and the ICU nurse that he was going home and instructed the radiology techs to call him as soon as the radiologist dictated the report.

I went to Radiology. The techs told me the system was still down. I could stand it no longer. I asked for the doctor's telephone number and called him again. He shouted, "Do you expect me to stay at that hospital 24 hours a day?"

"Yes, if it takes it to take care of your patients."

"Well, I called Diane Solomon, now let me talk with the tech." As the tech spoke with him, I could tell by the expression on her face that he was also angry with her.

In a short while she politely spoke, "Sir, Mr. West is my boss, he requested your number and I had to give it to him. Goodbye."

Rather than report the neurologist to the Chief-of-Staff, I con-tacted the patient care supervisor and asked her to page Dr. Fox, hoping he had not left on vacation. In a few minutes she had Dr. Fox on the phone ready to speak with me.

I tried to remain calm as I took the telephone, "Hi, Dr. Fox. Thanks so much for calling."

"That's what I'm here for. The nurse told me what happened. What would you like for me to do?"

"If at all possible, I would like for you or one of your associates to come look at the scan and examine Betty."

"I'm on my way."

I realized even more how important it is to have a doctor that is very ethical and has the patient and family's interests and concerns foremost in their thoughts and actions. Even though Dr. Fox was probably packing for his vacation, he came immediately when he was notified there were concerns about Betty. I knew he would have done the same for any of his patients.

Though the evening had been most unpleasant, I did not regret insisting that Betty get good medical care. All families should insist on the same care, particularly when the patient cannot speak.

During this wait I called June and Gene Prater and they immediately came. We were sitting at the station outside the ICU when Dr. Fox arrived. He immediately asked the nurse to get all of Betty's scans. She had already requested them from radiology and in a matter of minutes he was looking at them. "I cannot see any change in this scan from the scans done a few days earlier." Looking more intently at the most recent scan, he commented, "I do see a small area on the left side of the brain that I did not see in the earlier scans." Looking directly into my eyes, he spoke, "I'm sorry but I am certain this is a second stroke." Putting the scan that had been made on the past Thursday on the view box he commented, "Yes, here it is, It just shows up better on this scan tonight." He assured me that treatment would have been the same but that it did explain some of the effects that Betty now was having. I told him that Diane also had viewed the first scan but did not see the second stroke on the left.

Dr. Fox stayed with Betty for quite some time. He ordered an additional medication for seizures. I expressed my appreciation to him for coming but he merely said it was his job. Very firmly I stated, "I do not want the other doctor on her case again." He agreed.

I called Diane and gave her the report from Dr. Fox. I asked if I should call the other doctor and tell him he was released from the case. She chuckled. "I think he already knows it. He called me and inferred that he was off the case and began to tell me about you. I informed him that I had known you for years and knew that it was right for you to demand that he look at the films. In fact, because he is now off the case, I would tell him what he should have done. He should have never left the patient when he insinuated that she was getting worse."

Dr. Fox's progress note that evening stated, "Prognosis is guarded."

The next morning when the internist, Dr. Shallin, examined her at 6:30 a.m., he agreed her prognosis was not good. Betty could not speak or follow simple commands. He discussed the CT findings and Dr. Fox's impression. We also discussed that she was not to have CPR.

The next day was uneventful and on Wednesday morning, one week from the day the strokes occurred, Betty was transferred from Intensive Care into a private room.

Chapter 3:

Finding God on a Three-cent Stamp

♩♪

M oving out of the ICU was a bit frightening to me. While in the unit, Betty could have a nurse within seconds. Although her new room was close to the nurses' station, it was certainly not like ICU. If no one was with her, she could not get assistance. However, I decided to make the most of it. I went downstairs and got the stereo from my office. Betty would now be able to listen to CDs. I hooked up the stereo and immediately the CD player jammed. I could not get the CD released.

Gene Prater appeared. "Gene, you're just the one I need. Somehow I have jammed a CD in the player."

"Sorry Louis but I probably can't help you. June refuses to allow me to work on that type of equipment."

"Oh, come on, Gene, I promise I won't tell June. I have confidence that you can get it going. Betty needs to hear the CDs."

Grinning he replied, "I'll risk getting into trouble with June in order to help Betty." In a few minutes, he had disassembled the unit, released the CD and reassembled the unit. Praise the Lord! I started the Christian music CDs and kept them playing constantly.

The next few days dragged by. There were no significant changes in Betty's condition. The doctors determined that it would be better to insert a "peg tube" into her stomach surgically rather than using the tube in her nose for her nourishment. After consulting with a gastroenterologist, the doctors scheduled the procedure. Prior to the procedure the doctor visited with me and explained what he would do. I liked him immediately. He was empathetic and assured me that the tube could be removed when it was no longer needed. He also advised that sometimes the patient was not a candidate for the procedure and he would not know for sure until he attempted it.

Fortunately it was successful. We no longer had to be concerned that the nasal tube would become displaced and have to be reinserted.

The following Sunday, one of Betty's brothers came to visit. When I told Betty that Hank was there, she reached up with her right arm and hugged him. It was an emotional moment for Hank and me. After Hank left and I had gone home, I received a call from another of her brothers, Jerry. He stated that he had also come to see Betty but did not awaken her. I assured him that she would have known him. He did not think so.

The next days were very disturbing for me. When Betty was in ICU, the nurses were extremely careful not to speak negatively about Betty in our presence. They were compassionate and loving to both of us. However, some of the medical-surgical nurses did not hesitate to give negative opinions. They made unacceptable comments about Betty's condition that certainly should not be made in her presence.

We have no idea what the patient can hear and understand even though they appear to be asleep or unconscious. I rarely heard a positive expression from the nurses. Some were obviously unhappy that she was their patient. Their eyes, their looks of frustration and impatience were disheartening to me. I hoped Betty did not sense these mannerisms as much as I did. They showed very little respect to either of us. I hoped they did not treat other patients and family members as they did Betty and me.

I was sure they were capable of caring for patients and family members and I could not understand or tolerate their lack of caring. I wondered if it was because I was a Vice President. I knew that it was not uncommon for some employees to look at management in a different light. I made certain that I never demanded something that would not have been given to any patient or family member and always tried to thank them for caring for Betty.

It was most upsetting when I would tell Betty's nurse that she appeared to be in pain and needed medication. It was not uncommon to have to tell them more than once before they responded. I could see them sitting at the nurses' station laughing and talking. On one occasion Betty's nurse responded, "You know, we have other patients." I should have reported the lack of care and concern to a nurse manager.

After Betty had been on the medical surgical unit a few days, a social worker told me they were going to have a case conference pertaining to Betty and would like for me to be present. I reluctantly agreed. When I walked into the small conference room there was standing room only. I had never seen some of the people who were present and wondered who they were. Soon after I arrived, Dr. Shallin, the internist, arrived. I wanted to run. He would not have been in the meeting unless it was very serious. I knew I was not going to get words of encouragement.

The meeting started and various staff members gave their negative assessment of Betty. I had seen improvement in her but I was the only one who had. After all, they had read her chart. Dr. Shallin, her internist spoke very authoritatively. "She is not aware of anything and cannot follow the simplest commands." Nurses chimed in. I listened for a few minutes and then I forgot that I was a Vice President. I was the husband of Betty West. I knew I must speak up.

"I have never seen some of you in Betty's room and I am curious as to how you can tell me what she can and can not do when you have never seen her." Turning to Dr. Shallin I challenged him. "It is strange that Betty will respond to me and will not respond for you. You only see her in the early morning when she is still asleep."

Despite my intervention, it appeared that almost all agreed that Betty was not a candidate for rehab and that she no longer qualified for acute care. I knew they wanted me to say that I would take her to a nursing home. I refused.

Jackie McRoberts, highly respected for her knowledge and abilities as the director of Inpatient Therapy and one of my directors, was present. Jackie had previously told me, "I know you have a lot of people with you now; however, just know there are a lot of us in the wings ready to do whatever you need done."

Now Jackie spoke in support of Betty and me. "How can we say that she does not qualify for rehab when we have never done an assessment on her? Before any decision is made, therapy needs to do an assessment." Everyone in the room became very quiet.

One by one they began to speak.

"You're right."

"Good idea. When can it be done?"

At last the meeting was adjourned.

Patients and family members need to know to **Speak Up** if they have a concern about patient care. In March 2002, the Joint Commission on Accreditation of Healthcare Organizations, the accrediting agency for healthcare institutions, together with the Centers for Medicare and Medicaid Services launched a national campaign to urge patients to take a role in preventing healthcare errors by becoming active, involved, and informed participants on the health care team. The program commonly referred to as the **Speak Up** campaign features brochures, posters, and buttons on a variety of patient safety topics encouraging patients and family members to **Speak Up**. We had already posted many posters throughout the hospital, including patient rooms, in support of the campaign. Unfortunately serious and sometimes fatal errors are made in hospitals. Most everyone has heard of the wrong leg being amputated or even surgery done on the wrong patient.

This campaign has significantly improved the error rate nationwide.

The Commission also implemented several new procedures to help reduce the error rate. Some of those procedures were highly resisted by some members of the medical staff and clinical employees throughout the nation. Nevertheless, they were written as standards and whether they were liked or not, they had to be implemented if the facility was to be accredited.

If facilities choose not to be accredited, they must still be certified by the Centers for Medicare and Medicaid Services. If the facility loses its Joint Commission accreditation, Medicare will send a team of surveyors to the facility. Depending on the seriousness of the deficiencies, the surveyors will attempt to work with the facility. If there is no cooperation, reimbursement is withheld, and patients are transferred to another facility. These regulations apply to any facility that treats Medicare or Medicaid patients, including nursing home facilities.

Along with many other responsibilities, I was the Joint Commission coordinator for the hospital. I welcomed the **Speak Up** campaign with open arms. Excellent policies and procedures are worthless if they are not implemented.

After the meeting, I returned to Betty's room. I wanted to cradle her in my arms and protect her. Soon I realized that two therapists were at the nursing station. The nurse did not know I could hear her remarks. "You can assess her if you want to, but there's nothing there."

After the therapists did their assessment, I waited. The next day I was told that Betty could not sustain the rigorous regimen for rehab. What should I do? I kept hoping and praying for a miracle. Even though Jackie McRoberts told me that Betty did not qualify for rehab, no one approached me to let me know when we would need to move her.

Later that afternoon, Jamie told me a rehab nurse had told her that Betty no longer qualified for acute care, nor rehab, and we would need to move her. It was upsetting to me that a nurse who had no authority to tell us anything, because Betty was not in rehab, would tell my daughter this instead of telling me. In doing so, the nurse completely ignored the Patient Privacy Act that protects patient information. I had never given permission to provide information pertaining to Betty to anyone but myself. I wanted to be the one to give the family information concerning Betty.

Jamie was visibly upset. The nurse had never met Jamie and could not have known that she was my daughter and whether I wanted Jamie to have that information or not. She also gave this notice in Betty's presence. I could only imagine what Betty's thoughts must have been if she understood what the nurse had said. Hospital personnel are taught to never assume that the patient cannot hear or understand what is being said. I discovered who the nurse was and immediately demanded that she never be allowed in the room again. I emphasized that no one had my permission to speak to any of my children or anyone else about Betty's condition. The director for the Rehab unit contacted me and apologized.

Although I was not enjoying these challenges, I was learning. I learned that we, as hospital staff, never know what is going on with family members. I remembered the old adage, "Until you've walked

a mile in my moccasins, you have no idea what is going on with me."
I had seen and been with family members who were angry. Because
of what I was experiencing, hopefully I would never be critical of
family members or patients who exhibited anger or impatience.

The next day the social worker, Rhonda Chambers, approached
me again. "Betty doesn't qualify for rehab at this time but I believe
she will qualify for long-term acute care."

"What is that?" I asked.

Rhonda explained there were facilities in Austin that specialized
in care for medically stable but complex patients that need extended
medical and nursing care. Long-term-acute-care (LTAC) hospitals
provide this level of care for patients like Betty that are too ill for
discharge to a nursing home, an acute-care rehabilitation hospital or
their homes. I asked Rhonda to proceed with this possibility.

The next day Rhonda, always positive and encouraging, visited
with me. "A nurse from the LTAC facility will need to do an assessment to be certain Betty qualifies. If she qualifies, your insurance
will cover most if not all the expenses." Although I knew Betty
could not stay in the Georgetown Hospital, it did not keep me from
wishing that she could. I did not realize at that time how mentally
and physically exhausted I was. Many times I prayed that I would
awaken from this horrible dream and we would be back in our
home in Taylor safe and secure.

That evening when I reached home I noticed a front-page news
article stating that the first class stamps were increasing to 37
cents. I thought, *Great. I have 34-cent stamps, bills to pay, and no
three-cent stamps. If I don't have enough to be concerned about,
now I have to deal with three-cent stamps.*

The next morning I drove by the Georgetown post office to get
stamps. However, the parking lot was crowded and I decided to
come back later. When I reached the hospital, I checked on Betty.
No noticeable changes. I went to my office.

Before long, Sam Schultz came in. I told him of my frustrations
about what to do with Betty. He immediately responded, "You're
fretting about all of this too much. You will know what the right
decision is when the time comes. You just need to relax. By the
way, I knew you would probably have to go stand in line to get your

three-cent stamps so I have brought you some." He handed me several stamps.

All at once it hit me, if God cared enough to give me three-cent stamps. He would certainly take care of everything else. Tears came to my eyes as I shared this revelation. Sam smiled. "We didn't buy these. We had already bought stamps and someone gave these to us. We don't need them." Sam was obviously sent by God to hold me up and encourage me at a very crucial time. That evening when I went home, I stuck three-cent stamps on all the mirrors in the house as well as the refrigerator. They continue to be a constant reminder that God cares and will see me through any situation.

That same morning I went to visit with Ken Poteete, the hospital CEO. Because the hospital self-insures the employees and their dependents, I wanted to keep him informed. I was certain he would be more concerned that Betty received proper medical care than how much it would cost. He greeted me warmly and I shared our tentative plan with him. "Obviously Betty no longer qualifies for short-term acute care and does not qualify for rehab either. Social Services employees are checking into a long-term acute care facility (LTAC) in Austin." He replied, "We need to do what is best for Betty. I will help you in any way that I can." I knew that he would.

That afternoon, the nurse from the LTAC hospital came to Georgetown and assessed Betty. She stated that Betty certainly qualified for the LTAC hospital and that I should tour the facility. I made arrangements to go the next morning and asked Jackie McRoberts, the director of In Patient Physical Therapy to go with me.

Specialty Hospital of Austin is located on the fourth level of North Austin Medical Center in the northern part of Austin. As Jackie and I rode up the elevator I was very apprehensive. When we entered the facility, the nurse that assessed Betty in Georgetown greeted us. She toured us around the patient area and introduced us to the staff. Two employees in whom I was most interested were Kim the Speech Pathologist and Oscar the Physical Therapist. They would be the individuals directing Betty's care. I liked them. They were young, energetic and positive. Jackie expressed satisfaction with what she observed. I made the decision. We would bring Betty as soon as possible.

Upon my arrival in Georgetown, I went immediately to Betty's room. I explained in detail what we would be doing. She gave little response. Nevertheless, I was relieved. It was as if a great load had been lifted. I was ready to move on.

That night as I prayed, I asked for God's protection over Betty. I asked Him not to let anyone come into her room that He did not specifically send. I wished that I had asked Him that before. There had been a few employees in the past few days that we could have done without. I felt at peace after having prayed for specific individuals to care for Betty. I was excited to see whom God would send.

Chapter 4:

You Are Her Voice

♪♫

O n July 5, 2002 the EMS personnel arrived about 9:00 a.m. to transfer Betty to Austin. I chose to drive our van and meet them at the hospital.

As I got off the elevator on the fourth floor of North Austin Medical Center, the nurse who had come to Georgetown to assess Betty greeted me. She took me to Betty's room and the EMS folks had just gotten her in bed. The patient rooms were nice and large. Outside the rooms was a very large area where patients and visitors could sit and where the therapists and doctors did their paperwork. I knew that Betty's doctor was to be Dr. Teresa Pham, an internist. I saw a young lady go into Betty's room, and I assumed she was Dr. Pham.

In a few minutes she came out of the room and headed towards me. Smiling, she offered her hand, "I'm Teresa Pham. I'll be Mrs. West's doctor. Do you mind if I ask you some questions?"

"No, I will be happy to answer any questions you have." I immediately liked her. She was very compassionate and apparently very knowledgeable. We talked for some time and she told me what to expect while Betty was a patient. She then went back into Betty's room to thoroughly examine her.

While Dr. Pham examined Betty, a gentleman came to me and introduced himself. He said he was a counselor and asked if I would mind him going in to see Betty for a few minutes. I assured him it would be alright. I thought to myself, *What a wonderful man*. He assured me he wanted to be friends and if I needed any help to please let him know. After Dr. Pham left Betty's room, he went in for about three minutes, smiled and told me he would see me later.

Later, I received a $150 statement from him. My response to him was that he should forget about his charge because I was not paying him to look at Betty. There was no way that he could have made an assessment of her. He could have been a friend but he obviously made the decision not to be. I should have been suspicious when he made his request. Betty could not speak. How was he going to be able to evaluate her? This was the beginning of a pattern that I soon recognized from other "counselors." If he had been able to document that Betty was depressed, there would have been no end to his "counseling sessions." Because it is a known fact that almost all stroke victims will have depression, Betty was already taking an anti-depressant.

Soon the therapists came. Oscar, the Physical Therapist, got Betty out of bed and into a chair. He worked with her awhile and then put her back into bed. The Occupational Therapist came and both of them worked with her. In Georgetown, the therapists used a Hoyer lift to transfer Betty from the bed to her chair. A Hoyer lift consists of a sling that is placed underneath the patient and a crank that is used to lift the patient and transfer the patient into a chair or bed. Oscar transferred Betty without a Hoyer lift. At the time, Betty was considerably overweight. It was amazing to see him work with her. Oscar and Kim worked together as a team to prepare Betty for a rehab facility. I was beginning to understand the advantage of having Betty in a facility where the employees were accustomed to working with long-term patients.

The nurses were all very gentle with her and asked me about the polymyositis. They admitted that they were not familiar with it but wanted to learn. Betty was placed on an airbed exactly like the one she had in Georgetown.

Because Betty was admitted on Friday, she received no physical therapy over the weekend. The therapists demonstrated how to do range of motion with her arms and legs. This consisted of gently taking Betty's limbs and moving them to the height recommended by the therapist and then gently laying them back on the bed. After the demonstration, the therapists observed as I did the exercises to be certain I understood. These exercises kept Betty limber and also assisted with her muscle tone and circulation. I wanted so badly to see some movement of her left side. The right side had plenty of movement; however, it was mostly involuntary.

I hooked up the CD player and started the Christian music. The nurses commented that the music was very soothing and produced a peaceful atmosphere in the room. They assured me that when I was not there they would keep it playing for Betty.

Jamie came on Friday evening. It was so good to have family present. Mark, Dawn, and Sam Schultz called often to check on us. Because Betty could not speak, I longed for communication and visits with friends and family.

On Saturday after admission to LTAC, Jamie and I helped Betty do her exercises. She would respond to us but could not speak plainly. We sensed that she thought she was speaking so that we could understand. She continued to get all her nourishment and medications through the peg tube.

Betty's nurse was a young male. I felt awkward about discussing it with the supervisor but I knew that I must. I explained that Betty was a very modest person and would feel very uncomfortable with a young man taking care of her personal needs. They were all quite understanding—actually more than I realized. They interpreted my concerns to mean that no male could work with Betty alone. I had to correct that misconception quickly.

Monday came and so did the therapists. It was good to have them back. I felt much more comfortable when they were on the unit. Oscar came fairly early and he and the Occupational Therapist, Kim, dressed Betty in one of her patio dresses. She looked so pretty. It was wonderful to see her in a dress instead of a hospital gown.

The Speech Pathologist also worked with Betty. She reminded me that although Betty had a stroke on both sides of her brain, the right side of the brain had significantly more damage than the left side. Research has shown that the left side of the brain controls the speech in 97% of right-handed people. The pathologist had a box with all sorts of "tools" such as toothbrush, small clock, a ball and other items that she left in Betty's room. She instructed me to work with Betty during the day and on weekends.

During the therapy session, Kim, the Occupational Therapist, suggested that Jamie could assist her while she was working with Betty's motor skills. "Betty, take the ball out of my hand and give it to Jamie." Betty gave Kim a blank look. Kim explained again, "Betty, I want you to take the ball out of my hand and give it to Jamie." Betty glanced down at the ball, looked up at Kim, and then jerked her head in Jamie's direction as if to say, "She's right in front of you. You hand it to her yourself!" All of us got a big laugh and Kim decided to switch to another exercise.

In addition to working on Betty's motor skills, the therapists also worked on her cognitive skills. The therapist would hold up two objects, such as a water glass and a tissue box, and ask Betty to point to the water glass. Then they would hold up two different objects and repeat the exercise. The therapists worked diligently with Betty for quite some time and then let her sit in the large area outside her room.

After the morning session, I was concerned that Betty couldn't tell a toothbrush from a pencil and could not speak except with guttural sounds. I silently prayed that she would at least pick one correct object. I was concerned they were going to tell me she was not meeting her goals and we would need to leave. I did not realize we had just begun on a very long journey of bringing Betty back. It would be many weeks before she could select the correct objects. But I was a fast learner. I worked with her every moment I could.

When Dr. Pham came to Betty's room later that day, she told me Betty's CK test result was 50. I exclaimed, "50?" Dr. Pham assured me that was correct. "It can't be," I replied. "You need to get it repeated. It was 250 when she had the strokes and she has not had IVIG since then."

"I've already had it repeated and it is 50," was her firm reply. I'm sure she could see from my expression that I still did not believe the report. Then it hit me. God was answering my prayer. I had prayed for God to relieve the polymyositis so Betty could have therapy and that's what He had done. I was almost overcome with this great report.

After we had been at the Specialty Hospital approximately a week I summoned the courage to ask if I could bring Pepper, Betty's Sheltie dog, to see her. The supervisor questioned me about Pepper and then said I could bring her if I took her straight to Betty's room. She cautioned me that other family members and patients would probably want to pet Pepper and that would not be permitted. I agreed.

I brought Pepper to see Betty on the following Saturday afternoon. Pepper was so beautiful as she pranced into the hospital. People stopped to ask about her and commented on her beauty. I was so proud of her. I placed her on Betty's bed and told her that Pepper had come to see her. Betty immediately reached out with her right hand and began to stroke Pepper's fur. I asked, "Does Pepper's fur feel soft?"

"Yes."

I wanted to shout and cry at the same time. That was the most intelligible word she had spoken since June 13. I immediately shared with Betty's nurse what had happened. Smiling, she responded, "Bring Pepper every day you possibly can and let her work with Betty."

By Monday morning word had gotten around that Betty had spoken an intelligible word. The Speech Pathologists were ecstatic. I felt like a proud daddy whose child had just spoken his first word. However, I realized Betty's word was far more important. Kim remarked, "I know the speech is in there. We just have to get it out."

I naturally assumed my name would be next. About two days later Betty spoke her second word: "Oscar." There were times that she would call for Oscar. I cared for Oscar too so I did not become jealous. Had he been thirty years older I might have been concerned.

To prevent Pepper from being at the hospital for long periods, I would take her back home and then return to the hospital to be with Betty, a sixty-mile round trip. Because I had plenty of paid time off, I chose not to go into the office every day so I could help with Betty's rehab.

One afternoon Sam called and said he would be by the Specialty Hospital around 5:00 p.m. to take me to supper. I told Betty and she seemed pleased. Sam arrived and joked as usual with Betty and then he told her he wanted to take me out for awhile. She consented. As we were leaving, Sam informed me that we would be eating at the Olive Garden. I assumed we would eat and then he would take me back to the hospital.

After we ate he remarked, "I'll give you two choices. We can either go to the mall or Starbucks before I take you back to the hospital." Sam knew I love to shop and also that I like Starbucks. I knew Sam was a devoted family man and that it was a sacrifice for him to do this. Normally, he would have gone straight home from work and spent the evening with his family. I also knew he did not like to shop nor did he drink coffee. I told him it was not necessary to do either but he insisted. I chose the mall.

He did a good job of making me feel he was enjoying strolling around the mall as much as I was. It was a very relaxing evening and one that I badly needed. Even though it was difficult to leave Betty, I needed this kind of break to recharge my batteries so that I could be a better caregiver and advocate for her.

Almost every day there was a battle with the insurance company to keep Betty in the hospital. Betty had to show continuous improvement to qualify for more approved days. We were so fortunate to have excellent therapy personnel to help her reach her goals and document her progress. The case manager at the hospital was very helpful and encouraging. She would come to me and say, "I have Betty approved for three more days." I prayed that Betty would show greater signs of progress. I knew that her recovery was going to take a long time without a miracle. I soon learned that miracles happen with or without a timeframe. The fact that Betty could breathe and participate in the therapy was a miracle.

Betty had been at the Specialty Hospital for only a short time when some dear friends came to see her from Oklahoma. Sonny and Jane Terral lived across the street from us in Luling, Texas in 1966. We lost contact with them for many years and finally one day in 2001 they unexpectedly showed up in Taylor. We remained in close contact thereafter. They came to visit on a Sunday afternoon just as Gene and June Prater were leaving after one of their regular visits. I had become accustomed to Betty's condition and appearance and I did not realize for quite some time how the sight of her affected the Terrals.

Late that afternoon I explained that I needed to go home to check on Pepper. I thought they would leave also. However, they said they wanted to stay awhile with Betty. They shared with me later that because there was such a marked difference in Betty's appearance from their last visit that they were concerned she was actually near death at that time and wondered if I was in denial.

One morning as I entered Betty's room, her nurse was standing by her bed. As I greeted Betty, her eyes opened wide and with perfect speech she said in a very disturbed voice, "Wrong medicine! Wrong medicine and you check it out!"

I immediately asked the nurse what had happened and she denied knowing anything. I kept quizzing her and finally she said, "I was talking with another nurse about Betty's feeding tube and maybe she misunderstood." I demanded to speak to the charge nurse. Finally we determined the two nurses were discussing Betty's feedings and did not realize she could understand them. Apparently no error was made, but Betty had real concerns. As I walked outside the room, the Speech Pathologist exclaimed, "I heard her. I am so happy! Well, I'm not happy that she thought she got the wrong medicine, but I am so happy she spoke. I knew speech was in her. It will come out eventually."

Betty stayed in the Specialty Hospital for three weeks and continued to show slight improvement. We rejoiced with each positive sign.

The caseworker called me into her office and advised me that Betty would need to leave the hospital by July 29. My first thought was, *That is our 41st anniversary.* It had finally happened. The day I had dreaded had arrived. Ordinarily it would have been good news for Betty to be discharged on our anniversary. However, I had no idea what I was going to do. It was obvious Betty had not progressed enough to be transferred back to the Georgetown hospital for rehab.

"Do you have any suggestions for me?" I asked the caseworker.

"Actually, Betty qualifies for a skilled nursing facility," she responded.

I was ecstatic. "Great! Johns Community Hospital in Taylor has swing beds, which is the rural hospital equivalent of a skilled nursing facility."

Smiling, the caseworker said, "Let me check with the insurance company to see if that hospital is an approved provider."

I sat in the visitors' lobby and waited for her response. Soon she returned. "No, Johns Community Hospital is not approved but I have some facilities in Austin." She gave me the names, addresses and directions how to find them. She called the facility that appeared to be the most appealing and made an appointment for me that afternoon.

While driving to the facility, I prayed that God would let me know immediately when I found the right place. As I drove up to the facility, I observed that it was well maintained and the grounds were attractive. I was encouraged—until I went inside. The interior was very depressing and shabby. I wanted to run but I knew I needed to check out every possibility. The administrator toured me through the facility. The rooms consisted of two beds, two little bedside tables and two small wood chairs. He insisted I meet the Director of Nurses. As we entered her office, she was in the process of redoing her makeup and continued to do so as we talked. I didn't need to ask God if this was the place. I had known when I entered this was not the right place for Betty.

As I drove back to the Specialty Hospital, I continued to pray that God would provide the perfect place for Betty. I made it a point not to talk with the caseworker when I returned. I was afraid to tell her that I had not found a suitable skilled nursing facility.

There were serious doubts Betty would qualify for the Georgetown Rehabilitation Unit. However, the department director had been requested to arrange an evaluation for her.

The following morning the nurse from Georgetown Rehab came to assess Betty. She was the same nurse that had told Jamie that Betty was not qualified to stay in the Georgetown Hospital in June. I had asked Jackie McRoberts the director of Inpatient Therapy in Georgetown to be present also. After the assessment, they agreed that although Betty had made improvements, she did not qualify for rehab.

After they gave their report to the caseworker, the caseworker informed me that the insurance company had called her that morning and approved Johns Community Hospital in Taylor for skilled nursing. Somehow they had overlooked it the day before. My hopes rose. I was getting to the point of not being overly optimistic because I did not wish to be disappointed. I asked the caseworker to contact the director at Johns Community Hospital and see if they would take Betty.

The possibility of moving Betty to Taylor was exciting, not only because she would be located so much closer to our home but also because I had been the administrator at Johns Community Hospital from 1969-1986. Even though it had been many years ago, I still knew several of the hospital staff and administration. I liked the idea of a "home team" that already knew Betty and me.

The following morning, before I left for Austin, Barbara Maruska, whom I had known for many years and was now the nurse in charge of the skilled nursing unit in Taylor, called to tell me that she, the Director of Therapy, and the Nursing Director had met and agreed to "give it a shot." "We can't promise anything but we will certainly do all we can for Betty." Barbara explained that unlike most skilled nursing units, Betty's room would be in the same section of the hospital where the acute care patients were kept.

I asked, "Are they semi-private rooms?"

"Oh, we will put Betty in a private room. She certainly qualifies for one."

I was so grateful to hear a friendly voice speaking positively. I assured Barbara that we would start making arrangements for the transfer.

I was anxious to get to the hospital and share the good news with Betty. I asked the caseworker what we needed to do for the transfer. She assured me that she would take care of everything and not to worry. Dr. Pham told me that we would transfer Betty the following Monday.

As I entered Betty's room the next morning, I could hear gurgling sounds in her chest. I immediately contacted her nurse. "There's nothing wrong with her chest; it's perfectly clear," she snapped.

The therapists came and they were also concerned about the gurgling sounds. I assured the therapists that I had spoken with the nurse about the sounds and she insisted that Betty's lungs were clear. I assumed when Dr. Pham made rounds that she would examine Betty. However, Dr. Pham did not make her usual rounds. Betty continued to get worse and I continued to try to be diplomatic with the nurse. Finally, about 5:00 p.m., I could stand it no longer. I demanded that the nurse get the Cardiopulmonary Therapist immediately to assess Betty. When the therapist entered the room she immediately took charge. Hearing the gurgling in Betty's lungs, she ran from the room and I could hear her telling the ward secretary to page Dr. Pham immediately to come see Betty West. In the meantime the therapist began checking Betty's oxygen saturation and attempted to suction the mucous from Betty's throat.

Dr. Pham arrived quickly and asked me to step out of the room while they worked with Betty. I was angry with the nurse because she had ignored both Betty and me all day; however, I was more upset with myself for not doing what I knew should be done. As I sat in the day area of the unit I cried. After all Betty had been through it appeared that I was going to lose her now simply because I didn't push.

Soon a lady came to me and introduced herself as the hospital chaplain. I was certain the ward secretary had paged her. Placing her arm around my shoulder she asked, "May I pray for you?"

"Yes, thank you very much for coming."

When we finished praying, she commented, "I suppose you have a very large support group from your church in Taylor."

"No, most are working and the older friends don't drive in Austin."

After the chaplain left, the unit manager came to me. "Is there anything I can do?"

"No, I am very upset that something was not done for Betty earlier in the day and now it may be too late. It was very obvious there was something seriously wrong. The nurse ignored her for hours." The manager immediately went to her desk and picked up the telephone. I knew, from being in healthcare for many years, that the unit manager knew she should call someone from administration.

She was on the telephone briefly and came back to me. "The system director has offered to come if you would like to see her."

Sarcastically, I responded. "Oh no, I certainly don't wish to disturb her evening." I wanted to say "If I were the system director I would come to the hospital immediately." Betty had been a patient in the hospital for three weeks and I had never seen the system director. I had no idea who she was.

The unit manager continued, "I want to assure you that we will have an experienced RN with her tomorrow."

"What about tonight?"

"We are having a special ICU nurse come in to be with her tonight."

I thanked her and she assured me they would do anything within their power to help.

Eventually, Dr. Pham came from Betty's room and sat beside me. She placed her arm around my shoulder, "I believe she is going to be alright. I'm having a chest x-ray done to see if she has aspiration pneumonia. The Cardiopulmonary Therapist is going to have to suction Betty through the nose which is very unpleasant for Betty but we have to get those fluids out of there."

Dr. Pham then gave me advice that I had already known but seemed to have forgotten. "I know you are blaming yourself for what happened. Let this be a lesson to you. Betty is going to require months of treatment. You are her advocate. She cannot speak for herself; that is your job. In the future, when you know something is wrong, you must **speak up**. Here is my pager number. If the nurse won't page me, you do it. Remember, Louis, wherever you are, you are her voice. Don't ever hesitate to **speak up**. I do not believe that Betty has pneumonia but I will write an order for an antibiotic as a precaution."

I did not want to go home that night. However, the nurse assured me she would call if there were any changes. I also spoke with the Cardiopulmonary Therapist on the night shift and was satisfied that he would be able to take care of Betty.

After that incident, I questioned the advance directive. I knew that Betty did not wish to be resuscitated if there was no hope of recovery. However, selfishly, I knew I did not want to lose her. Again, I made a decision to always honor what I believed Betty would want whether it was my desire or not.

The next afternoon our grandson Bryan was supposed to go to a church camp. However, after he was already on the bus, he changed his mind and got off. He told his mother, "I'm going to stay with G-Pa." I was so glad that Bryan stayed. I knew he would be a tremendous help to me and we would be a comfort to each other.

Chapter 5:

Everybody Plays

♪♪

M onday came and Betty had recuperated enough to leave Austin. Many of the staff came to tell her goodbye. They had grown attached to her in a short while. Several commented about her sweet spirit and told her how much they had enjoyed her music. Many hugged me and wished us well, speaking positive words of encouragement. When the EMS personnel came, they asked if anyone would be riding with Betty. I told them "no." In a few minutes, Bryan asked if he could ride with G in the ambulance. The paramedics agreed that would be good. Bryan was ecstatic and held her hand as they made the trip back to Taylor.

As we entered the hospital in Taylor, I saw familiar faces. Several of my long-time friends from the office and nursing staff came to greet us. They were quite somber. They had no idea how improved Betty was in comparison to her condition immediately following the strokes. They would tell me later their thoughts were, "What does he expect us to do for her?"

Betty was admitted to room 205. My thoughts went back to over twenty-five years before when we opened the new Johns Community Hospital. Little did I dream at that time that the most important person in my life would be a patient in the facility with a very critical illness.

A few minutes after we arrived, a pleasant and friendly gentleman with a brown ponytail entered the room. "Hello, I'm Dr. Scott Farquarson. Everyone calls me Dr. Scott." I immediately liked him. He gave Betty a very thorough physical exam and asked several questions. Before he finished, the door opened and a giant of a man who literally filled the doorframe ducked his head to enter the room. Dr. Scott introduced him as Bill Robinson, Occupational Therapist.

Bill also began to assess Betty and read the notes that had been sent by the staff from the Specialty Hospital. After several minutes he commented, "I'm through with my part of the assessment. Other therapists will be by in a little while to finish the complete assessment." No one else came that afternoon.

The next morning, I went by to see Betty and then drove the twenty miles to my office in Georgetown. Later that afternoon, our daughter Dawn, who had driven up from Houston called. "Daddy, aren't they supposed to be doing therapy with mother?"

"Yes, why do you ask?"

"Well, a therapist came by and said that Mom was too sleepy to have therapy."

I was livid and my thoughts were not pleasant. Why did they think we brought her to Taylor? It certainly wasn't for her to sleep. Did they not realize that we had to get her ready to go back to Georgetown for actual rehab?

Although she was supposed to have rehab in Taylor, skilled nursing is not nearly as advanced as an actual rehab unit. If she did not show signs of improvement, she could not stay in skilled nursing either. She would have to go to a nursing home or I would have to make arrangements for her to stay at home with caregivers.

Although I have long-term care insurance, Betty did not qualify medically for insurance of that type. I would have to pay out of pocket for all of her care whether it was at home or in a nursing home. We would not qualify financially for Medicaid and I knew Medicare would not pay for care at home or in a nursing home except for some skilled nursing needs. I would be able to pay for her care for a few years, but what would happen after that?

I drove the twenty miles back to Taylor. I went into Betty's room and the nurse confirmed that no therapy had been done that day because Betty was too drowsy. I asked for the Rehab Director. "Mike is over at the outpatient therapy department. I can give you instructions how to get there." I immediately drove to the outpatient therapy office. I jumped from my car and stormed into the office.

I immediately confronted the astonished receptionist. "I'm Louis West and my wife is a patient in the hospital and I need to see the Rehab Director."

Trying to calm me she replied, "He is at a nursing home doing treatments and will be back around 5:30." I sat down to wait.

Soon Bill Robinson, the Occupational Therapist who had evaluated Betty upon her arrival at the hospital, came into the lobby and warmly greeted me. "Why are you here?"

"I'm here to see the therapy director."

"Is there something I can do for you until Mike gets here?"

"No, I want to speak with Mike."

Bill pursued the subject. Big mistake. I unloaded on him in the presence of the patients who were waiting for their treatments and the office personnel. Among other things, I told him that we did not bring Betty there to sleep but to have therapy. After I talked for at least five minutes non-stop, Bill invited me to come into another room and wait for Mike. I'm sure he wanted to get me away from the other patients and family members in the waiting room.

In approximately ten minutes Mike Thompson appeared. He asked how he could help me. I was most unkind. I unloaded on him, too. "Perhaps I made a mistake in bringing Betty here because she is not receiving therapy."

He attempted to explain. "Most families get upset with us if we make a patient work that is sleepy and tired."

I interrupted him, "You have probably never met a family member like me and you may never see another. Unless you begin therapy with Betty, I will transfer her to another facility."

"Will you give us another opportunity?"

"I will give you one more chance. I will also promise you that I will not be difficult to get along with if you work diligently with Betty. However, if you do not, I will be extremely difficult. I am embarrassed to say that I was the administrator here for seventeen years. I hope you can prove to me that the hospital still has an excellent rehab department."

Probably Mike and others assumed my anger was because Betty was suffering from a stroke. That was only partially the reason. The real reason was because I could still hear Dr. Pham's admonition to me, "You are her advocate. She cannot speak for herself. You must speak up." I knew Betty would want to be awakened.

Mike asked what they were supposed to do if they could not awaken her. "Get ice water, wet a cloth, and bathe her face until she responds. That is what the therapists did in Austin."

I was told several months later by Lisa Jeffery, who was one of the therapists, that when she heard about me, she thought, "Oh no, I'm working Saturday morning." Saturday, when Lisa came into Betty's room I was not there. She thought, "Well if I'm lucky I will be through and out before he gets here." She wasn't that fortunate. However, she said she was pleasantly surprised to discover that I was very nice and helped her with Betty's treatments. I never had to bring up that complaint again and all the therapists became like family to Betty and me.

I resumed working at the Georgetown hospital each day until about 2:00 p.m. at which time I would go to see Betty. The therapists tried to be encouraging but I could tell they felt like Betty was not doing well. Each day I would get a report on how she had done. Almost every day I was told they had to bathe her face in ice water and there was still very little response. After she had been in Taylor about two weeks, another problem arose.

One day during therapy, I noticed little blisters on Betty's back. Everyone who looked at the blisters had a different idea. Some thought they were shingles, and some thought they were caused by the air mattress she was lying on. I researched "shingles" on the Internet. From the description, it appeared that Betty had shingles. She had shingles a few years before in her ear. Fortunately she had gone to the doctor and he immediately had diagnosed the problem. He gave Betty an injection that solved the problem. He had cautioned her that had she been a little later coming in, the injection would not have helped. I was determined to talk with Dr. Scott about the blisters even though he had told the therapists that it was not shingles.

About this time, Barbara Maruska, the nurse in charge of the unit, notified me that we needed to have a family conference regarding Betty. How well I remembered the conference that we had in Georgetown.

The next afternoon, Dr. Scott, Lisa Jeffery (one of the Physical Therapists), Bill Robinson (the Occupational Therapist), Leslie (the Speech Pathologist), the director of nursing service, and Barbara Maruska met with me. The meeting was not as tense as the previous one. We discussed Betty's lack of progress. Barbara explained Betty would need to start making significant progress soon or the insurance company and Medicare would deny the claim. Dr. Scott was very supportive and suggested that maybe Betty was overly sedated. He said he would adjust her medications and see if that would help. Leslie, the Speech Pathologist, felt the therapists were expecting too much too soon. Bill understood but was concerned that progress was not happening. Lisa stated that she had seen some positive changes during therapy sessions. Barbara was concerned that we were going to use all of the skilled nursing days allowed by Betty's insurance. She suggested sending Betty to a nursing home for awhile. I disagreed. Dr. Scott summarized the discussion and stated that he believed if he could reduce some of Betty's medicines that she might progress.

Although this meeting was not as depressing as the Georgetown meeting, I was still disappointed. Dr. Scott assured me that he was positive Betty did not have shingles. This was a welcome relief. I did all I knew to do. Eventually the blisters disappeared.

After the meeting, I talked with God. I explained that I knew He had heard the conversation and that only He could help. I was very appreciative of Dr. Scott for wanting to give Betty more time. Leslie, the Speech Pathologist, explained that because Betty had a bilateral stroke, the therapists and nurses should not expect her to progress as quickly as a person with a single stroke that only affected one side of the brain. I appreciated Leslie for her concerns and respected her vast amount of knowledge. She also shared that it would probably be in the second six months after the stroke that Betty would get more speech.

As I walked back into Betty's room, I sat down next to her. She was apparently asleep. I silently prayed for her.

The next day as I walked down the hall towards her room, one of the therapists jubilantly called to me, "Betty did better this morning than any day since she has been here."

Almost immediately Leslie came around the corner of the hall grinning. "Betty stayed awake for her entire speech session today." I was elated and so thankful. God had heard and answered another prayer for me. He assembled a marvelous team of therapists, nurses, a speech pathologist, and a most competent and loving doctor for Betty.

That night after Bill finished Betty's treatment, I walked out into the hall with him. With a serious expression, he looked at me and said, "I know what you want, but it isn't going to happen."

Grinning mischievously, I responded, "Wait and see."

He replied, "I don't understand you. If I were you, I would be very angry with God."

I laughed. "Why? God did not cause this to happen to Betty."

"I know, but He allowed it to happen,"

Looking deeply into Bill's eyes, I quietly responded. "God's ways are not my ways. There are many times I do not understand His ways. However, I know that He has a plan for Betty and it will be good. I don't want to be angry with the only One who can help her." Our conversation appeared to be getting too serious for Bill, and at that time we said goodnight and he left.

The following days Betty was able to participate in the therapy. Her progress was slow, but sufficient enough that it appeared there would not be a problem with Medicare.

Although Betty's speech was improving, it was still very difficult to understand her. When she became more alert, she asked me repeatedly for something, but I just could not understand what she wanted. She repeated the same word to Jamie over and over and Jamie could not understand her either. We were all frustrated. We knew Betty needed something but we couldn't understand what that something was.

Dawn came for the weekend and Betty's eyes lit up. She stared directly into Dawn's face and repeated her request. Dawn got it. "You want your deodorant?" The relief on Betty's face was precious. As Dawn applied the deodorant, she reminded me, "Daddy, remember years ago Mom had me promise her if the day ever came when she could not take care of her grooming, which included plucking her eyebrows, I would take care of her." Betty knew that fashion-conscious Dawn would not disappoint her.

From that day forward, I made sure Betty always had deodorant and used the Estee Lauder Beautiful body powder she loved. Whenever Dawn was able to visit, she made sure Betty's nails were trimmed and her eyebrows were well groomed.

Betty always recognized me and I would talk with her as if she had never had a stroke. I told her any interesting news concerning our children, grandchildren and our friends. I talked with her about the weather and any topic that I believed would interest her. I would play the balloon game with her.

As part of her therapy, the therapists had her bat a balloon back and forth to help her eye-hand coordination. This was an enjoyable time and Betty was very good at it. The years she had spent playing tennis obviously helped her with this. She loved batting the balloon so that I would have to really reach for it.

Almost everyone who came into her room had to play the balloon game. No one was exempt. One morning when Dr. Scott came to check Betty she told him she wanted to play the balloon game. He tried to make excuses but she lowered her head and raised her eyes firmly to his. "Everybody plays." He reluctantly agreed. He very gently batted the balloon to her as if she were a five-year-old girl. With one swoop of her right arm she sailed it back to him. He missed it. He realized he was not playing with an amateur and did not have to make allowances. With a determined look, he increased the speed but was badly beaten by a bed-ridden lady who had sustained a bilateral stroke a few months prior.

Late one afternoon Betty and I were batting the balloon. As I stood at the end of the bed and slammed the balloon back to her, she had to reach far to the right to hit it. I felt badly that I had hit it too far to the right. However, the balloon sailed back to me and I missed it. I jokingly said, "You won't give up will you? You never quit until you win!"

She smiled her lopsided smile and replied, "That was good, Louis. Put it on the wall." Suddenly I realized the impact of those words. She wasn't about to give up on anything until she won the battle. Later at home I made a large sign and hung it in her room that proclaimed "Never Quit Until You Win."

Chapter 6:

The Queen

♪♪

B ill Robinson, the Occupational Therapist, appeared to be even more determined Betty would progress after his remark that I was not going to get what I wanted. He spent considerably more time with Betty in the evenings. I usually watched closely as he had her do various exercises because I knew that I might have to help with those when she went home.

One evening I was reading instead of observing. I was not really paying attention to his instructions to her. After awhile, he told her to show me what she could do. I put the book away. "OK, Betty, show Louis how you can lift that left leg." With his coaching she slowly lifted her left leg off the pillow about four inches. I was speechless and overcome with emotion. She had not moved her left side since the strokes. I bragged on both of them. Then he encouraged her even more. "Watch this." He touched her left arm and she began lifting it off the pillow. God was using Bill to reach our goals.

I expressed my appreciation to Bill again. I did not bring up our previous conversation and his pessimism. It was obvious that he was allowing God to change his attitude.

Betty was able to do these feats for a few days. After that period of time she was no longer able to move her left limbs without assistance. We never knew why she could no longer move her left arm and leg. It never seemed to discourage Betty. She had already accomplished far more than the doctors had believed possible.

As I had shared with Bill earlier, I do not understand the ways of God. I continued to trust Him and believed that He had a perfect plan for Betty and it would be good. Of course, I wanted her totally healed but if He chose not to heal her, He would still be God and I would trust and love Him.

It was good to see Bill giving credit to God when she would improve. He eventually started wearing a leather bracelet with WWJD on it. I asked what it meant. "What Would Jesus Do?" he replied quickly. God was continuing to use Betty to bring others to Him.

Although the walls of her room were made of painted cinder-block, we tried our best to make it look homey and comfortable. Bryan and Caitlin loved to win stuffed animals for Betty and we used those to decorate the room. The therapists hung signs with the day of the week and the date written on them. These signs kept Betty oriented to the passing of time.

Had I been able to see into the future, we would have decorated her room with pictures of our house, both inside and out, as well as pictures of our children and grandchildren. In addition to the cute animals and pretty pictures, Betty needed to be reminded of people and places that she had known before the strokes. Unfortunately I did not know that at the time, and we decorated her room the best we could.

The therapists' goal was for Betty to be able to take care of herself. Each day they sat her on the side of the bed to help her practice her balance and strengthen her core muscles. They continued to do the range of motion exercises. Other family members and I did the exercises with Betty when the therapists were not there. Sometimes the therapists would take her to the gym, which was on the other side of the hospital. They would put her on a tilt table to transfer her. She hated it and made guttural noises going down the hall to show her dislike. The tilt table was an important part of her therapy though. Using the table, the therapists were able to tilt Betty upright so that she was putting some weight on her legs.

Everyone at the hospital loved Betty. She began to regain her sense of humor and kept them laughing, even though her speech was severely limited. The therapists doted on her and called her "the Queen." Leslie, the Speech Pathologist, began coming three times each week to work with her. Bill worked with Betty during the day for his sessions and would come back at night and work with her again. He assured her that he had already punched out and was on his own time in the evenings. After a hard day of therapy, some-times Betty would hear Bill coming in the evenings and pretend to be sound asleep. She could not fool Bill. He would walk into her room and loudly tell her it was time to do more work.

It was obvious the therapists had taken on a challenge. Whether they collectively agreed to do all they could to rehabilitate Betty or whether it was each one silently taking on the charge, I never knew. They shared with me that at noon and during breaks their conver-sations centered on Betty and what she had done that particular day. I recognized very quickly God had sent an entire squadron of angels to minister to her.

The nurses as a whole were also very attentive to her. She never lacked for love or attention. While all of this was happening I con-tinued to play the Christian music and scriptures.

The hot days of summer began to turn into fall. Jamie came for Labor Day weekend. Betty was sitting in a large lounge chair beside her bed with Jamie and me sitting close to her. We were talking with her and she would respond as best as she could. For no apparent reason, Betty lightly kicked me on the leg. I said something to her in a joking tone. I then told them about when I was in high school and I was walking down the hall with a friend of mine. All at once someone kicked me in the seat of my pants. I turned around and no one was there. Because I'm a little slow at times, it took awhile for me to figure out that it had been my friend, Joanna Pettit, swinging her foot up from behind and kicking me with her heel as we walked next to each other. When I finished the story, Jamie and I laughed. Betty kicked me again and clearly said, "He can't figure out who did that either." Then she began to laugh.

One of the nurses heard us and came to see what was going on. At that time Betty had not laughed and had rarely smiled since the strokes. The nurse saw Betty laughing and ran to tell others of the miracle. Soon, other nurses came to the room hoping to hear Betty laugh. However, that moment was gone except in our memories.

That incident assured me that Betty's personality had not changed. Various doctors had warned me that after a stroke or other traumatic brain injury the patient's personality can be com-pletely changed. As Betty began to communicate more clearly, it seemed to me that she was the same person she had been before the strokes. After she demonstrated her wit that Labor Day, I was certain that she was still the same woman I had married.

Betty had been asking for our son, Mark. He was teaching at the Federal Law Enforcement Training Center in Georgia. We arranged for him to come for a short visit. Before he arrived, our good friend Tony Haley from Harlingen came. Betty thoroughly enjoyed her. Tony was still in town when Mark arrived.

Betty brightened when Mark entered the room. It was a particularly joyous occasion because he had not been home since the week before the strokes. The days passed too quickly and soon Mark and Tony were both gone.

One afternoon as I was sitting by her bedside, Betty quietly called me, "Louis?" I responded and stood beside her. "Tell me about it. Tell me about the stroke. Where was I when it happened?" Although she probably had heard the therapists and nurses use that word, it was a word that I had avoided since the emergency room. I did not know how she would react when she knew.

I said, "You want to know about the stroke?"

"Yes," she said quietly. "Tell me everything."

I began telling her about what had happened. I had to stop at times to cry. She would tell me it was okay and that I could tell her later. I wanted to finish what I had started. So amid tears, I described in detail all that had occurred since June 12. After I finished, she quietly asked, "What about the shot?"

I explained that she had slept most of the afternoon of the strokes. When her nurse would check her, she was apparently asleep. The "shot" must be given within three hours of the stroke to be successful. Because she was sleeping, the time of the stroke was unknown. It was not until the nurse discontinued the IVIG, that she realized Betty's condition.

TPA can also cause severe bleeding no matter when it is given. Therefore, doctors must weigh the benefits each time. She said, "I understand." I put my arms around her as best I could and cried. She was unable to have that release.

On Betty's birthday, September 25, I walked into her room and there was a long banner across the wall, "Happy Birthday Betty." It was very nicely done and Betty was very pleased. The hospital staff had arranged for it.

Our children and grandchildren sent cards and many staff members also brought cards. I gave her two pretty patio dresses and despite the fact she could not eat, it was a joyful day.

Therapy continued every day except Sunday. The therapists began teaching Betty to use her power wheelchair. She had been so adept at it before the strokes. However, at this time the controls presented a real challenge for her. The therapists were young and brave. It frightened me to see Betty wheeling around. She had told me before we married that as a younger person she had loved to drive fast. I think she was now attempting to relive those times with her chair. I cautioned the therapists about her steering and reminded them that the chair had cost over $6000. I suppose I thought the chair might be damaged but that Betty would not be injured.

One evening I came in and there was white paint on the side of the chair. I did not react well. I wanted to know which therapist had allowed it to happen. Betty could not tell me. Soon Bill Robinson, the Occupational Therapist, entered the room. Without a greeting I started fussing at him that someone had gotten white paint on her chair. After I finally stopped, he mischievously grinned and spoke, "Betty ran into the wall." That conversation abruptly ended. I determined that I would be more cautious before I started accusing someone again.

The power wheelchair posed other dangers. The therapists would sit Betty in the chair to give her an opportunity to get out of bed. It was important to allow her to change positions frequently. This stimulated her mentally, as well as increased her circulation and relieved pressure on her body to prevent bed sores. Many times I would visit with her while she sat in the chair. The first few times she was put into the chair, a mischievous twinkle would come into her eye and the fingers of her right hand would inch toward the controls. Unless someone moved quickly, the chair would screech to life and lurch toward the foot or shin of an unsuspecting visitor. It only took a day or two before the therapists and I realized that if we wanted to keep Betty stationary that we needed to tape down the controls.

One Saturday afternoon, I needed to go into Austin. I spoke with Ernie, her nurse, whom both of us loved and trusted. Betty had long ago gotten over her timidity with a male helping her. He assured me he would watch her closely while I was gone. When I returned a few hours later, the sight that confronted me upon entering her room was unbelievable. There were about six pillows thrown all over the room and she did not have a sheet over her. I was infuriated. How quickly I had forgotten my lesson about the wheelchair. I immediately turned on her call light and Ernie entered the room. I began chastising him for not watching her as he had promised. He tried to explain that he had just been in her room fifteen minutes before but I would not listen to his explanations. We got the pillows picked up and placed around her. Ernie apologized and left the room.

I thought to myself, "I'll bet that never happens again." In less than an hour, Betty began pitching pillows. I was amused but embarrassed. I knew I had to "eat crow." I picked up the pillows and placed them on her bed. I walked up to the nursing station and spoke to Ernie. "I'm sorry for what I said awhile ago. I know you take good care of Betty and I want to apologize."

"Did she pitch the pillows again?" he asked smiling.

"Oh yes," I replied. Hopefully this time I had learned my lesson about jumping to conclusions.

Betty and I had our share of confrontations with various nurses who still tried to give Betty medications by mouth. Although Leslie, the Speech Pathologist, had written a note in her chart in bold letters, "DO NOT GIVE ANYTHING BY MOUTH," it was obvious that some either could not read or would forget.

On one occasion, a doctor who was taking call for Dr. Scott argued with me that it would be okay to give some pain medications by mouth. Again, I stood my ground and was Betty's advocate. I tried to be nice and explain Betty's condition but could see that I was not convincing the doctor. Sternly I spoke again, "I am telling you, do not allow anything to be given by mouth unless the Speech Pathologist is present and I am holding you solely responsible for the consequences if you do."

"Well alright," she snapped. "I'll write the order." Even after this, I had to be on the alert with some nurses who still insisted on giving Betty medications by mouth. Eventually Dr. Scott ordered a sign to be placed near her bed, "Nothing by Mouth unless Speech Pathologist is Present."

Leslie, the Speech Pathologist, was excellent with Betty. She had Betty working on "Peter Piper Picked a Peck of Pickled Peppers." Early one morning before leaving for the office, I suggested we work on her speech. I asked her to repeat the one about Peter Piper. She started out with "Peter Piper picked a peck of pickled peppers. Where's the peck of pickled peppers Peter Piper picked?" She stopped suddenly and looking up with the twinkle in her eye and the smile that only she could give, suddenly stated very emphatically, "I never stole his peppers, did you?" Then she snickered. Each time I thought about it during the day, I laughed.

Throughout all the months after the strokes we received many cards and letters from friends and relatives. We also received many from total strangers who were friends of friends and relatives. I would read each of them to Betty. One day a beautiful bouquet of flowers was delivered. The card only read, "From your secret admirers." It was handwritten and I tried to determine who had written it. Being a highly curious individual, I finally discovered that Jo Lynne and Charley Williams had sent the flowers. Jo was my assistant for several years when I was the hospital administrator in Taylor. They are precious friends and I knew they were praying for Betty. A network of friends and relatives who provide support is crucial for the patient and family. It would be extremely difficult to get along without that care. I vowed if I ever knew a friend or relative who needed support that I would make every effort to fill the role. I understood now what the doctors meant when they would say to someone, "Betty has a large support group and her husband is the biggest supporter."

October 10 was my birthday. As I entered Betty's room on my way to work that morning, I noticed a large banner across the wall, "Happy Birthday, Louis." She smiled and said, "They made it for me." She was so proud she had been able to tell the employees about my birthday and they had done this for her. She had insisted a few days before that I buy a new coat for my birthday. To please her, I went to Austin and bought a nice coat. I wore it that morning so that she could see it. As I strutted around the room, pretending to be a model, she smiled.

We also had arranged for Betty to have a haircut that morning. Mary Dominguez, who had cut her hair for several years, was coming to the hospital to cut it for her. This would be her first haircut since the strokes.

That afternoon when I went into her room she handed me a beautiful birthday card and had tried her best to sign it. It was a card exactly like she would have picked for me. There was also an African violet on the little table for me. I asked who got the card for her and she said, "Mary." I explained that I would give Mary the money for the card and plant. Betty became somewhat upset and let me know not to do that. She then told me she had gotten the card herself from Wal-Mart, which was located within walking distance of the hospital. I asked how she got to Wal-Mart and she said that Mary and her husband had taken her. I asked how they took her and she replied, "In their van." I continued to quiz her. I assumed that Mary and her husband had a handicapped-accessible van and they had loaded Betty into it and taken her to Wal-Mart. I was not pleased that someone would take Betty out of the hospital without my permission.

I immediately went to the nurses' station and quizzed the nurses about it. One of them said, "That's her story and we're not interfering with it." I demanded to know the facts. The same nurse finally admitted, "Well, a guy named Sam came and helped her." Now I knew. Sam Schultz had come and helped her get the card. I promised the nurses I would not tell Betty that I knew the true story.

Later that evening as I was in Betty's room, Sam Schultz walked in, greeted me and then went over and kissed Betty on the cheek. "How're you doing?" he inquired.

"Fine," she answered. They acted as if they had not seen each other in weeks.

Sam told me he wanted to take me out to eat for my birthday. I agreed. We told Betty goodbye and that we would be back before bedtime. As we were walking out of the hospital, I shared with Sam that I knew he had been instrumental in helping Betty and that I would not let her know. I asked him how he had arranged it because his home was in Round Rock over twenty miles from Taylor.

Knowing my curiosity and that I would not give up, he finally confessed. "Well, I knew your kids were not going to be able to come for your birthday, so I figured I should help Betty. I came over last week and we made our plans. I drove over this morning and parked where you could not see my car. I waited until you left the hospital and then I came in with the card and plant."

Smiling, I replied, "Sam, I don't have the words to express my appreciation from Betty and me. No one else would have thought to do what you did. You are very special to both of us."

We went to the new restaurant in town that was in an old rail-road car and had a delightful dinner. What a friend!

The month of October went quickly. Leslie, the Speech Pathologist, made arrangements for Betty to get a modified barium swallow in the Round Rock Medical Center to assess her ability to swallow. The hospital in Taylor did not have the equipment to perform the test. The procedure was scheduled for 8:30 a.m.; therefore, I arrived at the hospital earlier than usual that morning. Leslie was already there, and Betty was dressed and ready for the ambulance. The crew arrived and transferred Betty to the stretcher. She was excited. The crew was great with her. I rode up front with the driver and the other paramedic sat in the back with Betty.

When we arrived at the hospital, Leslie was waiting for us. After I completed the necessary paperwork, Betty was taken to one of the radiology rooms. The radiologist and the therapist were very considerate and patient with Betty. Because Leslie did not work at that facility, she could not do the procedure but stood next to the therapist who did. They began to give Betty small spoons of thickened barium. My heart was beating rapidly. What if she couldn't swallow it? She did. I watched the screen as the barium entered her mouth and went down her esophagus into her stomach.

They gave her another spoonful of barium, followed by a pill coated with barium. Down the hatch it went. Thank you, God. There were a few minor challenges, but Leslie was elated.

Leslie explained it would now be safe to give Betty some foods by mouth if the foods were pureed. Previously she only had been allowed a few bites of ice cream given by Leslie. Betty would even be able to handle thickened juices, but not thin liquids such as water. Thin liquids posed a greater choking hazard.

Betty was exhausted when we returned to the hospital in Taylor. All therapy for the day was suspended. That did not deter the therapists from coming by and congratulating Betty on her exam.

The countdown began for the day when Betty would be transferred to the Rehab unit in Georgetown. The therapists became even more intense with her therapy. They did not want any questions about Betty being able to tolerate the increased therapy in rehab.

Three days before Betty was to be transferred, the rehab nurse from Georgetown came and did the assessment. She said there would be no problem for Betty to be transferred.

Chapter 7:

Squeaky Wheel Gets the Grease

♪♪

On November 5, Dawn's birthday and almost five months since the strokes, the ambulance came to transfer Betty to Georgetown. All the therapists came into the room and said their goodbyes and blessings. Nurses came and told her what a good patient she had been. Dr. Scott came and hugged her and told her how proud he was of her. He said again, "Your husband would not give up. You have indeed received a miracle."

As I followed in my van behind the ambulance taking Betty to Georgetown, I was reminded that we had come full circle. We left Taylor on the morning of June 12 for Georgetown. After the strokes, we went to Austin. We then returned to Taylor and now we were returning to Georgetown.

When we reached the Georgetown Hospital, we were taken directly to the rehab floor. Betty's large private room was ready.

Soon a nurse came and did Betty's assessment and paperwork. This assessment must be done when a patient is admitted to the hospital. A Speech Pathologist brought her a soft lunch and assisted her with eating. Even though they were nice and I was back in the hospital in which I worked, I missed the familiar faces and surroundings at the Taylor hospital. I began to be apprehensive. What if they expected too much of Betty? I would never forget the patient conference we had soon after the strokes. Now, Jackie McRoberts, the director of Inpatient Therapy, was on vacation. In the past I could always go to her if I had questions or concerns. Who could I turn to while she was out?

I went to the van to bring Betty's power chair upstairs. The easiest way to move it was to ride in it. As I reached the elevator, I heard a familiar voice behind me. It was Mary Walker-Chyle, wife of Valerian Chyle, MD who was medical director for the Cancer Treatment Center. Mary questioned why I was in a wheelchair. I explained that we had just brought Betty for rehab and that I was taking her chair to her room. Mary asked for an update on Betty's condition and told me to let her know if she could do anything for us. Then I proceeded upstairs.

Early that afternoon, a large bouquet of beautiful yellow and white daisies arrived. The enclosed card read, "From your secret admirers. Our prayers and thoughts are with you." I never knew for certain but had strong suspicions that the flowers were from the Chyles.

The rest of the day was uneventful. That evening there was a knock at the door. It was Bill Robinson, the Occupational Therapist, from Taylor. I jokingly said, "You've missed Betty already haven't you?"

With a grin, he replied, "Just checking to see that everything was going okay." He visited with Betty and then I toured him around the Rehab unit.

The next day, Thursday, was also uneventful. The therapists would get Betty into a geriatric wheelchair and see how long she could sit. I asked Betty if they were doing therapy and her reply was, "Not like in Taylor." I was frustrated and disappointed that apparently she was getting very little therapy and we had already been in rehab two days. I questioned the social worker that was managing her case. Her response was that the goal was to get Betty to the point that she could use her power chair at home.

That night as I drove home, I began to be apprehensive that anything was really being done for Betty. I knew I must do something as her advocate.

Friday morning, I sent the following email to Danica Sims, the director of outpatient therapy:

This is Betty's third day here and we are very disappointed with the lack of therapy. Since Jackie is not here, I will appeal to you. Very little is done except putting her into the chair. They do minimal range of motion with her legs but

Betty tells me it is very little. Obviously the range of motion with her arm is so little that she does not even classify it as therapy. She is accustomed to very aggressive therapy from the Taylor therapists. We are wondering where all this aggressive therapy is that we had been told about. We obviously did not bring her here to stay in bed and sit in a chair. I can tell you more frustrations if you wish to hear. I have decided that I am going to meet with her therapists today and find out why she is not getting therapy that she obviously needs. From what the social worker told me yesterday, they have set a goal of sending her home with the power chair. That obviously is not our goal. The left arm is ignored by nursing and therapy. At the other facilities we were told to keep it on a pillow in order to decrease tone. That is not done here. Disappointed? Yes.

Within ten minutes, I received the following email from Danica:

Jennifer and Sally will be contacting you. This will help them clarify goals for her. I know that the first day is just evaluation and there has only been one day of treatment. Some of that is just finding out what she is able to do. I know that they will work hard with her.

I had also sent the email to Sam Schultz. Within a short while, I received the following email from him:

You can call it whatever you want, "back to the basics," "blocking and tackling," etc.

Bottom line is this. You are her advocate. You have to be her voice. You have to be heard.

Squeaky wheel gets the grease.

Set your expectations and then communicate them with both the therapists and with Ron, the director. He needs to be involved too. Tell them that you expect to be kept apprised of her therapies and her progress.

Have you gotten her medical record from Taylor? Has it been requested? Certainly the therapists should see the Taylor therapists' notes. Tell them to arrange a call between some of her key Taylor therapists and the ones who will be seeing her here.

If you want weekend therapy, you better tell them and how much therapy you expect.

It's a whole new ballgame buddy. The Taylor game is over. Now you're playing Georgetown. Get back into the batter's box and hit another home run for that special partner of yours. Remember that SHE is counting on you.

You should map out your daily expectations for her stay and tell those who will control it. Make sure they know that you don't have unlimited days that you are here. Explain to them the continuum of care. LTAC to Taylor, and now that she is here this is when the most progress should occur.

I know that you are a great communicator. You can give this entire message in a motivational or rallying tone, but with an underlying expectant tone.

You've done the right thing so far by talking with Danica. Remember the trouble you get in with assuming. Be prepared to have to tell them EXACTLY and SPECIFICALLY what you want done each and every hour of the day.

Hope this helps.

Sam

About 9:00 a.m., I made my way up to the third floor rehab therapy office. All the therapists were present. Ron Weaver, the administrative director for the Rehab Unit was also present. I explained my frustrations and disappointments. They told me the plans they had for Betty on that particular day. It sounded as if she would be busy. However, I could tell that they did not believe that she would make a great deal of progress.

She was kept busy that day. I discovered very quickly that the spokespersons for the unit would be the Speech Pathologist and the psychologist. I never understood why these individuals were the ones who would be telling me what Betty was doing and when she would be leaving. As far as I could tell, all the psychologist had done was to spend a few minutes with Betty and try to convince her that she was depressed.

After a few days, the social worker also began to talk to me about how I planned to take care of Betty at home. I finally realized that they did not believe she was going to make a great deal of improvement. I was grateful that at least they never mentioned a nursing home to me.

Late one evening I was in my office and Dr. Anisa Godinez, the medical director for the Rehab Unit, came in. She was obviously upset and near tears. "I am so sorry that Betty is not making the progress that you expected."

I sincerely replied, "I do not blame anyone and it is certainly not your fault. You have worked very diligently with her."

Trying to smile, she spoke again. "May I hug you?" As she wrapped her arms around me, I wanted to cry but did not. She continued speaking, "Betty will be going home for Thanksgiving."

Those words sounded so final. This should have been a happy time for me but instead I was very concerned. What would I do with Betty? Who would I get to stay with her?

For the next several days, Dixie Wellhouse was Betty's Physical Therapist. She is an older lady and Betty loved her. Betty would do things for Dixie that she would do for no one else.

The Rehab Unit had an actual kitchen so that patients could learn to function in a kitchen much like home. Betty was obviously not able to participate in the cooking and cleaning like a few of the patients. However, the therapists would sit her at a table much like a home situation. They would place a mirror so that she could observe herself eating. The mirror made it easier for her to determine where her mouth was. Betty would state that she did not want the food even before tasting it. I asked why. She said she did not know what she had on her plate. Because all her food was pureed, everything looked the same except the color. I had to guess at what each food might be. I suggested to the dietitian that she put little labels on each food so that patients would know what they had on their plate. She said she thought it would be a great idea and they had never tried it before. The idea worked. Betty began eating well. Because she could not read the labels, we would tell her what she was eating.

One day after lunch I went to visit with Betty. I could sense she was unhappy. I asked what was wrong. "They wouldn't let me eat my ice cream."

"Why?"

"Because I didn't eat all of my lunch."

After inquiring, I discovered it was her Speech Pathologist that had refused her. This woman might have been an excellent thera-pist but in my opinion did not have a clue about taking care of an adult stroke patient. I wanted to report her to Jackie, the Director of In-patient Therapy, but I thought better of it. I knew we would be leaving soon and that the therapist was pregnant and did not plan to return after the birth. Now I was ready to make plans to take Betty home. If the lady had just realized how long we had worked so that Betty could eat ice cream, maybe things would have been different. Those who work with adult stroke and head injury patients should realize they are not children and should treat them as adults.

The last week in the unit, Dixie Wellhouse, the Physical Therapist, worked diligently to teach me to transfer Betty from the wheelchair to the bed and from the bed to the chair. I learned very quickly that it was not as easy as it appeared. Dixie showed me how to use the sliding board but also let me do a few pivots with Betty. Pivots were more difficult. Because Betty did not put weight on her feet and legs, I was actually lifting her.

The social workers pressed me about how I was going to care for Betty at home. I told them I planned to hire a caregiver. They gave me names of individuals in the Taylor area. Unfortunately, I knew very few of them and the ones I knew, I did not want to care for Betty. The caregiver would be one of the most important members of Betty's team.

I contacted a lady and had her come to the house for an interview. She had been sitting with someone who had recently died. I realized very quickly that although she was apparently a nice lady, she was not someone who would be able to care for Betty.

I also called the hospital in Taylor and told them I was looking for someone and to contact me if they knew of anyone.

The following night as I was driving home, I prayed candidly. I learned many years earlier that I can depend upon the scripture, "God will supply all my needs according to His riches in glory by Christ Jesus. Philippians 4:19. I stressed to Him that I needed a caregiver quickly.

I had been home about five minutes and the telephone rang. I answered, "Hello."

"Hi, I'm Pam White and my daughter, Christy, who is a nurse at the hospital, told me that you need someone to help with your wife."

After asking a few questions, I learned that her husband was a paraplegic having sustained a spinal cord injury in an auto accident several months prior. She had been his caregiver and now he was able to stay home alone. She transferred him from a chair to the bed and back. She was accustomed to bathing him and provided complete care. She shared that she also worked weekends in Austin with an elderly lady. I agreed to an interview the following Saturday night after she returned from Austin.

The following week Dr. Godinez called and said she had contacted Dr. Fox to see Betty since he had not seen her for several months. She asked him to contact me and set a mutual time for the evaluation.

That evening Dr. Fox paged me. I returned his call. He asked, "When will it be convenient to visit with you and Betty?"

I replied, "Just give us a time that is best for you."

"Will Saturday at about 1:00 p.m. be okay?"

"Great." I realize I had missed talking with him. Dr. Fox is a role model for doctors of any specialty.

Saturday afternoon about 12:45, Betty was eating her lunch and I heard Dr. Fox at the nurses' station asking for Betty's chart. I walked out and greeted him. "She is eating but you're welcome to come in the room."

"I just want to review her chart. I'll be in when she finishes."

In about five minutes he walked into the room. Although the nurse assistant was helping Betty, Betty was actually feeding herself. Dr. Fox walked over to the bed and Betty extended her right hand, "Hello, doctor. Thank you for coming to see me." It was a "Kodak Moment." The expression on Dr. Fox's face was of complete surprise and it was apparent he was delighted. He made small talk with Betty and then continued to review her chart while she ate. She finished shortly and the nurse assistant left the room.

Dr. Fox expressed his amazement with her progress, "Betty, I have been so concerned about you. We know now that the stroke was caused by the Gamma Globulin. I have been trying to determine how we were going to treat you now that you cannot have Gamma Globulin. Now, as I look at your chart, I see that you are pain free with just a Duragesic patch and your CK is perfectly normal. I will have to tell you that I cannot give you a scientific answer as to what has happened with you."

Betty raised her right hand and said, "It's God."

Dr. Fox smiled and said, "I agree. You have received a miracle."

As he continued to visit with her, he laughed and said, "Betty, as I came into the room, I intended to ask you simple questions such as, 'Do you know where you are? What day is this? Is the sun shining? What is your name?' It is obvious by your greeting and the way you handle that right hand that I don't have to waste our time with such trivial questions."

He visited with us for over an hour. It was moments like this that I felt so inadequate in expressing my appreciation to him. I did not think of him as just Betty's doctor but as a close friend who had given of himself to help Betty and me. As he prepared to leave, I told him that it was customary to take a picture of those who had been especially helpful to Betty. Betty had made that request for some time and wanted to be included in the picture with the individuals. Dr. Fox's response was, "I will have my picture made if you will let me do the posing."

"That will be fine. Just let me know when you're ready."

He walked around to Betty's right side and picked up her arm as if she had won a boxing match. "I want my picture made with the champ. Betty is truly a champion."

Saturday night Pam arrived as scheduled. When I met her at the door she radiated a countenance that I knew only God could give someone who had been through what she had. We visited for awhile and agreed that she could work temporarily to determine if caring for Betty was something she would want to do on a full time basis. "We will be bringing Betty home next Wednesday and I will need for you to start the following Monday morning." She agreed. Home Health therapists would be here also and I planned to take off work for the week. If necessary, I could be off longer.

I was excited to tell Betty about Pam and she agreed that it appeared God had answered my prayer.

As the day for dismissal came, I became more confident. On the day before dismissal, one of the nurses showed me how to test Betty's blood sugar and how to give her fluids and medicines through her peg tube. I had seen them use the peg tube for months but never imagined I would need to know how to use it. The most difficult thing I had to learn was how to put a brief on Betty. I also had to learn to empty the catheter bag and clean it. Although I had done these procedures many years before when I worked as an orderly and medical technologist, it was quite different when I realized I would need to perform them for my wife.

Chapter 8:

Getting Equipped

ℐℛ

A few months before the strokes, we had made an application to a Texas state agency to make our van handicapped accessible to accommodate Betty's increasing disability as a result of the polymyositis. I had no idea that there was an agency that would assist with this unless you were destitute. However, when I began seriously checking out various options, the owner of one of the "handicapped" stores told me that help was available through the state agency. If you find yourself faced with this situation, I recommend finding a reputable company and ask for references before proceeding further. Just because a company does a large amount of advertising does not necessarily mean they are the best company to assist you. Texas had a long waiting list. The goal is to get people back into the community.

We had a lift in the rear of the van that we used to raise and lower Betty's empty power chair prior to the strokes. However, she was still mobile to some degree at that time. The plan was to lower the van so it would be simple to get Betty in and out. When we first made application, she was number 100 on the list. Very few accommodations were made each month. Periodically we would check the status and her number was still high on the list. Therefore, when she was discharged from rehab, we had no way to transport her. The approval process often took as long as a year, so the van was not yet handicapped-accessible. I was concerned as to how we would bring Betty home. The social worker told me there was a taxi company in Austin who had handicapped-accessible cabs. She made the arrangements for a cab to be at the hospital at 2:00 p.m. the day before Thanksgiving.

A few days earlier the durable medical equipment company had brought Betty's bed, Hoyer lift, and other necessary items and put them into place at the house in Taylor. I had made a thorough inventory as to what we would need. I bought a new extra-wide recliner so that Betty could sit next to the grandkids when they were visiting. I also bought a baby monitor so that I would be able to hear her at night from my bedroom. I realized that I would need a good blender in which to puree her food and extra-long twin sheets for her hospital bed.

When the bed arrived, I thought the bed looked very high in comparison to the hospital beds and wondered if I would have a problem transferring her. In hindsight, I should have said something right away, but I was not sure. I assumed that the durable medical equipment company personnel would know what was needed. That was a big mistake. Never assume anything. My friend Sam had warned me many times about my assumptions. I might learn some things quickly but not in this instance.

Wednesday came. Betty was happy but I sensed that she was a bit apprehensive. I had no idea of all the thoughts that were going through her mind.

We went to the lobby about 1:45 p.m. I had asked Jamie to come from Houston because I did not want to be at home alone with Betty. Dawn, Bryan and Caitlin would be coming late Wednesday night from the Dallas area. The appointed 2:00 p.m. hour came and no taxi. Time continued and still no taxi. A nurse assistant stayed with us in the lobby. She went back upstairs and asked the nurses to call the taxi company. When she returned, she reported there had been a bad car accident on IH-35 and the cab was delayed. Finally at almost 3:30 we saw him drive up. He apologized and told us that he had taken the side roads to get around the collision.

The taxi driver was competent and courteous. I learned as we drove towards Taylor that he owned the vehicle. About half way to Taylor, Betty became very restless. I asked her what was wrong and she said the belt was too tight. Thinking it was the seat belt, the driver said he could do nothing about it and she would just have to tolerate it. She kept telling me the belt was too tight. I continued telling her that it had to be tight in case of an accident. She finally made me understand. It was not the seat belt but the gait belt that we had put around her waist to help us transfer her from the bed to the wheelchair that was too tight. We had tightened it when we took her to the taxi and forgot to loosen it. I felt guilty for being so careless with her. I should have checked all the belts when we put her in the taxi.

When we got to the house, Betty did not recognize it. She kept insisting that this was not her home. I wheeled her into the house, hoping that the familiar furnishings would jog her memory, but she had no recollection of anything. This was traumatic for me. I can only imagine what it was like for her. She had been so excited about coming home, but home was not a place that she remembered. I began to get some idea of the damage the strokes had caused to her brain.

If we had placed pictures of the outside and interior of the house in her hospital rooms after the strokes, would she have remembered the house? I don't know, but it seems likely that it would have helped her. We just had no way of knowing that this part of her memory had been lost.

As Jamie and I took Betty into her bedroom, it was very obvious the bed in Betty's room was much higher than the hospital beds I was trained to transfer her on. The mattress was much thicker and presented a real challenge for getting her into bed. Jamie and I worked with the sliding board but finally decided I should just attempt a pivot. This was not easy. It took Jamie's assistance to get Betty into the bed. I knew we would need a new bed but also remembered the next day was Thanksgiving and everything would be closed.

Dawn, Bryan and Caitlin came that night. Betty was delighted to see them. Dawn brought some pies that she had made for Thanksgiving. We were prepared to have a good Thanksgiving despite the conditions. We had so much for which to be thankful.

The Home Health nurse came early Thanksgiving morning and made her assessment of Betty. She advised they would be making frequent visits for awhile until Betty was stabilized.

Dawn and Jamie prepared a delicious lunch. We set the table in the dining room and fixed a place for Betty in her wheelchair. When the food was ready, we got out the new blender and attempted to puree some green beans for Betty. The green beans swirled into the bottom of the blender and stuck under the blades. Pureeing food was not as easy as we had thought. The blender did not work to puree small amounts of food like Betty needed. We did the best that we could but we knew we needed another solution. It would have been helpful if the Rehab Unit had included a course on the proper pureeing of food.

At lunch I wheeled Betty to her plate. Almost immediately, she vomited. I felt so sorry for her. We took her back to bed and finally got her situated. I had no idea why she had gotten sick. I assumed it was the stress of coming home. However, she continued to be nauseous. I called the Georgetown emergency room and the charge nurse told me she would get the doctor to prescribe some Phenergan for the nausea if we could come pick it up. Because it was Thanksgiving, all the pharmacies in Taylor were closed. Dawn graciously drove to Georgetown and picked up the suppositories. The suppositories helped Betty get over the nausea. It is difficult to anticipate all the needs for patients when they are dismissed from the hospital. Therefore, I recommend that the family members speak candidly with the doctor, particularly about nausea, if their residence is more than five miles from the hospital.

Dawn, Bryan, Caitlin, and Jamie left for home on Friday. That afternoon Betty became very nauseated again and I knew something was seriously wrong. I checked her blood sugar and it was 45. I panicked. Instead of giving Betty some sweetened apple juice by the peg, I called 911. I had never called that number before. The paramedics came quickly and rechecked her blood sugar. They got almost the same results as I had. Because I had been a med tech years before, I felt confident of my results. I told the paramedics that I would give her some apple juice by peg and recheck it. I did this and very soon her blood sugar had risen to almost normal and she appeared fine. They left and assured me that I was correct to call them.

I began to check her blood sugar quite often after that to make sure it was within normal limits. Within a few days, it was obvious she did not need medicine to control her blood sugar. It had returned to normal and never gave her any more problems. Before discontinuing the medicine, I talked with Dr. Shallin, her internist, and he agreed to discontinue it. God had answered another prayer.

The following day, my sister Laverne and her husband Dorris came from Denton. They not only came to visit but also brought boxes of goodies. Weldon and Emma Jo, my brother and sister-in-law, had sent so many good treats, including fried apricot pies. Emma Jo is the champ in making pies of any kind. Laverne and Dorris were so helpful that weekend. The love they showed Betty and me was immeasurable.

Monday morning after Thanksgiving, Pam White came to start her care-giving duties. Soon the therapists arrived to begin Betty's therapy. They worked diligently with her and told me they wanted to teach her how to dress herself and use the bedside commode. They also said they would teach Pam and me to transfer Betty and they would contact the durable medical equipment company about the mattress. They also discovered that the Hoyer lift that we had would not work properly. This meant they had no way to get Betty in and out of the bed. The bed was too high to safely do a pivot.

A week went by and we still did not have a suitable mattress for Betty and the Hoyer lift that was brought was too wide to go through the bedroom door. Betty had to stay in bed the entire time because we could not transfer her. These experiences taught me that when equipment was brought to the house I needed to test it to make sure it was something we could use before I let the company personnel leave the house. We never did receive a suitable mattress from the durable medical equipment company. Eventually, we got a working Hoyer lift and I got a suitable mattress from the Georgetown Hospital.

After the first week of Home Health Therapy I overheard the Physical Therapist say that they were going to dismiss Betty. I asked her about the statement. She said their goal had been to help Betty learn to dress herself and use the bedside commode but they were not being successful. I told her those weren't exactly my goals. She asked me about my goals. I told her that eventually I wanted Betty to be able to walk. She said, "Well, then we need to change our goals." I was so frustrated that the therapists had wasted a week trying to get Betty to learn to dress when that was not important to me at all. I wanted Betty to walk. Hopefully the therapists learned to include the patient and family in setting goals.

The therapists asked me to place a large mirror at the end of Betty's bed so that she could see herself in the mirror. Fortunately we had a mirror in the closet. I began to get the tools to hang it. Betty asked, "What are you doing?"

"The therapists want me to put the mirror at the end of your bed so you can see yourself."

"I don't want a mirror." I tried to explain that it was necessary.

She responded, "Louis, this is our home. It does not belong to the therapists. Do not put that mirror on the wall." I should have picked up some clues to alert me to the fact that Betty felt she had no control even in her own home. I learned that later. I should have included her in making decisions that affected her or our home.

The therapists began working with Betty to get her to stand at the kitchen sink. This was very difficult to do. It was not only hard for Betty but also difficult for the therapists. They taught me how to do this also. If Betty "stood" for thirty seconds I was delighted. We teased Betty that if she stood long enough at the sink that she could do dishes.

No one ever suggested that we get a standing frame for her. It was many months later that I asked about getting a standing frame. I discussed it with Jackie McRoberts, Director of In-Patient Therapy at the Georgetown Hospital. She thought it would be a great help to Betty. The doctor wrote the order and we had no problem getting the insurance company to pay for it. It was a great help to Betty. We put the frame in a large room that we did not use. We would put Betty into her wheelchair and roll her into the room where the frame was. The frame had belts that we hooked on to a "vest" that we had placed on Betty. We used a lever to lift Betty into a standing position. We would time her to determine how long she was capable of standing. It was excellent for her circulation and also helped the muscles in her legs. Her weight was on her legs but with the straps attached securely there was no danger of her falling. We always stood close to her to make her feel confident and safe.

After a few weeks, the therapists discontinued all therapy except for speech. However, Pam and I performed range of motion exercises with Betty and practiced her balance by sitting her up on the bed and leaning her from side to side. We faithfully exercised Betty every day. I was not giving up.

Chapter 9:

The Daily Routine

☙❧

P am and I entered into a daily routine of caring for Betty. When I woke up, I would go into Betty's room and she would usually be awake. Through her peg tube, I would give her the medicines that needed to be given on an empty stomach. Then I would check her blood pressure, pulse, and other vital functions to make sure that everything was within normal range. Next I would turn her body onto her side or back (depending on the position she had slept in) to prevent pressure sores.

When Pam arrived, she would fix Betty's breakfast. Betty liked Cream of Wheat with fresh fruit pureed and mixed into the cereal. I would puree batches of fruit to keep in the refrigerator for Betty's breakfast. Pam would sit Betty up in bed and Betty would feed herself from an over-bed tray table. On the table was a mirror so that Betty could watch herself as she ate. I eventually bought large plastic aprons to fasten around Betty's neck and cover her clothes. These aprons were easy to clean and had large pockets at the bottom that would catch falling food.

After breakfast, Pam would crush Betty's medications that required a full stomach and "feed" them into the peg tube. Then Pam would sponge-bathe Betty and put lotion all over her skin. Betty's skin was fragile and the lotion not only moistened her skin, but the application stimulated Betty's circulation. During the sponge bath, Pam would check Betty for pressure sores.

Part of Betty's grooming regimen included brushing her teeth. When Betty first came home from the hospital, at the instruction of the rehab staff, I bought an electric toothbrush for her. She hated it. I did not realize how irritating the sound and the vibration were for her until she asked Dawn to hide it from me. From then on, we went back to a normal toothbrush. Another lesson learned.

Keeping Betty's hair clean was a challenge because she could not shower. Occasionally, we would back her wheelchair up to the kitchen sink to wash her hair. We also used dry shampoo powder that we could brush into Betty's hair to keep it clean between washings. Whenever she needed a haircut, we would have a stylist come to the house to cut and style her hair.

After the bath, Pam would dress Betty for the day. Unless Betty didn't feel like it, we always dressed her in regular clothes so that she would realize that it was daytime. We knew she would feel better if she was dressed and groomed well. Before the strokes, Betty never went anywhere without lipstick. Once Betty was home, we put lipstick on her every day. I became quite the lipstick expert.

If the weather was nice, Pam would transfer Betty from the bed into a wheelchair and take her outside for a walk around the neighborhood. We always made sure that Betty was wrapped warmly and protected from the sun with sunglasses and a hat with a brim. We also put sun block on her face and hands. Betty's right leg would flail involuntarily, so we used an ACE bandage to secure her leg to the wheelchair. This prevented her from being injured because sometimes her leg would flop out and hit the wheel of the chair or drag on the ground. She did not like the ACE bandage but I assured her that it was only for safety purposes.

Betty loved these walks. She gave her regal, queenly wave at all of the cars that drove by and the people in their yards. If they didn't wave back she would say, "They didn't wave." For the most part though, people that saw her on a regular basis would stop and say hello and visit with her for a bit. Many of the healthcare workers had referred to her as the social butterfly because she was always so friendly with everyone. Betty liked to vary the route of her walks so that she could see different sights and different people. Before the strokes, she had enjoyed driving country back roads and it was apparent that her love of exploration had not diminished.

After a walk, Pam would transfer Betty back into bed and work with her range of motion and balance. Then Pam would turn on a Gaither Family DVD for Betty to watch. Betty loved the Gaithers. We had every DVD that they had made and we both enjoyed watching them over and over. If a Gaither video was not playing, Betty enjoyed listening to other Christian music CDs. Unless Betty was sleeping or visiting with someone, we kept her surrounded by joyful sounds.

For lunch, Pam pureed a meal for Betty. Betty had the option of eating lunch and dinner either in her bed or at the dining table. Very often, she chose to eat at the table. She didn't like for people to watch her eat, so if she had visitors, she would eat in her room.

The first week that Betty was back from the hospital, one of the therapists told me to use a hand blender to puree Betty's food. This tip was a Godsend that I wish had been imparted to me before I brought Betty home. Using the hand blender, we easily pureed small amounts of food. Plus, it was easy to clean. It can be purchased at most stores that sell kitchen supplies.

Through trial and error, I discovered that I could puree anything that I made for myself to eat and feed it to Betty. All I needed to do was to add extra liquid. For example, if I made a roast, I would add extra gravy and puree the roast for Betty. Mashed potatoes and pureed green beans were a staple. If I made enchiladas, I would add extra enchilada sauce and/or beef or chicken broth and then puree. I would cook a steak for her and puree it in hot beef broth. I used the broth because it was more nutritious than water and had more flavor. In this way, almost anything could be pureed and I didn't have to make special food for Betty. Also, she could still enjoy the food that she loved.

On one occasion I decided to make lasagna. The recipe called for eight layers. It took almost all of one Sunday afternoon to prepare it. Even though it was delicious, I decided it wasn't worth the effort. I would rather have spent that time with Betty. After that I cooked frozen lasagna and pureed it with extra tomato sauce or broth. On one occasion a visitor was discussing food with Betty. Betty replied, "Louis is a good cook and he has no fear. He will try anything." There were many times that I would bring Betty into the kitchen when I was cooking. I would ask for her opinion to make her feel a part of what I was doing. She also was an excellent cook and often would tell me how to fix a certain dish. On occasion I would call June and Gene Prater and ask them to come for lunch or dinner. They never refused the invitation as they were usually planning to come for a visit anyway. June is an excellent cook but doesn't really enjoy cooking. She is too busy helping other people with their needs, and so is Gene.

After lunch, Pam would give Betty her noon medicines. Then, if Betty felt well, Pam would use the Hoyer lift to move Betty from her bed into her recliner in the living room. Although Betty had not had any bad experiences with the Hoyer, she was always afraid of falling. Many times she made a strange sound to show her fear and dislike. After she was in her recliner, she forgot about the unpleasant sensation of transferring her from the wheelchair to the recliner. Moving her back into the wheelchair was a greater challenge. If Betty had ever known how I dreaded that process for fear of letting her slide out of the chair, she probably would have always refused. I never let her slide out of the chair but there were times that I had to use every muscle in my body to keep her safe. Usually I wore a short-sleeved shirt and shorts when caring for her. Often visitors were present when I did the transfer. Sometimes I heard them remark to each other, thinking I could not hear, "Look at the muscles in his legs." Okay, I will admit that made me feel macho. I would have much rather to have developed those muscles at the gym rather than lifting Betty. However, I never complained about caring for her. I felt it was a precious privilege to do so.

In the living room, Pam might read to Betty or just visit with her. Sometimes a visitor would come by. If Betty wanted to, Pam would take her for an afternoon walk or just take her to sit outside. We were always careful to give Betty as much control as possible. We asked her what she wanted us to do, rather than telling her what to do. This was very important because she had so little physical control. We wanted her to feel like a consenting adult rather than an invalid or a child.

If Betty stayed in bed, Pam or I would turn her every hour or so to prevent pressure sores. It was amazing how quickly and easily these sores would appear and in the most unexpected places. She had a bad pressure sore on the bottom of her left heel. The therapist worked on this pressure sore and we also propped her left ankle up on a pillow to relieve the pressure.

I usually arrived home by 5:30 p.m. Pam would leave at that time and I would begin Betty's evening routine. I fixed Betty's supper for her and visited with her while she fed herself. After we both had eaten, I would put on a Gaither video for her or she would doze while I did laundry or other housework. I kept the baby monitor on in her room so that I could hear her if I was on the other side of the house.

Sometimes I would transfer her into the living room so that I could play the piano for her. One of her favorite songs for me to play and sing was *Have I Told You Lately that I Love You*. She also enjoyed *Joy Comes in the Morning*.

At her bedtime, I would transfer Betty back into her bed, undress her, and put on her nightgown. I made certain that all her clothes were pretty. I had shopped for her since we had married. Any time we transferred her or dressed her was a good opportunity to sit her on the side of the bed and work on her balance. After she was dressed for bed, I washed her face with a damp washcloth and brushed her teeth. I also put lotion on her to protect and nurture her skin. Then I administered her bedtime medicines. I always prayed with Betty before I turned out her light for the night. We had bought a touch-lamp so that she could turn a light on and off herself with her right hand, but she never had the motor control to actually use it.

On the weekends, I cared for Betty by myself. Jamie came often and Dawn came whenever she could. It was always good to have the extra help. I would cook some of her favorite foods during the weekend and freeze them. She was not hard to please but always complimented whatever I cooked.

Soon after we came home from rehab at the Georgetown Hospital, we attempted to attend our local church. Charley and Jo Williams, our dear friends, would rent the local hospital's handi-capped accessible van and take us to our church. At that time our van was not handicapped accessible. However, it was difficult for Betty to sit in her motorized chair for long periods of time. After a few trips, we gave up on that idea. For the first few months Betty was at home we had very few local visitors including church friends. This bothered me but it did not seem to bother Betty. Because we were unable to attend church, I longed for Christian fellowship.

I always prayed with Betty before she went to sleep. She had been such a prayer warrior and I knew even though she could have positive thoughts of God, she missed having the ability to verbalize her praises. We always prayed for the people serving in the military. I never told her of all the bad things that were going on in the world. I knew it would trouble her greatly. She had enough to be concerned with now.

Christmas is my favorite time of the year. I was so thankful Betty was home. As a special gift to Mark and Cheryl I told them we would fly them home if they could make the arrangements. Betty was the one who made that suggestion to me. It actually was more of a gift to us than it was to them. Cheryl and the children had not seen Betty since the strokes. Soon after my proposal to them they confirmed they could come. I also told them they were free to visit with Cheryl's family as well. We had an extra vehicle they were welcome to use.

It was always my job to decorate for Christmas. It was especially fun because I would bring Betty into the living room and play Christmas music while I decorated. The house was totally decorated when Mark and family arrived. It took portions of three days to get all the decorations up.

Time passed quickly and Christmas arrived. Our children and grandchildren were all with us. I didn't have to cook. Cheryl, Dawn, and Jamie took care of all the food. Betty appeared to be so happy.

Several months after we came home, we had a call from our church asking if we would like visitors. That was a welcome call. Steve and Trish Sorensen started coming to visit every Wednesday night. This was a wonderful time each week. They were so helpful and a blessing to both of us. Trish, a hair stylist, eventually began to style Betty's hair. Also, Ron Neel and Joyce Israel would visit. Betty loved for them to sing for her. Kathy Zrubek also would visit and read scriptures to Betty. June and Gene Prater who lived in Georgetown came almost every weekend and sometimes during the week. I determined during this time that if in the future I ever knew of someone who could use a visitor, I would make every effort to visit.

In late February of 2003, Lisa Jeffery, one of Betty's therapists in Taylor, called and asked if she could come by after work. We were delighted to see her. She visited with Betty for awhile and finally stated her main reason for coming. She said that she had agreed to run in a marathon for the American Stroke Association in June in Hawaii. She told Betty that she had made such an impact on her life that she would never be the same person again. Therefore, she wanted permission to run the marathon in honor of Betty. Her goal was to raise $5,000 for the American Stroke Association. Naturally, both Betty and I were pleased and Betty gave her permission.

Lisa had never run a marathon before. In fact, she was not even a regular runner. As she was training, when she started thinking, "I can't do this," she would think of Betty and think, "Yes, I can do this!" and keep running. She made frequent visits to tell us about the progress she was making in preparing for the run and also raising the money. She did well with both.

In March of 2003, our good friends Mildred Fulfer and Tony Haley came from Harlingen. We were delighted to have them. They were very encouraging to Betty and me. When you are confined to your home almost continuously, it is so good to have visitors.

It was physically tiring for me to take care of Betty and work full time at the hospital, so I hired another caregiver to assist me in the evenings and on the weekends. On one occasion Pam could not work and this lady filled in for her. That morning I got a frantic call from her that Betty had slipped from her chair to the floor. I told her to call 911 to assist in putting Betty back to bed and I drove home to check on her. Very soon thereafter Betty told me to let the lady go. I asked why and she said, "She treats me like I am in a nursing home. I know I am in my home and I don't want to be reminded of a nursing home." I told her to give me some specifics. She said, "Can't you see?" She comes in and says, 'It's time to get up and eat supper. It's time to go back to bed.' and on and on. She does not ask what I would like. I have no control." I talked with Pam and she agreed that she would like to have more hours. Therefore we ended the other relationship. Betty was not a demanding individual. My motto was "Whatever the queen wants, she can have if I can get it."

It was helpful to have Pam working extra hours in the evenings, but I still had full care of Betty on the weekends. Betty did not like for me to leave her. Her insecurity battled with her selflessness at these times. She knew that I needed to take breaks and get out of the house some, but she was nervous if I was not around. She trusted me to take care of her in a way that she trusted no one else. I did not want to leave her either, but I knew that I needed these times of refreshment so that I could be a better caregiver for her. If I did not take care of myself, I could not take care of her.

Chapter 10:

Who Are You?

⟨J⟩

One Sunday afternoon in the spring I was transferring Betty from the bed into her wheelchair. I never knew what went wrong, but she ended up on the floor. I eased her down and knew that she was not hurt. She was making all sorts of sounds of distress, however. I told her that I was going to get Laine Holman, our neighbor from next door, to help me get her back in bed and that I would be right back. Laine immediately came with me. When I opened the front door, there was silence. Betty heard us talking and began making sounds of extreme distress. As we rushed into her bedroom she immediately stopped her sounds, casually lifted her hand in a wave, and said, "Oh, hi, Laine, how are you?" It struck me as being so funny that I had to compose myself before we could lift her back into bed.

Betty began to have frequent urinary tract infections (UTI), which were very hard on her. Dr. Shallin referred her to a urologist in Round Rock. Dr. Freidberg was very personable and I could tell he was very interested in Betty's progress. He told me that I should learn to observe her well enough that I could tell if she was developing an infection without having to have a urinalysis done. The symptoms were fever above 101, pain in the kidney area, and/or mental confusion. I assured him that Betty would not become confused. He told me that it was not unusual for someone to become confused if they had a severe UTI or any other infection.

In early June 2003, one Sunday afternoon Betty felt extremely warm. I checked her temperature and it was almost 102. I immediately suspected a UTI. Our van was still not handicapped accessible at this time. When we needed to take Betty to the doctor, I would pay Pam extra for taking Betty in her van. I called Pam and she agreed to take Betty to the hospital in Taylor. I called Dr. Freidberg's answering service and was told his associate was on call and that he would call me back very soon. The associate called within ten minutes. He told me to take Betty to the hospital and that he would call ahead and give the orders for a catheterized urine specimen and culture and sensitivity. He also told me he would prescribe Cipro, a strong, general antibiotic, until he got the culture report. Because it was Sunday evening, I knew that all the pharmacies in Taylor were closed. I called Manny Garcia who lives in Taylor. He is a registered pharmacist and works at the hospital in Georgetown. He had previously been director of pharmacy in Taylor when I had worked there as administrator. Manny assured me that he could get some Cipro from the Taylor hospital.

After a 24-hour incubation period, Betty's culture was positive. However, the organism was resistant to Cipro, so Betty required a different medication.

Betty began to have frequent urinary tract infections. I dealt better with the infections when they did not cause mental status change. However, more and more frequently, the infections caused severe mental status change. Betty would not know where she was and would also make remarks that were not typical of her at all. I encouraged her not to say those things, but it was to no avail. Sometimes she did not know who I was. I had no idea how to deal with someone who had mental status change. This was something that I felt would never affect Betty.

On one occasion she asked me, "Who are you?"

I was distraught. "I'm your husband!"

"No, you're not."

"Yes, I am! We've been married for over 40 years."

"No, you're not. We picked you up on the side of the road."

"I'm your husband!" I protested.

"You're cute," she grinned.

Later she admitted that she had been just teasing me. That occasion was comical, but when she really didn't recognize me it was not. Because of the frequent urinary tract infections, her recovery progress had not only stopped, but she was obviously regressing.

Two days before Lisa was to leave to run her marathon in Hawaii, Betty and I invited all the Taylor therapists to the house for lunch to wish Lisa well. We had a very good time with them. Everyone was happy that Lisa had raised over $5,000 and was physically ready for the run. She completed the marathon and enjoyed it so much that she now runs on a regular basis.

In the latter part of May we received a call that they were ready to install the lift apparatus in the van. Originally, the plans were to actually lower the van. However, further review revealed that their first recommendation would not work on our van. I was very disappointed. However, the owner of the store we were using had another idea and it would not interfere with the van. It is called a Turny. The front passenger seat was completely removed along with the electrical wiring to the seat. The Turny was then installed. It was a leather seat almost exactly like the original seat. However, the entire seat would swivel. Using the control buttons the seat would swing outside of the van and then lower to the height of a wheelchair. This allowed us to easily transfer Betty from a manual wheelchair into the van. We would roll the chair alongside the Turny. Then, using a transfer board, we would slide Betty into the Turny seat. We would then use the control panel to raise the Turny and then swivel it into the regular seat position, fasten the seat belt and we're ready to roll. When we first used it, there was a representative from the State Agency present to be certain that I could transfer Betty. I asked if I could have Pam help if necessary. She replied, "I don't care how many people you use as long as I see that you know how to get her into the van." It was definitely easier to have Pam's help.

Soon after we had the van modified, Betty wanted to visit her older sister, Mildred Schill who was in an assisted living facility in Brady, Texas, which is about 150 miles from Taylor. Early one summer morning Pam and I placed Betty into the van and drove to Brady. Betty did fine until the return trip. Approximately 100 miles from Taylor, her hips began hurting. We stopped at a Dairy Queen and took her inside for ice cream. I gave her some pain medication and she did fine the rest of the way home.

The Turny seat in the van made life so much better for Betty. We took shopping trips to Austin and Round Rock. On one occasion we took a trip to Katy to visit Jamie. Betty did fine. When we arrived at Jamie's, she chose to lie down rather than sit in the recliner.

Other times when we would be out driving, she would almost beg me to take her to Dallas to see Dawn, Bryan, and Caitlin. I did not feel confident about driving that far with her and I knew I would have to bring her home by bedtime. She could not tolerate a regular bed.

Mark and Cheryl and their family came in the early part of the summer in 2003. Cheryl and the children stayed while Mark went back to Georgia to work. Cheryl has other family members and friends in the Austin area and they also visited them, so they were not with us all the time; however, we enjoyed them when they could be with us.

Mark returned to Texas mid-July. Betty was not doing well and it helped to have family present. About August 1, they left our home and went to Cheryl's folks before returning to Georgia.

Jamie brought one of her friends home for the weekend. On Sunday morning it was obvious that Betty was very ill. She was vomiting and I suspected that she had another UTI. We got her into our van and started for the emergency room in Georgetown. Just as we drove into town, she vomited. Unfortunately, I was not prepared for this. I stopped the van, tried to clean her as best as I could and proceeded to the emergency room.

They took her to a treatment room as soon as she was triaged. The doctor ordered lab and x-ray studies. After we had been in the room for over an hour, Mark walked in. It was so wonderful to have him close. Jamie had called him and told him where we were.

The tests showed that Betty had a raging infection again. The doctor prescribed medications for nausea and an antibiotic for her until the culture reports were available. We told Mark goodbye and took Betty home.

In the latter part of July 2003, Betty had an appointment with her neurologist, Dr. Fox. He was delighted to see her and expressed how well she appeared. I assured him she was not progressing; in fact she regressing. I gave him several examples and told him she was also having frequent UTIs. He continued to be encouraging. I finally said, "You don't understand. She is going backward."

I believe he almost lost his patience with me. He looked right at me and said, "You would be going backward too if you had a urinary tract infection. I'm telling you, she is going to be alright. She just needs to get over this infection." I knew I had been reprimanded. Here I was, thinking that I am God's man of faith and power, and it takes a medical doctor to tell me that my wife is going to be alright. I remembered the times I had told everyone Betty was going to be alright, no matter what they said.

At first I attributed all of the depression to the UTIs. I should have realized that it was also caused by her condition. Betty had depression and also anxiety. Several times Betty became so anxious that her whole body would shake. I would lie in bed with her and hold her in my arms and pray that the anxiety would pass. I also was afraid of giving her too much anxiety medication. One night I called a pharmacist friend because I was so upset. He assured me that I could give her four or five times the prescribed dosage of that particular medication and it would not hurt her. I did. I didn't give it as one dose but several doses over a period of about two hours. She finally became calm.

Betty and I had decided to remodel her bathroom so that it would be handicapped accessible. I began looking for contractors to give us a bid. It was obvious that some had no idea what to do and others didn't seem to want the job.

I checked with Jackie McRoberts, director of inpatient therapy regarding a contractor for the bathroom. She gave me the name of one that had left his business card with her. I called him and we arranged a time that he could come look at what we wanted done with the bathroom. Robert Siemens came to the house the following week. He appeared to understand what we needed and how to make it happen.

Within a few days he brought us a copy of the plans he had drawn and his quote. After discussing it for a few days, we accepted. Robert told me that he would be able to start within ten days. In the meantime, I would need to empty Betty's closet because it would be incorporated into the new bathroom.

I began to look for available space to put everything that was in Betty's closet. Her clothes could be moved into a nearby closet in another room and I would have to find space for all the boxes that were on her shelves, which contained mementos from years past.

As we prepared for the new bathroom, Betty's urinary tract infections began to reoccur and she began to have more severe mental status changes. She would tell me that she knew she was dying. I attempted to encourage her but usually started crying myself. She insisted she needed to start telling everyone goodbye. I asked where she was going and she told me that I should know that she was dying. I asked her if God had told her this and her response was "No." I asked her not to tell me those things because it was depressing to me. She would say she was sorry but would soon forget. I did not realize that she had no control over what she was saying.

I must say there were times I felt sorry for myself. I probably needed an anti-depressant at the time but did not recognize the symptoms or was too proud to admit it. Soon after Betty's strokes, my doctor prescribed Trazadone for me. The main complaint I had was that I would awaken at 3:00 a.m. and was unable to return to sleep. I had no idea that was a symptom of depression.

Construction was to begin on the bathroom about August 14, which was on Wednesday. The Sunday morning before, I realized that I needed to finish unloading Betty's closet. As I was sitting in her room, she began to tell me again that she was dying and needed to tell everyone goodbye. I began to cry. I silently prayed to God. "God, have I misunderstood you all along? Are you going to take her home soon? If so, why haven't you told me? If you are not, please give me peace about it. If you are, please tell me somehow so that I can begin to adjust accordingly."

My thoughts and prayer were interrupted by quietness and the realization that I could no longer hear the washing machine in the utility room. I walked out into the room and moved the clothes over into the dryer. As I turned to leave, I noticed a large filing cabinet. I decided that I needed to check its contents so that I could get it out of the way to make room for the boxes from Betty's closet. I opened the top drawer. There was a large brown envelope. I brought it into the kitchen and placed it on the table. I started to dump it into the trash but decided better of it. The first item I picked up was a letter. It was very nicely done on thick, dark cream-colored paper with brown calligraphy. My thoughts were to throw it into the trash. Then I realized there was four more just like it. I decided to check it out. I began to read:

Little One,

Be patient. I will bring to pass all that I have promised. What now seems to you as needless delay—even a back-ward move—is actually an important step in the necessary process.

Child, the pains of healing are similar to the pains of the earlier difficulty—but with one significant difference...They are the result of the steady flow of my Life which is—even now—reversing the damages you have asked Me to mend.

Keep your eyes on Me, for I know an important principle you have forgotten. Often what is quickly acquired is also quickly lost. Therefore—rest! I AM laying a solid foundation which CANNOT be moved.

Faithfully,
Dad

I was stunned and I began to weep uncontrollably. Without a doubt I knew that God orchestrated the letter for me. At the bottom of the letter was written in very fine print:

"Excerpt from the upcoming book <u>From the Father's Heart.</u> Copyright 1988 Charles Slagle. All rights Reserved."

The words in this letter meant absolutely everything to me. I went into Betty's bedroom and read the letter to her. The infection had caused problems with her mental status; therefore, the words meant nothing to her. However, I felt as if I was under a huge weight and it was crushing the life out of me. Now that weight was gone.

Early that afternoon our friends June and Gene Prater came to visit. They had been so faithful to assist us in any way they thought would make things easier for us since Betty had had the strokes. I showed them the letter and they agreed that it was indeed written for my benefit. Gene immediately remarked, "Oh, the book is by Charles Slagle." Then I remembered that Charles and his wife, Paula, had spoken at our church many years before. Charles told the congregation about his upcoming new book and suggested that we pick up a copy of one of the letters as a souvenir. Apparently, I didn't hear the word "copy" and took enough "copies" for Betty, each of our children, and me. I had placed the copies of the letter in the filing cabinet and had not looked at it again for at least fifteen years.

The next day I searched the Internet for "Charles Slagle." I discovered his website and copied his email address. I wrote him an email telling him what had happened with me in regards to his letter. I also asked his permission to use his letter in my book. The next day I received the following response:

Hi Louis,

I was deeply touched by your letter and in an interesting way. God used that old "Be Patient" message He spoke to me so long ago yet again yesterday, as I read the contents of your email. Our heavenly Father is amazing, isn't he?

I'm praying that your dear wife soon will experience again the Lord's healing touch and that His Spirit somehow will impart powerful encouragement and lasting joy to her weary heart. And to yours as well.

Yes, please be at liberty to include this Father's heart message with your new book. I'm glad you feel that it will be of value. I'm recovering right now from brain surgery for the removal of a tumor in my left acoustic canal. All went very well, and the attempt at hearing conservation (for the left

ear) has gone well too, praise the Lord. Dizzy as daft duck, but the surgeon says will go away in time.

God bless you, Louis! Your letter was a true blessing to me.

Yours with sincere love and prayers,
Charles

The realization at how awesome God is began to dawn on me. To think that Charles had written that letter at least fifteen years before, had not thought of it in years, and that it had been in our filing cabinet for fifteen years unread was astounding to me. God had known when He instructed Charles to write that letter fifteen years earlier that both Charles and I would need it at the same time.

When I shared this experience with our children, Jamie immediately responded, "I have that book. Dad, you gave it to me when I went away to college in '89."

The day before the remodel project was to begin, June and Gene, along with their robust grandson Keith, who was visiting from California, arrived to help move Betty's bed and furnishings into the spare bedroom. I was all primed and ready to get started, but Gene informed me that they would not need my help. The three of them could manage very well without me and they were not going to take a chance of my hurting myself in the process. No amount of arguing would change their minds.

The next day Robert and his assistant, Mark, arrived to start renovating the bathroom. After they came, I went to work in Georgetown.

Each day when I came home I would check the progress. They were certainly creating a lot of dust but they were trying to keep it contained to the area in which they were working.

Betty said it did not matter to her what color was used so Jamie and I picked a soft shade of green for her bedroom and a matching shade for the bathroom. Robert told me he would order the paint on the following Monday.

On Friday of that week Mardy Yonikas, one of the ladies who had been present for the healing service right after Betty had the strokes, came by my office with a pretty heart-shaped prayer pillow that she had made for Betty. Betty was very appreciative of it and we laid it on her bed. About midmorning on Saturday she picked it up and held it to her. "This is the color I want," she emphatically stated.

"For what?" I asked.

"For the room."

I explained that we had picked a soft green because we thought that was what she wanted. "No, this is what I want," she said. It was a very pretty shade of pink.

We had also picked green tile for the bathroom. I nearly panicked. I called Robert and asked if he had picked up the paint. He said he was picking it up the following Monday. I told him to hold off for a couple of days because Betty had made some changes. I called Dawn, who was living in Dallas, and asked her to find some paint with a shade of pink and tile that would match. She loves to shop and she went on her mission. Before long she called me back and told me the paint color number and the tile number. I had samples of paint and tile at home and I showed them to Betty. "That's what I want," she said.

The bathroom and bedroom were completed in about four weeks. They were very attractive. June and Gene with another of their grandsons, Adam, came and moved all the furnishings back into the room. They asked if I had anything else that needed to be done and I told them that the blinds needed to be installed but I didn't have the heart to ask them to do that too. They could not be stopped. They hung the blinds also before leaving for the day.

We decorated Betty's walls with Thomas Kincaid prints. Jamie made a bouquet of dried roses that we hung on the wall next to her bed. Later we realized that we should have changed out the pictures and other items in her room much more often. She spent a lot of time in there and had to look at the same things day in and day out. She eventually asked us to move the rose bouquet because she kept counting the roses in it over and over again.

The morning after the bathroom remodel was completed, as I left for work, I told Betty and Pam that we would give Betty a shower when I got home that evening. I was looking forward to her being able to have a shower. She had only bed baths since the stroke. I could hardly wait for the day to end so that I could go home. When I arrived home, we dressed Betty in a robe to wheel her to the shower. From her wheelchair, we transferred to her shower chair that also could function as a bedside commode. We then removed her robe. Betty was very apprehensive and I assured her that we would be careful. That did not ease her apprehensions. I tested the water, got it to a good temperature and started letting it flow over her. She did not like it. I tried to convince her that she was alright, but she wanted me to stop the water. I reluctantly agreed. I had no idea that she would not enjoy it. However, she did not and said that she did not want another shower. I assured her that it would be better the next time. We tried it again the next day and it was not any better. After the third day I told her we would not give her a shower for awhile. I realized showers were out.

Chapter 11:

Ups and Downs

eℐℐ

B etty continued to have frequent urinary tract infections. Pam and I were doing everything possible to keep her from getting sick. We were very careful to clean her catheter bag twice daily and took many other precautions. We made sure that our hands were clean when we touched Betty. We were also careful that the catheter bag and tubing never touched the floor. Dr. Freidberg, her urologist, was also concerned and was doing all he knew to do to prevent the infections. He was always complimentary to Pam and me for our care of Betty. It seemed the worst type of infections were yeast infections. She eventually started taking acidophilus to try to keep her urine more acid-based. This did seem to help.

Towards the end of 2003 Betty began to have spasms in her right leg and foot. Dr. Fox said she had restless leg syndrome. I began to research on the Internet to try to find something that would help her. She was now on another medication for this new problem. I discovered that Botox had been used successfully to treat the same type of spasms that she was having in her leg. She also had problems with her right arm. I sent a note to Dr. Godinez, her rehab doctor, asking if Botox might help. She immediately called me and said she believed it would. Botox could be injected just under the skin in very small doses in her leg, foot, and arm. We made the appointment to see Dr. Godinez.

As we entered the exam room, I noticed a monitor at the end of the exam table. With her equipment, Dr. Godinez could tell exactly where to inject the Botox. Betty said it was not painful. Dr. Godinez told us that it would be about three weeks before we could notice improvement. Betty's right leg and foot had become so bad that it was difficult to get her into the car. I thanked Dr. Godinez and told her how much I appreciated her. She said, "You know, I am only an instrument of God."

In about three weeks, just as Dr.Godinez had said, there was marked improvement in Betty's arm and leg. Our insurance company had said in the beginning that it would not pay for the treatments. Dr. Godinez wrote them a letter explaining the research that had been done. After that, we had no problems with the insurance company.

In December, my nephew Allan, who lived in the Gainesville, Texas area, was diagnosed as terminally ill with colon cancer. Although, Allan is my nephew, he is six days older than I am and we had grown up together. (I tried to make him call me "uncle" but he wouldn't do it.) I knew that he did not have long to live and I wanted to see him. I broached the topic with Betty and she told me she did not want me to go. She was insecure when I was not around and the idea of my going over 200 miles away caused her much anxiety.

I called Jamie and asked if she could come to stay with Betty while I was gone. She could, so I approached Betty again about the trip. I assured Betty that I would leave very early in the morning and would come home the same day. Jamie and Pam would be with her the entire time and I would not stay overnight. She still was reluctant to let me go, but I told her, "I have to go."

Jamie and Pam took care of Betty while I was away, and I was able to see Allan. I was so glad that I had taken the trip. I would have always regretted not getting to see him again. It also taught Betty that I could be away from her and that she would be okay. She still didn't like for me to go far though.

Even though Betty was not making progress, I never lost hope that she would totally recover. I knew she was tired, but I kept telling her I was not tired and that it was a privilege to take care of her. Despite my doing everything that I could for her, the depression became worse. At times she would have panic attacks. She would shake so much that at times I would crawl up into the bed with her, hold her and pray. She was on various medications but nothing seemed to help.

I made another appointment to see her neurologist, Dr. Fox. After his exam, he told us that he really needed help with her medications for depression. He assured us Betty's depression was not psychological, but a chemical imbalance caused by the strokes. He recommended that Betty see a psychiatrist. He told us that he believed Dr. Alam would be able to help her.

In a few days we received a call from Dr. Alam's office and made an appointment for Betty. When we went into her office, I immediately felt at peace. She was a very caring person and I knew in an instant that she would do anything she could to help Betty. It took several weeks before the medications that she prescribed began to help. She explained that some of the medications had not originally been made for depression but for seizures. Over time they had discovered that they were very good for patients suffering from the type of depression that Betty had.

It was good to have control over the depression. Betty seemed to have more energy and began wanting to go outside more. However, before long, we had another challenge. She began to lose her appetite. We began supplementing her diet with tube feedings. I had a talk with the dietitian at the hospital and she suggested talking with the doctor about giving Betty megase to stimulate her appetite. I talked with Dr. Shallin and he agreed. After about a week of taking the megase, her appetite improved and we stopped the tube feedings.

Within a short while after that challenge, we noticed a sore on her left leg. We realized that a patch that the doctor had ordered for the severe pain in her knee had caused it. I contacted Home Health and a therapist began coming at least three times each week to dress the wound. It was beginning to heal when we noticed a red spot on her bottom. Despite all we could do, it also became a sore. The therapist taught Pam and me to dress the wounds on the days that she did not come. I thought this would be just a temporary setback, but it did not prove to be that way. It seemed that we would get one sore healed and another would start. I looked forward to the time that we could take Betty on another trip, such as going to see Jamie, again. Betty would tell me that she did not believe that she could stand the trip even if she did not have the sores. I did not realize how badly she felt.

In the beginning of the summer of 2004, Betty was so weak she could not hold her head up while she was sitting in the van. This made it very difficult to take her out. About the only place we went was to see one of her many doctors. I kept waiting for a miracle from God. I was not giving up although I did not see Betty improving.

Chapter 12:

Believing by Faith and Not by Sight

JP

In July 2004, Pam and I took Betty to see the psychiatrist for a monthly checkup. Betty could hardly sit up in the van. On the return trip as we neared Taylor, I asked her how she was doing. She almost fell over and called "Louis." She immediately began to shake violently. I was scared. I pulled the van to the side of the road and Pam jumped out and opened the passenger door. I realized I should not have stopped but should have gone directly to the Taylor hospital. I told Pam to get back in the van and I drove as fast as I dared with the horn blaring and the hazard lights flashing.

Cars pulled over to the outside lane for us except for one. He would not budge. However, I managed to get around him and continued on towards the hospital. Pam was crying and reaching up behind the seat trying to hold Betty's head up. I continued calling, "Jesus, Jesus, Jesus. Betty, I speak life to you and not death. You will not die. Jesus, Jesus, Jesus." She appeared to have died. I kept calling on Jesus and kept saying, "I am believing by faith and not by sight." She began breathing sporadically.

As we got closer to the hospital, I remembered the telephone number. It had not changed since I was the administrator there several years ago. I dialed the number and told the operator who I was and that I was bringing Betty in and to have the Emergency Room notified. As we drove up to the emergency entrance, three nurses were waiting outside for us with a stretcher and also a wheelchair. One nurse opened the passenger door and literally lifted Betty into the wheelchair by herself. She told me later that she had no idea how she did it alone. Betty gasped for breath and began breathing more normally. They wheeled her into the emergency room and put her onto the exam table. She was hooked up to monitors, and an I.V. was started to keep her vein open.

I thought Betty had experienced another stroke. Tests showed the possibility of a heart attack. The doctor asked that the Georgetown Hospital be contacted and requested that they fax over the last electrocardiogram that Betty had there in 2002. Within minutes it arrived. After comparing the new electrocardiogram with the one from 2002, the ER doctor told me there were definite changes suggestive of a heart attack. Betty would need to be transferred to the Georgetown Hospital so that a cardiologist could evaluate her.

I explained to Betty what was going to take place. She did not seem alarmed. As soon as the ambulance arrived, Pam and I left. Pam went to our home to take care of Pepper and I left for the hospital in Georgetown. From my cell phone, I called Jamie and asked her to call Mark and Dawn. I also called June and Gene Prater and Sam Schultz. Normally, I would not have been able to talk without crying, but I felt a peace all around me.

When I arrived at the Georgetown hospital, June and Gene were there. We went directly to the second floor and waited for the ambulance. I assumed Betty would be admitted to ICU. In a matter of minutes, Sam arrived and told us that he had seen the ambulance crew taking Betty to a room across from the nurses' station. As soon as they had her in the bed, I went in to see her. I only stayed a few minutes because the nurses were attending to her. As June, Gene, Sam, and I sat at the end of the hall, Betty's internist, Dr. Shallin, arrived. I began telling him what happened. Before I could finish, one of the nurses ran from the room and shouted, "Dr. Shallin, we need you now!" I ran after him. When we entered the room, I looked at Betty and saw a replay of what had happened out on the highway. She was having a seizure. It did not last long and Dr. Shallin continued asking questions about what had happened. Betty was started on an anti-seizure medication immediately.

After more tests, Dr. Shallin said he believed that Betty had had a heart attack but would not know definitely until the next morning when her enzymes would be checked again. I encouraged the

Praters and Sam to go home. I stayed for quite awhile. The nurses assured me they would call if there were changes in her condition. I should have remembered the incident in the hospital in Austin and stayed at the hospital because Betty could not communicate. However, the nurses kept emphasizing they would call me if there was a change in her. I should have also asked Dr. Shallin why Betty was not admitted to ICU.

I arrived at the hospital early the next morning and the nurses told me that Dr. Shallin had examined Betty and would return to visit with me. It was obvious that Betty was not doing well. The nurse told me that Betty had had some choking spells during the night and did not rest well. I asked why someone did not call me. The nurse did not give me an acceptable answer. I was not happy and I'm sure the tone of my voice and my expression left no doubt about it. I wondered just how much Betty had been neglected throughout the night. I felt guilty that I had left her.

Soon Dr. Shallin arrived. With a very concerned look he told me, "Test results along with my exam confirm that Betty has had a heart attack. I'm not certain of the severity. I have called Dr. Garland and asked him to examine her." Dr. Steve Garland is a cardiologist who is also on the staff of the Heart Hospital in Austin.

About mid-morning Dr.Garland came. As he entered the room, I sensed he was also very concerned. He shook my hand and asked, "Can you tell me exactly what happened yesterday?" I gave him all the details. He began to question Betty but she was unable to respond to his questions. As he examined her, he remarked, "We're going to need to transfer her to the Heart Hospital for a heart cath procedure." After he told me all the tests that needed to be done, he asked, "How do you feel about the tests that I've mentioned?"

"I want her to have anything she needs. My faith is strong and I believe she will come through this. However, neither of us want her to be placed on a ventilator for a lengthy period."

Dr. Garland then proceeded to do a thorough examination of Betty. As he examined her left leg, I noticed he kept moving his hand around over various parts of her ankle. He appeared to be extremely concerned. He asked me to hold Betty's left leg in a different position. He felt again and I knew he was trying to detect a pulse. He asked me to place my hand on Betty's ankle. I did but could not feel a pulse either. "Louis, there's no pulse in her left leg. We've got to transfer her to Austin Heart Hospital as quickly as possible or she is going to be in even greater trouble." With that comment, he left the room to contact doctors in Austin and let them know he was transferring her immediately. Soon the nurses began coming into the room to prepare Betty for the transfer. I explained to her that she was going to be transferred but I did not tell her the seriousness of her condition. I do not believe she was able to comprehend Dr. Garland's comments.

Within a few minutes there was a constant stream of employees coming to tell me they were praying for both of us. It was comforting to know that I had so many loving friends at the hospital who were willing to do anything possible to save Betty's life.

The EMS personnel arrived quickly. I was asked if I wished to ride in the ambulance with Betty. I declined because I knew I would need the van in Austin. I assured them that I would follow them closely.

I called Jamie and asked her to contact Mark and Dawn about the transfer. Dawn was in the process of selling her house in Frisco so she could move to Katy to teach. She said that she would be home as quickly as possible. I discouraged her and Jamie from coming until the next day, which was Friday.

I prayed all the way to Austin that God would work another miracle for Betty. He had been so faithful to hear and positively answer so many of my prayers.

Nurses were waiting for Betty when we arrived at the Austin Heart Hospital. Betty was immediately taken to a room and a young nurse quickly began to do an assessment and prepare her to be taken to surgery for the heart cath procedure. The nurse also attempted to find a pulse in Betty's left ankle and leg. Excitedly she exclaimed, "I feel a pulse!" I asked her to mark the spot so the doctor would know exactly where it was. As she felt over other parts of Betty's leg and ankle she assured me there was now a strong pulse. I was so grateful to God for giving us another miracle.

Soon the doctor's assistant arrived. He said, "I understand there is no pulse in her left leg." I told him there had not been, but the nurse had found a pulse. He reached over and touched Betty's leg and ankle in several places. Smiling he said, "She has the pulse of a seventeen year old." He told me they would probably not do the heart cath until the next morning. He left the room and no one told me when the procedure would be done. Later in the evening, the nurse finally told me that Betty would have the heart cath the next morning at 8:00.

The doctor ordered blood work to be performed that evening before the heart cath procedure. After one nurse assistant stuck Betty three times, I told her she was not going to stick her again and to get someone who was competent. She left and came back with another person. I quizzed her and she assured me she did not think she could hit Betty's vein but was going to try. I told her she was not going to practice on Betty. Finally a nurse from the emergency room came and drew the blood.

Sam Schultz and his three children came late that evening. As we were visiting, a young lady came to the room, announced that she was from the business office and that I needed to pay the $250 deductible for Betty's insurance immediately. She acted as though she believed that I had no intention of paying. I told her that I had company and that I would be down to the office later. She did not move. Rather than create a scene, I handed her my credit card and she left. I discovered later that incident was mild in comparison to what Betty and I would endure while at the Heart Hospital.

I stayed until quite late that night, but after being assured that I would be called if there were a change in Betty, I went home. I assured Betty that I would be there early the next morning.

Friday morning as I entered Betty's room, I immediately sensed that she was very upset. June Prater was there and told me that the nurse could not find a vein. At that time there were two individuals trying to start another I.V. I told them they were not going to stick her again and to get someone who was competent. Soon a nurse came from the emergency room and started the I.V. Assuming that the hospital was a specialty hospital, I was shocked at the incompetence of so many nurses and techs. After that incident I realized that I should have never left Betty during the night. I felt guilty for not being there earlier that morning.

About 8:00 a.m., Betty was taken to the heart cath lab. After the procedure, she was returned to her room at approximately 9:30

a.m. The nurse who came with her told me the doctor would be in later to talk to us. I asked what was found. The nurse responded, "We did not find anything."

Time passed and still no definite report from the doctor except for the short response that the nurse had given. I could stand it no longer. I asked to speak to the Chief Nursing Officer. The response was, "She's on vacation. What do you want?" I told them I wanted a report on what was found regarding Betty. Finally a person entered the room and told me that she was the charge nurse for that unit. I told her that I was very disappointed in the lack of information. She told me that the doctor had other patients besides my wife. I told her that surely he could send a message to tell me what was found. She proceeded to tell me that was entirely out of the question and that I would be told when the doctor had time. I then asked to see the CEO. The reply was, "On vacation."

It was nearly 1:00 p.m. when the doctor came. He told me that Betty definitely had a heart attack and that the back side of her heart was damaged. He also told me that he had requested another cardiologist to come in later to explain our options.

His report was far different from the report the nurse had given me that morning. "We did not find anything."

By this time Jamie had arrived. I expressed my frustrations to her. The other cardiologist did not see Betty on Friday. I continued to be amazed at the lack of communication with the patient and family.

Betty was reasonably responsive fairly soon after the procedure. She had no appetite, however, which concerned me. I tried to get her to eat some Cream of Wheat that I had brought from home and fixed in the hospital microwave. It was obvious she could not eat the food that was brought to her. This seemed to be of no concern to anyone except Jamie and me.

Late that night after Betty was asleep, Jamie and I drove to Taylor. Dawn and her children were coming to the hospital the next morning.

Jamie and I arrived at the hospital early Saturday morning. About mid-morning the other cardiologist came into the room. He explained that the back side of Betty's heart was damaged but he felt that it would heal. He told us that she could be treated with medications or they could implant a pacemaker-defibrillator. He asked which method I though Betty would prefer. I knew that Betty was not capable of making that decision. I asked him to explain what results he thought each one would provide. He seemed genuinely concerned that he wanted to make the right decision. The problem we encountered was that these doctors had not seen Betty prior to the heart attack. They did not know how well she could communicate and what a wonderful personality she had. They could only see a lady who was almost non-responsive to everyone.

I asked the cardiologist, "If Betty was your mother, what would you do?"

He looked very surprised and said, "That's a difficult decision to make. I would need to think about it."

I said, "We need to think about it too." After discussing the options, Jamie and I agreed that Betty would do better with the medications. After we told the cardiologist our decision, he told us that Betty could go home after lunch. Later that afternoon, he told us he agreed with our decision.

We took Betty home in the van. We had to get her in bed quickly as it was almost time for the pharmacy to close. The doctor had given her several new prescriptions. I did not feel good about all the medications she would be taking. I also resolved that I would contact the Nursing Director and the CEO of the Austin Heart Hospital and register our complaints. Several years later I was a patient in the Heart Hospital. It was under new management and I received excellent care.

Earlier in the day, I had tried to call Betty's niece, Dr. Diane Solomon, in San Antonio. She was at a conference in Dallas. However, her husband Dale called her and told her that I had called and gave her Betty's recent history and what the doctors were advising. Although Diane is a neurologist, she was in a meeting with several well known cardiologists. She immediately told them that she needed some advice concerning her beloved Aunt Betty.

After we arrived home, Diane called us and reassured us that we had made the right decision and also assured us that God was with us.

Betty was very quiet and almost non-responsive at times. I was not sure that she understood all that had happened. I wasn't sure myself. I was positive that God knew exactly what had happened and that He would take care of us. I was reminded many times of this in the next weeks and months, as I would look at the three-cent stamps that I had placed on various mirrors in the house. If He cared enough for me to provide the three-cent stamps, I knew that He would take care of Betty and me.

Chapter 13:

Despair and Disappointment

ƆƖƤ

Betty's neurologist, Dr Fox, wanted to make certain that he did as much as possible for her. He scheduled her for an EEG on July 28, 2004. As the technician was hooking her up to the many wires, Betty seemed to be apprehensive. Attempting to make her feel more at ease, I said, "Betty, I know you are apprehensive with all that is going on with you. You have had so many traumatic experiences; it is certainly understandable for you to be apprehensive."

She gave her funny little grin and immediately replied, "Yes I know. I married you." With that comment Betty started laughing and I thought for a minute the tech was not going to be able to continue because she too was laughing so hard. I attempted to shame Betty for making such a remark. I even reminded her that the next day was our forty-third wedding anniversary but I was not successful in making her ashamed. Her ability to find humor in adverse situations had always been one of her strong attributes. I loved her even more if that was possible.

I returned to work the following Monday and we began our usual routine at home. Pam came each day to care for Betty and I would take care of her when I got home and on the weekends.

The following weeks were not good for Betty. She began to lose her speech. I thought she just didn't try hard enough to form the words and requested that a Speech Pathologist check her. After working with her for several sessions, I was told that she just did not seem to have the energy to form her words. I was not about to give up. I asked if we could try the Biographical System for her. This is a special computer used to retrain stroke patients so that they can communicate. The company in

California offered to let Betty have a system at no cost for a few months to see if it would help. I received training with it and then began to work with Betty. We seemed to be making some progress but not as much and as quickly as I wished. I began to really push Betty to practice more and more. The more I pushed the more she rebelled. She kept telling me she was tired. I would not listen. I kept insisting that she work harder. I was frantic that she would not recover her speech. Finally I realized that I was expecting too much. I began to have her practice only five minutes each day. She soon gave up on that too.

By December 2004 Betty could only say a very few words. When we visited her cardiologist, Dr. Garland, he was shocked at her loss of speech. He ordered more blood studies and an echocardiogram. The echocardiogram showed that the heart had healed well. However, the blood test showed that her thyroid level was extremely low. He then referred her to Dr. Fain, an oncologist who was also a hematologist. He had more blood studies done and discovered that another test was extremely out of balance. He ordered medicine for her and Dr. Garland ordered medication for her thyroid.

I was sure the reason for her speech loss was because of the problems with her thyroid. I was certain that when the thyroid improved that she would have more energy and be able to regain her speech. After weeks of treatment, unfortunately that did not happen.

One night in late December as I was giving her bedtime medications and getting her ready for the night, she told me very plainly that she was tired and wanted to go home. Thinking she was confused, I assured her that she was at home. She looked at me with those beautiful, piercing, brown eyes and said clearly, "That's not the home I'm talking about." I did not need for her to repeat that statement. I understood perfectly. I asked her if she was talking of Heaven and she nodded her head affirmatively. I began to encourage her and told her that I was not tired and I loved taking care of her. I could tell that did not change her desires. I talked more about her thoughts, feelings and emotions. Finally, through tears, I told her I would release her to go home if that was what she wanted and what she also believed God wanted. She looked relieved. I was not. I knew I was not ready for her to leave me.

The next morning on my way to work, I prayed. I told God that I only released Betty to comfort her. I was definitely not ready for her to leave me.

That day as Sam Schultz and I went to lunch I told him of my conversation with Betty. I told him that I had believed that God was going to heal her and that I did not understand what was going on. He listened attentively as he always did. He was quiet for awhile. Back at the hospital as we were getting out of the van, he said, "You need to find the movie *Chariots of Fire*. You and Betty need to watch it. I believe there is a message in it for both of you." I told him we saw the movie many years ago soon after it was produced. "Watch it again," was his quick response.

"Can't you just tell me?" I almost pleaded.

"Nope," was his quick reply.

I was surprised to find the movie in a local video store. It probably had not been rented in many years. I explained to Betty that Sam thought we should watch it. That night after I had given Betty her meds and tucked her in for the night, I put the movie in the VCR. It was not easy for me to understand the dialect and even harder for Betty. She became rather agitated and I asked if she wanted me to turn it off. She nodded affirmatively.

After she was asleep, I took the video to my bedroom and watched it alone. I wanted so badly to find some answers. However, I saw absolutely nothing that I felt was a message for us.

I dreaded telling Sam that I did not see anything that I felt pertained to Betty and me. I knew he would tell me to keep watching it until I got the message. I was in for a surprise. He immediately explained it to me. "Remember the scene when the brother told his sister that he was meant for a purpose. I believe that God gives everyone a purpose and until that purpose is fulfilled they will stay here on earth. Determine what Betty's purpose is and you will know if she has completed it or not."

About three weeks later some dear friends and former pastor visited us. Bob and Claudine Little had been like family to us since we first met them in Luling, Texas in 1966. They had survived the long illness of Bob's mother and then the tragic death of their talented and beautiful sixteen-year-old daughter. I always marveled at their faith through those times.

I shared Sam's idea of having Betty and I watch *Chariots of Fire*. Before I could tell them about the scene that Sam felt was a message to us, Bob immediately began to share the exact scene that Sam had shared. He also talked about Betty's purpose. I was now positive that God was attempting to tell me something that was important. It was no coincidence that these two men whom had never met before and were very close friends of mine had the same message for me. At the time, I was not sure that I wanted to receive the message.

The following weeks Betty continued to let me know that she was tired and wanted to go home. I continued to try to encourage both of us.

I anxiously awaited improvement in Betty's speech. The improvement never came. In early March she had another visit with the cardiologist. He told us that her thyroid test was now normal. A feeling of despair and disappointment flooded over me. I had believed that if her thyroid improved that her energy would increase and she would be able to speak. To learn that her thyroid was normal and her speech had not improved was almost more than I could take.

While all of this was happening, the tension increased in administration at the Georgetown Hospital where I worked. I suspected that something was going on.

One day the CEO came to my office and motioned me to come with him. As we entered his office, he closed the door and we sat down. I could tell by his mannerisms that he felt uncomfortable. He immediately said, "Since you're old enough to retire, we're going to let you go. I've got to make some changes, so we're going to take care of you and go ahead and let you retire." I was numb. Thoughts raced through my mind. What about Betty? She was on our insurance plan and how could I continue paying Pam if I had no income? I had some retirement funds but I had no intention of retiring at this time.

After several days we came to a termination agreement. God gave me peace about it. I had no idea what the future held for us but I remembered the three-cent stamps that my friend Sam had given me. God would meet all our needs.

I did not realize that God was stirring my nest. All too often throughout our life we blame unpleasant situations on Satan when in reality God is making us uncomfortable because He has something far better for us. He is ready for us to use our wings and fly rather than stay in our warm and comfortable nest. I must confess, when you suspect that the person you have loved, adored, and been married to for almost forty-four years is probably dying, we tend to cling very tightly to our nest. In retrospect I know it was difficult for the CEO to terminate me. I had no idea what a blessing this would be for me.

I selected the day that would be my last at the hospital. I shared the date with very few. I had told everyone that I did not wish to have a reception and to please honor my request. I had been removing personal items from my office throughout the month of April. The final day arrived and I quietly went to those in administration and wished them well.

A positive side to this unexpected change was that I was able to spend more time with Betty. I never told her that I had been terminated. I knew it would upset her. I simply told her that I wanted to spend more time with her. Pam continued her regular hours with us and I tried to encourage Betty with her speech. She just could not improve.

About the middle of April I invited several of Betty's family to visit. This had become an annual affair since she had the strokes. Aunts, uncles, cousins and brothers all came. I enjoyed preparing lunch for them. Pam and I dressed Betty in one of her nicest outfits and I applied her makeup, something I had learned to do soon after the strokes. It was a wonderful time for all of us. It was obvious her health had declined since our last reunion. Although it was not discussed, some shared with me at a later time of their concern.

Pam and I brought Betty into the living room after her lunch. She was absolutely beautiful and radiant. She was a favorite of almost all of her relatives including even second cousins. She could wear any color and look like the queen she was. Her beautiful brunette hair only had fashionable streaks of gray. Her olive complexion was flawless. Her beautiful dark brown eyes were flashing. I was so proud of her. I had vivid memories of the day I first met her over forty-four years ago. The family was impressed that we could maneuver her around in the lift so easily. We carefully lowered her into her recliner and she smiled as only she could. As each said their goodbyes, I secretly wondered if this was the last time that all of us would be together on earth.

Unfortunately, on this special day we had major plumbing problems. The plumber was present when the relatives began arriving. The washer drain was not functioning in the utility room. The plumber gave me the bad news that he could not repair it and that I needed to call a company who had more sophisticated equipment. After everyone left, I called a larger company and they sent a plumber immediately. After doing some tests he determined that it would be a major job that would probably take at least four or five working days. They began work the next morning. They were extremely considerate of Betty and tried to keep the dust and noise to a minimum. The job was even more than they had originally anticipated and it took over a week to complete the repairs.

Around the latter part of April I attempted to give Betty her medications through the feeding tube. It was totally plugged. I tried to open it to no avail. When Pam came I asked her to try. She was unable to do so. I called Home Health and was told if we couldn't get it open they probably couldn't either. The nurse said she would call the gastroenterologist in Georgetown and ask what we should do. Soon we received a call from the doctor's office. They asked if we could bring Betty in after lunch. We took her to Georgetown and wheeled her into the office.

I wondered how they were going to do this procedure in the office because when the tube was originally inserted they had taken her to surgery. The doctor quickly explained that it was not a difficult procedure because they could use a different type tube this time. He asked me to assist him and it only took a few minutes to change the tube. I was so relieved and thankful that it was a simple procedure. The doctor said the tube might get stopped up again. If so, just call his office and they would change it.

It was nice to have doctors who had worked with me at the hospital on various projects. They were not just Betty's doctors, they were my friends and they all loved Betty. It was easy to see their admiration for her. She always thanked them for helping her and even as she lost her speech she would still attempt to tell them thanks.

Even though I was now home all day, it seemed that both Pam and I stayed busy. My worst time was after Betty was asleep at night. It was then that I would allow my mind to dwell on the negatives. When this happened, fear came quickly—fear of what might happen tomorrow or fear of what wouldn't happen. When this happened, I tried to think of God and all He had done and was continuing to do for us. As I would walk through the rooms, I would invariably notice the three-cent stamps that I had stuck on the mirrors and other objects almost three years earlier. Pam also put a stamp on Betty's sliding board. Our wonderful friend Sam continued to be a blessing to us even though he had a family of his own. Everyone needs a Sam in his or her life.

One of my biggest frustrations was mealtime. It would take approximately an hour for each meal. After Betty could no longer use her right arm, we had to feed her. We tried to laugh as often as possible. On occasions I would start the utensil towards her mouth while she had it open and just as it reached the intended destination she would involuntarily clamp her mouth shut. Or just as the spoon was almost to her mouth, she would make a quick turn of her head and the utensil would hit her chin or cheek. These moves were totally unintentional. She had no control over them. It was very obvious that she was totally and completely dependent on me. She trusted me to always do the best thing for her. I will rejoice when I reach that level of dependence and trust on God.

Betty's condition had deteriorated so much that it was now difficult for her to eat food. Many times we had to feed her a liquid nutrient through the peg. She had a very poor appetite. I knew she had lost a considerable amount of weight in the past year. However, it was impossible to weigh her. I tried to console myself by believing that she was getting enough nutrients.

Betty continued to develop pressure sores on her bottom. Just as we would get one healed, another would develop. The sores appeared despite the fact that we turned her frequently to relieve the pressure. We were no longer able to use the standing frame which was excellent for her circulation and muscles. The Physical

Therapist would come at least once each week to assess the wounds. Many times I thanked God for preparing me for such a time as this. Had I not been an orderly and also a military medic, I would have been helpless. Even though I had been in hospital administration for many years, I could not recall any administration friends who could do what I was now doing. God always equips us for what He calls us to do.

Betty also had developed sores on her ears. Her primary care physician referred her to a dermatologist. The dermatologist performed a biopsy of one of the lesions and when she received the report, she told us the sores were caused by pressure. She pre-scribed a medication for the sores and also gave us a suggestion. She smiled and said, "Go to a store and buy a large, soft pillow. Cut a hole in the pillow where her ear will fit. This should relieve the pressure on her ears so they will not develop sores." I did as I was told. I bought a foam pillow and Jamie helped me cut the hole. When we turned Betty on her side, we made sure that her ear was always resting in the hole. Betty's ears healed and never developed sores again.

Chapter 14:

Joy Comes in the Morning

♪♪

A s the days went by I tried not to notice the decline in Betty's health. She continued to attempt to tell me she was tired. I tried to ignore her comments. However, one Sunday afternoon as a Gaither video was playing, she became very restless and attempted to talk. The song that was playing was *Joy Comes in the Morning*:

> **If you've knelt beside the rubble of an aching, broken heart**
> **When the things you gave your life to falls apart**
> **You're not the first to be acquainted with sorrow, grief or pain,**
> **But the Master promised sunshine after rain.**
>
> **Hold on my child**
> **Joy comes in the morning,**
> **Weeping only lasts for the night.**
> **Hold on my child, joy comes in the morning,**
> **The darkest hour means dawn is just in sight.**
>
> **To invest your seed of trust in God**
> **In mountains you can't move,**
> **You have risked your life on things you cannot prove.**
> **But to give the things you cannot keep for**
> **What you cannot lose,**
> **Now that's the way to find the joy God has for you.**

Hold on my child,
Joy comes in the morning,
Weeping only lasts for the night.
Hold on my child, joy comes in the morning.
The darkest hour means dawn is just in sight.

When the song finished, I was near tears. I knew she wanted to tell me something and I was positive I knew what it was. I finally summoned the courage to ask. "Are you trying to tell me something about the song?" She nodded her head affirmatively. "Betty, are you trying to tell me again that you're tired and you want to go home?" I can still see those brilliant brown eyes looking deep within my soul as if she was looking for something special. I hoped she saw what she was looking for.

She nodded her head affirmatively again. "Have you lost hope that you will ever get well here on earth?" Looking at me for at least a minute and as if she dreaded responding, she finally nodded her head again. I began crying. I went to her and held her close. I told her that I had also lost hope and that if she wanted to go home that I would release her. Her body relaxed in my arms. The time that we had both dreaded had come. We had both finally agreed that she should be free from the things that had weighted her down for the last three years.

Memories flooded over me. As a newly married couple, at times I would think of the day when one of us would die and leave the other. I always hoped that I would be the one to go first. This day I felt as if someone was tearing my heart from my body. It hurt so badly. I believe at that time God let me have just a small taste of what He went through when His son was crucified.

I remembered an occasion months before as I was preparing Betty for the night she suddenly became very serious. She gave me one of her looks. Then quietly she said, "Louis." I had learned over the years when she called my name before speaking to me that she had something very important and usually something very serious to tell or ask me. This was no exception.

I responded, "Yes, sweetie?"

She quietly asked, "If I should go first, would you remarry?"

Without hesitation I said, "Absolutely not. We have had such a wonderful marriage and I would never be able to love someone else." She seemed satisfied. Then I asked, "If I should go before you, would you remarry?" Of course I knew what her answer would be before I asked. After all, she had experienced a massive stroke and a heart attack. She was totally dependent on me.

Her eyes and her mischievous smile flashed as she answered, "Well, probably." We both had a good laugh. It was so good to see her sense of humor was still alive and well.

However, now I did not want to be funny. This was serious business. We had both been very candid with each other. However, even though it was painful, there was still a sense of peace and relief. We finally had been very straightforward with each other and with God.

After I was able to talk again I asked her if she had seen angels in her room. She nodded and looked directly towards the end of her bed. "Is there just one," I asked. She nodded. "Is he standing at the end of your bed?" She nodded again. "Have you seen glimpses of Heaven?" Again, she nodded. How I wished she could talk! "Can you describe it for me?" She looked very intently and directly into my eyes. I knew that look. I had seen it before. If she could have spoken, I knew what her answer would have been. I had heard it too many times over the past forty-four years.

Her eyes were saying, "I knew you would ask, but I can't tell you because it is indescribable."

Chapter 15:

Why Don't You Speak to Me?

♪♫

The next day I was to have lunch with Sam. On my way to Georgetown it was all I could do to keep from crying. I had a Gaither CD playing. I cried out to God, "Why don't you speak to me? I need to know you are with me in all of this and right now I'm not sure where you are." Suddenly, Gloria Gaither began one of her wonderful messages...

Dear Child,

Lately I have noticed that the noise and pressures of the world and the demands of your commitments have left you exhausted and discouraged. I just want you to know that in it all I am with you. Draw from me; let me give you peace deep down where the world can never touch it. Make my words a part of you and they will make you strong. Whisper them to the morning; repeat them when the sun is low. Draw from them in the heat of the day. Now here are my words:

I have something very special for you—a gift. It is peace of mind and heart. And this peace isn't fragile like the peace the world gives. So don't let your heart be troubled and don't let it be afraid. Just remember that all I am and have is yours if you will just learn to trust me.

With all my love,
Father

Fortunately there was little traffic on the road. I began to cry. Peace flooded over me like I had never had before. However, the questions remained. What should I expect from God now? Total healing for Betty or should I prepare for her deliverance from all of this and allow God to take her to Him?

It was about this time when I realized I needed to see a grief counselor. I contacted our Employee Assistance Program and shared my concerns with them. They were very empathetic and told me they would schedule an appointment.

A few days later, as I dressed to go to my first appointment, two of my worst enemies, pride and doubt, raised their ugly heads. Why do you need a counselor? Why are you so weak? Aren't you a Christian? Christians should not need a counselor. What will your friends think? Look around and see all those people who have more problems and challenges than you do. You don't see them running off to a counselor. Don't you think God can counsel you? What will your family think? Why can't you just pray about it and let it go? You're going to hurt your Christian witness. The thoughts drowned out any positive thoughts.

However, I had made the appointment so I would keep it. One time was not going to hurt anything. Maybe God wants me to help the counselor because I am so strong. It's hard for me to admit that I, Louis West, need help.

I dreaded meeting the counselor. Maybe she would not be there. Wrong. She was right on schedule. I had to complete several privacy papers. The worst part of it was that I actually liked her immediately. Her name was Tammy. She was warm and friendly. She didn't stare at me as if I had mental problems. She started the conversation by asking me to tell her what brought me in. About half way through my reason for coming, I stopped and abruptly and asked, "You think I'm making all of this up don't you?"

She shook her head and said, "No, I am just wondering how you have survived for the past three years. If anyone has a reason to be depressed, you have several." I told her that I knew that God had been watching over me. She agreed. I was amazed that I could talk with her and cry very little.

She said I should quit bottling my emotions and learn to release them. I shared everything with her including my termination from the hospital. It helped to get a stranger's perspective.

The hour passed quickly and I wasn't through. I shared with her that I had a compelling need to write about whatever came to my mind regarding Betty and me. I had been sending regular emails to friends and family about Betty's progress and my feelings ever since she had the strokes. Tammy said, "I was just going to tell you that I always ask my clients to 'journal'. However, what you are doing is far better than putting it in a journal. You are actually writing to people who care about you and many of them are responding to you. That's great. Continue to write."

I also shared a dream that I had earlier that morning. I dreamed that Betty was comatose. I knew that she was dying. However, I had peace about it. Even after I awakened, I felt the peace of God. I had no idea what the dream meant but I felt it was significant. I was very thankful for the peace. It was that marvelous peace that passes all understanding that only God can give and I was learning that He gives that peace freely.

When I picked up Sam for lunch, I shared with him the conversation I had with Betty. I poured my heart out to him. I told him I did not understand why God had not answered my prayers the way I wanted. He listened attentively. I knew he would not condemn me for lack of faith. Finally he quietly said, "You just don't get it do you? God has allowed you three years with Betty since the strokes. He has allowed you to make some adjustments rather than taking her instantly. He has done many miracles for her." I don't remember what else he said. I just knew that peace once again came over me and I began to realize the next steps I needed to take.

Once again God was answering my prayer and giving me direction. Instead of condemning me, He was patiently guiding and revealing His perfect will for Betty and me. When will I ever learn to totally trust Him? Maybe never. Little did I realize at that time that

God was already preparing others and me for the future. The depth of God's love is so much deeper than my shallow thoughts.

After leaving Sam, I went to visit with June and Gene Prater. After small talk I told them of my conversation with Betty and also with Sam. I also shared with them the dream I had concerning Betty. They both told me they had felt the same way for some time. I realized the next step was to tell the children. Gene and June prayed for wisdom and peace for Betty, the children and me. I drove home with many thoughts rushing through my mind.

When I arrived at home I greeted Betty and Pam. I immediately went to my computer and sent the following words to Mark, Dawn, and Jamie:

I am going to mail each of you a letter tomorrow. You should receive it by Thursday or Friday. I did not want to send it by email. Love, Dad

I immediately began to write the letter.

Dear Mark, Dawn and Jamie,

I feel I need to let you know how things are really going here. I do not mean to be an alarmist and I know you know me well enough to know that I am not. This letter is about your mother. I am writing each of you and giving you my thoughts so that later you can't say, "I didn't know that or why didn't you tell me."

Several months ago while Betty could still communicate she let me know that she was tired. She also said, "I want to go home." Thinking there was some confusion, I said, "You are at home." She said, "I'm not talking about this home." We talked for quite awhile and through tears I told her that I was not tired and was not ready for her to go home. The conversation finally ended with my telling her she could not leave me. At various times later she would still say, "I'm so tired."

She has very little strength and it is difficult for her to sit in her wheelchair at times. Many days she does not want to get up. Granted this may all be tied to the thyroid deficiency.

She has been on medication and they will be checking that again this week with a blood test. There are times she apparently does not have the energy to eat so we supplement with the nutrient through the feeding tube.

I am going to be very candid with you. Some time ago I lost my hope. I never told anyone and still tried to believe that she would get better.

On one occasion some time ago when she told me again she was tired, I told her that I was not ready for her to go home but that I would release her if that is what she wanted and if it was what she believed that God wanted. The next morning on my way to work, I had a very candid prayer time and also told God that I was releasing her for Him to do whatever He wanted to do. Consciously or unconsciously, sometime after that I reneged on that statement. I realized I was not ready and began to look for signs of improvement. I'm sure that is also when the depression for myself began to manifest.

Last week in the counseling session with Tammy, I told her about all of this. She quietly asked me, "Have you given permission again to her?" I told her, "Yes, I have but I have not told Betty." She told me that I needed to tell her.

On Friday morning before my grief counseling session, I had a dream. I have only shared it with June and Gene this afternoon. I dreamed that Betty was in a coma and I realized the end was near. I awakened before that happened. In the dream I was not distraught or anxious. I was at peace because I knew this was what she wanted.

147

I have no idea what the dream meant if anything.

Yesterday afternoon while the song, Joy Comes in The Morning was playing, she became very intent and made many sounds and her eyes were flashing. I asked if she needed to tell me something. She shook her head yes. I began to go through questions. What she wanted to tell me was that she was tired, lost hope and wanted to go home. After a long talk, (I'm asking yes and no questions) I told her that I would give her permission to go home. She seemed to be satisfied with that. I know she is very concerned about me although I try never to portray that I'm tired, etc.

So what does this mean? I'm not sure. I will not attempt to convince you to release her but I am asking you to do that. Maybe we need to do that so that He can do a miracle or— maybe He wants to take her home. I also know that without a doubt if she could speak, she would also ask you to release her. I asked her if she had released herself and she shook her head "no." I asked if she wanted to and she shook her head "yes." So I prayed a prayer of release for her. I asked if she agreed with what I had prayed. She shook her head "yes."

For the past several days I have also had thoughts about a Victory Service for her. I believe God is preparing me for what is ahead in the near future. I do not believe that He will leave her in this condition much longer. She will get better or He will take her home.

I know this is hard for each of you as well. Just know that I love you and pray for God's peace. Thank you for your prayers for Betty and me.

Love,
Dad

Each day I tried to send an email to many of our friends and relatives. Many of them responded and said the messages were very helpful. I seriously believe the reason I wrote them was for my own benefit. They were healing for me. Many times they were serious and occasionally I attempted to add humor. The following is an example of one that I wrote during this particular time in our journey.

May 24, 2005

Today I had lunch with Sam. You must meet him some day if you haven't already. I told you he will tell you what he thinks and doesn't say nice things just because you would like to hear them. Don't get me wrong. Once in awhile he even says something nice to me. I can't remember anything right now but I'm sure he has sometime or other. I had to go to administration for a minute and on my way I met some of the therapists. Therapy Services was one of my departments. It was so good to see the ladies and they seemed pleased to see me. They told me how much they missed me and asked about Betty. Once you ever meet Betty you never forget her.

As I was getting gasoline today just before noon, Lisa Jeffery, a Physical Therapist here in Taylor who ran the American Stroke Association's Marathon in 2003 in Betty's honor came over and gave me a big hug. She was so saddened when I told her about Betty's decline in health. We stood there and cried. When I arrived at home after lunch, Pam was dressing Betty. Betty has been able to swallow the past two days but she continues to get choked pretty easily. It was hot here today and I was rather surprised that Pam was taking Betty out. However, Pam said it would only be for a few minutes. Betty and Pam left the house and in a short time Pam came into the house and said that Betty was sitting under the tree and that she wanted Pam to read the Bible to her. I have told you there are ways to communicate without words if you work at it. Pam is so thoughtful. If that had been me,

I probably would not have asked if Betty would rather sit under the tree. I would have just strolled her up the street. When it was time for Pam to leave, I went out and sat with Betty. It was nice sitting under the giant Burr Oak tree that I planted from an acorn in the early seventies. One of Betty's friends, Mary Ann Zimmerhanzel gave the acorn to Betty. The wind was just enough to keep us cool. The front flowerbed by the mailbox is full of beautiful pink, blue and yellow blooms including some native Primrose. There were also some bees searching for sweet nectar. Occasionally a bird flew over us. Everything I plant is for Betty. She loves flowers but is not a gardener. She dug up one of my beautiful Gerber Daisies several years ago because she thought it was a huge dandelion trying to take over the flowerbed. The daisy looked so pitiful lying wilted and chopped up on the sidewalk. I told Betty I could tell the daisy had died a horrible death. Betty promised never to get in the flowerbeds again. She was very good at mowing for which I was thankful.

I can't sit for long periods so I suggested to Betty that I trim her nails. I attempted to trim them a couple of days ago but it was difficult to trim them in the house because of the poor lighting. I have to be very careful not to cut her fingers. Because of Betty's low thyroid her nails became brittle and were splitting. The dermatologist recommended that I get Elon at the drug store and use it on her nails to soften them and keep them from splitting. It worked well. It takes just a tiny bit rubbed into each nail including the base of the nail. I was able to trim her fingernails easily. I will trim her toenails in the morning. For several years she has used Aquaphor on her nails and hands to keep them moist and soft. Our dear friend, Dr. Valerian Chyle, a radiation oncologist recommended she use it routinely.

Fortunately I learned early in our marriage to consult Betty about even minor decisions. Betty also did the same for me. We built our marriage as a true partnership. We tried to always include God in our decisions. Early in our engagement period I realized she had a very close personal relationship and walk with her heavenly Father. What an inspiration she was and continues to be for me. Betty was my most ardent encourager. I have always remembered how supportive and encouraging she was when I first mentioned in 1964 before Mark was two years old about returning to college to get my Bachelor's degree. Betty encouraged me even more in 1982 when I approached her about enrolling for my Master's degree. She often told me there was nothing I could not accomplish if God was in it. I knew she was a precious gift given to me by God.

Love,
Louis

On Friday May 27, 2005, Mark, who was teaching at the Federal Law Enforcement Training Center in Brunswick, Georgia at that time, sent me the following email in response to my letter to him, Dawn, and Jamie a few days before.

Hi,

I got the letter today. It was as I expected from some of your earlier emails. I know it was difficult to write and it is equally difficult to read.

This is hard to write too. I've had to stop 3 times already. We don't want her to be tired anymore either. We will do whatever she wants.

We were going to surprise you but I'll tell you now that we will be parked in front of your house sometime on Wednesday June 8. We are leaving very early this Friday morning and driving to Houston. We will spend the night with Jamie and then go to Lockhart to surprise everyone at Donnie's (Cheryl's Dad) 70th birthday party.

We will stay there until Wednesday and then come to Taylor. Cheryl has to be back at work Monday so we are driving her to Houston on Friday to catch a flight on Saturday.

The kids and I will be back in Taylor on Monday and leave for home on Saturday. We'll spend the night somewhere and be back at home on Sunday the 19th.

We can't wait to see everyone.

Love,
Mark

I was excited to tell Betty that Mark, Cheryl, Lauren, Kristen, and Colton were coming. I was glad he shared the news with us because it is good to anticipate something wonderful.

When I sent emails to friends and family, I attempted to have a positive message. I did not tell them how I really felt. However, I knew it was time to inform everyone of Betty's decline. Finally on May 30, I sent out an email to our family and very close friends who lived away. I determined I would wait awhile to notify everyone else.

I told them of the times Betty had told me that she wanted to go home. I reminded them of her loss of speech and the extreme weakness. I finally confessed I had lost hope as well. I described her condition in detail. I finally realized that I felt as if I needed their approval for what we were doing. I felt like a little boy telling his parents all the benefits of going to a major league baseball game before finally summoning the courage to ask, "Can we go?" I was concerned that they might not give their approval. I did not want them to think that my faith had weakened. I finally realized that it did not matter how they felt about me. I had to do what I believed God wanted me to do. I should not be trying to win a "faith" contest. If they were basing their confidence in God upon me, they were off base anyway. I shared with them that when she first mentioned going home that I told her "no." I explained that I had discussed my decision with the children and they were in total agreement with me.

I also shared with the family and close friends that I had shared my decision with her older brother, Jerry. His response was, "When she goes, all that I can say is 'thank God.'" He shared that it broke his heart to see her in this condition.

I finally asked them to release her also so that she could go home. My last paragraph was intended to assure them that we have not lost our faith and confidence in God, but that we were ready for His perfect plan to be fulfilled whatever that is. I spoke candidly of how God had been speaking and dealing with me for several weeks regarding her.

The following morning Betty slept until 9:30 a.m. Normally, she was awake by 7:00 a.m. Some of her medicines had to be given on an empty stomach so I gave those before 7:00 a.m. After I gave Betty the meds we had to wait for an hour before she could eat. She had not awakened by 8:00 a.m. so I gave her other meds with nutrient in her tube because those meds could not be given without food in her stomach.

When Betty finally awakened at 9:30 a.m., I prepared her breakfast of Cream of Wheat and pureed fresh fruit salad. The salad consisted of strawberries, apples, grapes and bananas. If fresh fruits were out of season, I would use frozen fruit. My brother Weldon and his wife Emma Jo had sent us some wonderful frozen peaches that were home grown. I had been saving them for a special occasion.

I decided that this was a special day so I added some of them to the salad. I told Pam they were specifically for Betty and that she and I would have to do without. However, I decided I probably should taste them to make sure they were good. Then I felt guilty and told Pam she could sample them also. They were wonderful. Later I gave Betty the peaches alone because they were so good.

This morning Betty had great difficulty in swallowing. She ate very little fruit and cereal. She continued to doze and keep the food in her mouth. I knew that was dangerous. I finally stopped trying to feed her and hoped for a better time. However, that did not happen. We saved the fruit for later. June and Gene Prater came to visit but Betty did not react to their coming. She continued to doze.

For lunch I prepared a wonderful pot roast with delicious gravy with which to puree Betty's food. We had the same scenario for lunch as we had with breakfast. She could not swallow and continued to doze.

Betty was unable to eat, so I fixed a plate of food for me. I usually ate my food in her bedroom. I enjoyed sitting close to her as often as possible. Even though many times she was sound asleep, I would fix my plate and take it to her room. In the mornings, I would fix a cup of coffee and sit beside her and hold her hand or pat her arm. It was very natural to want to be close to her. Somehow I knew these precious times were not going to last much longer.

On this particular day it was extremely difficult for me. As I was eating my delicious food and looking at her, my mind flooded with remembrances of the funny things she would say and I also remembered her sharp wit. Now she could not call my name plainly enough for anyone to understand except Pam and me. I cried unashamedly but I did not want her to see me crying. I can't explain why. She had seen me cry many times in the past months, but please, God, not today.

Betty dozed almost all afternoon. Around 5:00 p.m., I asked if she felt like getting up. She nodded. I dressed her in a hot-pink top and white pants. Cheryl, Mark's wife, had given her a sharp-looking straw hat a couple of years before. Betty had to wear sunglasses when we went outside because one of her medications dilated her eyes. She also wore white Keds with white socks. Of course, for her to be perfectly groomed, I applied pink lipstick. I knew Dawn, who had a degree in fashion merchandising, would have really enjoyed seeing her so sharply dressed.

The following day was similar to the previous day. Betty slept late again. She still had swallowing difficulties. Several months prior when she had this problem, the Speech Pathologist used an electrical device on her throat and around her mouth that stimulated the swallowing reflex. Betty hated the procedure and I wondered if I would be doing her a favor to request that it be used again.

She continued to appear to be very tired. I dared not show that I was also tired. I was not tired physically, but mentally. Sometimes I became tired spiritually also. I knew that God was my joy and my strength. However, there were times that I wanted to forget about being strong and just collapse. It was times like this that I could talk with Sam. I knew he would encourage me and not condemn me.

Although in my heart I knew no one would condemn me if I confessed I was tired, I wanted to be the one who encouraged everyone else. On various occasions, I told God I was tired. His response was always "My joy is your strength." I knew He would not allow more to be placed upon me than I could bear. I confessed this often. The joy of the Lord is my strength. He is my refuge during this storm in my life. He is my Rock. I will run to the Rock.

When I was a little child, a little baby in our community died. I wasn't for sure what death was at that young age. I can still see the dirt piled up around the large hole in the ground with a little white box somehow suspended over the hole. There at the graveside, the people sang Rock of Ages. Since I was a very young child, I thought they were singing Rock-a-Bye Baby. I remember singing at the top of my little lungs, "Rock-a-Bye Baby in the Tree Top, When the Wind Blows the Cradle will Rock." My mom frantically tried to "shush" me but I just kept belting it out. As I look back over the years at that incident, I wonder if God didn't use that moment to encourage the young couple that had lost their little one. It had to have brought a moment of joy to them or God would have closed my little mouth Himself. At least I have comforted myself with that thought.

I was born into a singing family. We weren't professional but all of us loved to sing hymns. My brothers played the guitar and harmonica. My Mom could play the piano but we did not have one at home at that time. We also had a large Victrola. This was actually a record player that worked by turning a crank as far as you could turn it. Long before I started to school, a neighbor man would come visit us and give me pennies to sing and dance while the record was playing. That was the closest that I ever got to a dance floor, as my parents did not approve of dancing. I wonder if they have seen me now when I dance before the Lord. Just Him and me.

Knowing that Christians all over the United States were praying for us was such a comfort. Many of them we did not know. However, as brothers and sisters in Christ, we don't have to personally know each other to weep with them and pray with them. We don't have to be members of the same denomination to have love for each other if we have the Spirit of God living within us. Prayer transcends all distance. I enjoyed reading their encouraging words and the love was so evident.

My friends Dorothy and Rod had prayed for us since Betty had the strokes. I worked with Dorothy at the Georgetown Hospital. When they retired they moved back to Iowa. They had just gotten settled when Rod had a ruptured aneurysm. He has been near death many times in the past years. However, each time God raises him up and he improves. The following is an excerpt of an email from Dorothy:

We are so sorry for what you are going through, both of you. It is so difficult to let go and yet there is a time. Betty has suffered so long and deserves the peace and contentment that is waiting for her. Reading your emails has brought us to see the love you two have for each other and the admiration we both have for you. I have often thought that it would be easier for you if Betty were in a nursing home. Yet I knew, you would not do this as you have enjoyed every moment you can spend with her. I feel our own experience has made us better people—more loving and considerate. I can see that it has given the two of you the closest and most loving relationship. You have many friends and you will make it through this.

I knew churches all over the country had us on their prayer list. At times someone we did not know would send us a personal note such as the ones below:

6-2-2005

Dear Louis and Betty,

I am so thankful we serve the Lord Jesus Christ, Jehovah-shammah—The Lord is There. May you feel a fresh touch from Jehovah-shammah for truly, He is there with you.

In Christ's love,
MB

7-29-03

Dear Betty,

What a joy and privilege to pray for you over the last year. I am praying for strength, courage and recovery. ALL our hope is in our precious Lord Jesus. He will sustain both you and Louis. May our Lord meet your needs with His abundance. Emma Jo and Weldon are dear, dear friends. God's richest blessings to you both. We care about you! Our prayers will continue from Temple Baptist.

In His Love

We also knew friends and family were praying for us. The note below is from my wonderful sister-in-law, Emma Jo West, wife of my oldest living brother, Weldon.

7-29-03

Dear Betty and Louis,

I just prayed for each of you, asking God's healing for you, Betty. You are so precious to all who know you!! Louis, you too are so precious to others also. May God continue to give you good health and strength beyond measure.

There are so many troubles and trials in this life. The best is yet to come for those who know the Lord.

Our prayer room is filled with many books of prayer requests of all kinds including the lost. So many.

Love you both,
Emma Jo

This is a portion of a letter I received on June 4, 2005:

We can only partially imagine how tired, weary and miserable Betty must be. Louis, I believe she has had a glimpse of Heaven (maybe more than once) and of course, she desires it. No doubt her rewards will be far beyond our comprehension, and just think of that mansion He has prepared for her.

God will continue to strengthen, guide and care for you. You could not have done the many tasks during these years except through God giving you guidance, strength and courage. God will never forsake you. Yes, He will have you prepared for what is to come, because you are one of His faithful children!!

That letter came just as I needed confirmation to discuss with Betty some things my counselor had told me I needed to do. Betty confirmed to me that she has had more than one glimpse of Heaven and she also had seen Jesus. Yes, it did make her want to go there. She let me know that she is no longer concerned about me because she knows that the Holy Spirit will comfort me. We were able to have a good five-minute discussion and I did not cry. No, Betty did not communicate with words other than yes and no and shaking her head. But, oh, those eyes...they said so much.

After our talk, I determined to let all those friends and relatives who had been praying for us know exactly what was now happening in our life just as I had previously informed close relatives. Therefore on May 30, I sent the following email:

This is the second most difficult email I have ever sent. The most difficult was one that I sent to the kids last week and told them I was sending them a letter. You may have picked up on some of my emails that Betty is not doing well. She told me in December as she was losing her speech that she was tired and wanted to go home. I told her she was at home and she said," It's not this home I am talking about."

Amid a lot of tears, I tried to convince her that she would get better. She did not agree but I did not give in and told her I was believing for a total healing for her. Then soon thereafter, she lost her speech completely. She also began to have difficulty with swallowing. After we discovered her thyroid was very low, I attributed everything to that. The thyroid is now normal through the use of medications and she has not improved. She is deteriorating. She told me about ten days ago through "yes," "no" questions that she had lost hope in getting well. She also agreed that she is very tired and wants to go home. I had to admit that I have also lost hope that she will recover. If you could see her being so miserable that she does not feel like getting up anymore, you would have a better understanding of where we are in this situation. I would go on forever but that is not what she wants. She wanted me to give her permission to go home. I did this about ten days ago. I had done it in January but it was words only. I could not let her go at that time. God has used these months to do more work in me to accept this and now I am at peace about her release. The kids know all of this and it is very hard on them as you can imagine. I believe they have released her or they will soon. Mark and family are coming next week. They had planned to surprise us but after my letter he told me they plan to come. I can hardly see as I am crying while typing this. I told Betty's brother yesterday afternoon about her wanting to go home. He said his response would be when she goes is "Thank God." He said it just breaks his heart to see her like this. She is beginning to sleep much more than usual. She did not awaken this morning until 10:00. Normally she would be awake by 7:00. Please pray that God will take her and she won't linger for months. She would not like that. I appreciate all your prayers but wanted you to know what we are praying about now. Whenever or however God takes her will be the best for all concerned. We have definitely not lost our faith in knowing that He loves us and has a perfect plan. God has been speaking and dealing with me regarding this situation very strongly for the past weeks. I believe He is getting me ready for her Homegoing. We love you. Louis

Later as I was going through some papers in my desk, among them was a single sheet and it was titled "Grief" adapted from Adolfo Quezada. I am not familiar with him and I'm not sure who sent the article. It answered many questions concerning grief that I had. It is printed below:

Such is the nature of loss that no matter how much time has passed, and no matter how much life has been experienced, the heart of the bereaved will never be the same. It is as though a part of us also dies with the person we lose. We will be right, but we will never be the same.

And so my old friend Grief drops in to say hello. Sometimes he enters through the door of memory. I'll hear a certain song or smell a certain fragrance, or I'll look at a certain picture and I'll remember how it used to be. Sometimes it brings a smile to my face, sometimes a tear.

Some may say that such remembering is not healthy, that we ought not to dwell on thoughts that make us sad. Yet, the opposite is true. Grief revisited is grief acknowledged, and grief confronted is grief resolved.

But if grief is resolved, why do we still feel a sense of loss come during anniversaries and holidays, and even when we least expect it? Why do we feel a lump in the throat, even six years after the loss? It is because healing does not mean forgetting, and because moving on with life does not mean that we don't take a part of our lost loved one with us.

Sometimes my old friend Grief sneaks up on me. I'll feel an unexplained but profound sadness that clings to me for days. Then I'll recognize the grief and cry a little, and then

I can go on. It's as though the ones we loved and lost are determined not to be forgotten.

My old friend Grief doesn't get in the way of my living. He just wants to come along and chat sometimes. In fact, Grief has taught me a few things about living that I would not have learned on my own. Old Grief has taught me, over the years, that if I try to deny the reality of a major loss in my life, I end up having to deny life altogether. He has taught me although the pain of loss is great, I must confront it and experience it fully.

Old Grief has also taught me that I can survive great losses, and that although my world is very different after a major loss, it is still my world and I must live in it. He has taught me that when I am pruned by the losses that come, and when I let go, I can flourish again in season and bring forth the good fruit that comes, not in spite of my losses, but because of them.

My old friend Grief has taught me that the loss of a loved one does not mean the loss of love, for love is stronger than separation.

I read this several times. It answered several questions that I had. Some of my thoughts and actions now made perfect sense to me. I really wasn't losing my mind. It continues to amaze me when God just shows up and meets my specific needs for that time. I am not surprised; I am amazed at His love for me. It is indescribable.

Chapter 16:

Releasing Betty

ℐℐ

B etty made no noticeable changes in the next few days. I would talk to her about Mark and Cheryl and the kids coming soon. Her eyes would become more alert and I knew she was anxiously waiting to love on them.

The day before their arrival, Betty had another surprise visit. Lisa Jeffery who ran the marathon in her honor in 2003 came. I did not tell Betty that Lisa was coming. When she saw Lisa, her eyes brightened like a three hundred watt light bulb. She tried so hard to talk to Lisa but the words would not come. This did not keep her from hugging her as best she could with her right arm. She had not forgotten the therapists who had worked so faithfully with her for so long and neither would I. I could only imagine what she was trying to tell Lisa. I'm sure she was telling her that she would be going to Heaven soon.

I had finally gotten to the point that I could talk with Betty about her desire to go to Heaven and be with Jesus. I would talk about various loved ones that were already there. I did not arrive at this point easily. I had to completely change my prayers, my thoughts, and my words. It had been almost three years since Betty had the strokes. I never had the slightest doubt that she would make a complete recovery until about three months previously. Yet as I looked at her, it appeared that God had a far greater plan for her than I had believed. He had also done a great work in me. Now I could accept the fact that He had a different plan all along. He was just so merciful to her children, grandchildren, and me to allow her to be with us for these three additional years.

When I think of the damage Betty's brain sustained with the strokes, I, along with her doctors and other medical personnel, are amazed that she lived through the first night. Then having the heart attack two years later and surviving was truly a miracle from God. Even though it was obvious to me that she was not going to recover, I could rejoice and give thanks because I knew that in Heaven she would have a completely new body. The peace that passes all understanding was mine again.

I was reminded of when my Mom had died in 1973. In her later years, she had dementia and was bedfast. I was very close to her as I was her baby of ten kids. It was very hard for me to give her up. As a child, I can remember dreading the day she would die. Living over two hundred miles away kept me from seeing her in the latter days as much as I would have liked. She was in pain and apparently did not know any of us. I could not understand why God did not take her. The last visit I made with her I told my family to call me when she died. I told her goodbye as best I could and left.

Days passed and she still lingered. Late the following Friday evening while walking in the neighborhood, I began grieving heavily. Finally I asked God why He wouldn't take her home. He didn't answer me so I continued to walk. In a few moments a thought came. I had not released her to God. Sadly, I had a very candid discussion with Him. I will never forget it. I told Him that I was upset because He continued to allow her to suffer. I knew she was ready. Then as if lightning had struck, I realized that five minutes before, I had confessed that I had not released her. While walking and crying I released her to Him. Within an hour we received a call from Wayne, my oldest brother, to tell us Mom had gone home.

The next time I saw her was at the funeral home. I hardly recognized her. The last time I had seen her she was in horrible pain and her body was emaciated. In those days, they did not know how to do pain management. Now she appeared to be no older than 60 years of age, although she was actually 80. Her skin was beautiful and soft. She even had a faint smile. What a transformation.

A few days after my mother's funeral service, Jamie, who was two, came to me. Looking up at me with those big brown eyes that were just like her mother's, she said, "Daddy, just think...

grandmamma can walk now." That was so comforting to me and I have remembered those words many times. God uses the little children to remind us of His promises.

Now the one I loved so much that I would gladly have taken her place through the pain and sickness was planning to take a trip. We both knew she had made all the preparations several years before as a small child when she accepted Jesus as her Savior. Because of Jesus, I knew Betty would walk again right beside my Mom.

I never took for granted that God had healed Betty of many diseases that modern medicine thought to be incurable. He had answered the prayer that I prayed the morning after she had the strokes. I am no better than any of His other children. God does not play favorites. Betty and I had prayed for years that He would take away the pain that she had. We never gave up. We never lost hope. We had agreed together. I believe that if a husband and wife can be in perfect agreement in prayer that God will answer. It may not always be what we want but it will be what is best for us. I had thrown myself upon Him and His mercy. I also had learned to remind Him that I really wanted what was best for Betty and what would bring glory to Him.

He honored my little faith when Betty could not talk or know what was going on. He remembered all the times that we had come to Him as one. God tells us that we will never have more placed upon us than we can bear. Betty had much placed upon her. She had Polymyositis, an autoimmune disease that some of the medical professionals, including some of the doctors, were not familiar with. I would give them a fast lesson so they would understand that it caused severe pain in her muscles and she had experienced it for several years. She had been able to walk but not well.

She also had neuropathy in her hands and feet so badly that at times she would scream with the pain. She had high blood pressure for which she had taken medication for several years. She also had Irritable Bowel Syndrome. If those diseases were not enough, after the strokes, she developed Type II diabetes. God healed all of those diseases. It is recorded in her medical records.

Because God had healed all of those diseases, it was difficult for me not to ask what we had done wrong. Why had He not healed her from all the damage that the strokes had caused? Was it something we had not done? I never asked God those questions. Up until a few months prior, I believed she would be totally healed. Did He know something and was just not telling me? Would I ever know the answer? Even though I never verbally asked those questions, I knew that He realized I was wondering. Betty always said I had more curiosity than anyone she had ever known. Because God formed me in my mother's womb, He knows that also.

It was good to have Mark and Cheryl and the children in the house. There did not appear to be any significant changes in Betty. She tried to talk with them but just could not. The day came when Cheryl would need to go to Houston to the airport. Prior to their leaving we left her alone with Betty. I knew she was telling her goodbye. I dreaded the day that I would have to do that.

Because Mark and the children had taken Cheryl to Houston to fly home, I was left alone with Betty much of the time, especially in the evenings. On Friday evening after I had finished giving Betty her tube feeding, administering her medicines, and praying with her, she went to sleep quickly. Because I was alone I decided to call Diane, Betty's niece who is also a neurologist and stroke specialist in San Antonio. Betty was Diane's godmother. She had visited us often through the years and I depended on her greatly when I just needed to talk with someone who understood our situation. I had also sent her the same letter I had sent the children. Normally I would have called her to give her that kind of news, but I knew that I could not handle that call emotionally.

As usual when I called her, her sweet voice calmed me. She is a very busy person but she always has time to talk with me. She is a mother of twin boys and also a younger boy. Her husband, Dale, is a very busy anesthesiologist. She immediately told me that she and Dale had planned to come to see us the next day however, two hours before my call they learned that Dale's mom was having a pacemaker implanted the next morning.

She immediately asked, "How's Aunt Betty?" I told her that I had some concerns along with some questions. She was very candid which is what I needed. She told me that she could not understand why Betty lost her speech again unless she had another stroke. I suggested that

I should have noticed some symptoms at the time. She agreed. She reminded me again that it was extremely rare for a person to live after the type strokes that Betty had in 2002. She said she believed that God was not through with her here at the time of the strokes and that Betty was a fighter. She also told me that because of Betty's high intelligence and being a fighter that she was able to learn to communicate again. Whatever caused her to lose her speech again last October had hit her very hard. Diane also believed that Betty could remember how hard she had worked to regain her speech and that she probably just did not have the energy and strength to do that again. Because Betty was ready for Heaven, she probably just told God, "I'm not going to fight any more. I want to go home."

We also discussed the strength it took her to survive the heart attack in July 2004. Then Diane asked the question that I had been dreading. "Uncle Louis, don't you feel it is time to contact hospice?"

"Oh, no, I think we're a long ways from that," I said. She told me that she felt I needed to discuss it with Betty's primary care physician or the neurologist. We continued that conversation. I was still hesitant. I knew what needed to be done before Diane had even mentioned it. However, I was not ready to admit that we needed to contact hospice.

Thoughts raced through my mind. After all, I wasn't tired. Pam and I could still care for her. Please God! Help me!

When someone is on hospice service everyone assumes that person is dying. I'm not ready for Betty to die. It doesn't matter that I have told her that I have released her. So what if the song says "Joy Comes in the Morning?" I can't be joyful if Betty goes on hospice. I can't imagine life without her. Can't you take me too? Why did I make this phone call?

Diane's sweet voice brought me back to reality. "Uncle Louis, just because someone goes on hospice does not mean they are going to die immediately. Hospice will be of great help to you and Aunt Betty."

"Yeah, I know," I muttered.

Diane gently responded, "You are so much further along with this process than most families would be. You do what you feel comfortable with."

I agreed with Diane. When I expressed my agreement, a deep peace fell over my entire being. At that time I knew that no matter what happened, God was with me and would shelter me. My next step would be to write each of her doctors a letter expressing what is going on with Betty. If they agree, we will proceed with hospice. Diane prayed for me and we said goodbye.

The next morning was June 11, 2005, which was the 44th anniversary of our engagement, I wrote the following letter to her primary care doctor and copied her five other doctors:

June 11, 2005

Dear Dr. Shallin:

I am also copying Betty's other doctors with this letter to keep all of you informed about her. I have recently spoken with Betty's niece, Dr. Diane Solomon in San Antonio. She is a neurologist. She suggested I contact you and that it might be the time to get hospice involved.

As most of you are aware, Betty began to lose her speech in October of last year. By January she could not communicate except with yes-no answers. After we discovered the thyroid was not functioning well, I attributed the speech problems and lack of energy to that. We had her thyroid rechecked toward the end of May and it is functioning normally. Her speech has never improved.

Betty told me in December that she was tired and wanted to go home. Thinking she had a UTI and was confused, I explained that she was at home. She replied, "I'm not talking about this home." I continued to encourage her and told her that I was not tired of caring for her and that I was still believing that she would get well.

A few weeks ago, she began to make the sounds that she makes when she really wants me to know something. I

began the yes-no questions. I definitely determined that she has lost hope of getting well, she is tired and she wants to go home. At that time, I will admit that I began crying. I told her that I had also lost hope of her getting well and that if she wanted to go home and she believed that was what God wanted, I would not stand in her way. At that time I told her I would give my permission for her to go.

She has limited energy, sleeps much more than she did and does not wish to get out of bed. This has been very noticeable for the past 2-3 weeks. Her vitals are good and her chemistry profile is normal. She still is able to eat pureed food. However, she does tend to get choked at times even with no particles of food in her mouth. I know that each of you have her best interests at heart. She has had a living will for several years and I want to honor it. I do not advocate stopping her nourishment and water and keeping her comfortable. She has an appointment with Dr. Fox on June 22. I don't believe she will be able to travel to see any of you much longer. I need your help with this. I have directed the letter to Dr. Shallin since he is her primary physician. As you may or may not be aware, I am no longer working at the hospital. You can contact me at home. My number is 555-1607.

Sincerely,
Louis West
Cc: Dr. Fox, Dr. Garland, Dr. Alam, Dr. Freidberg, Dr. Godinez

Monday morning I personally delivered the letters to each of the doctors. I decided against contacting hospice to give the doctors an opportunity to visit with each other or me.

The following morning as I was standing before my bathroom mirror it was noticeably quiet in the house. Pam was in Betty's bedroom and our precious Sheltie, Pepper, was napping. Pepper would go into Betty's room quite often and walk around the bed. It was if she knew something significant was going to take place. The only sound I could hear was the whirring of my electric razor. I was quietly praying and meditating. Suddenly I began to praise God for all His blessings and His great love and mercy towards Betty and me. All at once, He began to communicate with me in my spirit. It was as plain as if He were audibly speaking to me.

He said, "I want to speak with you. I know you have concerns about why Betty has not been healed."

I interrupted at that time, "I have tried to never question you and what you were doing."

He continued, "I want you to know that I have used her to strengthen the belief in others. It is not because of something you or Betty did or did not do. I have shown Betty glimpses of Heaven in the past and she made the decision at that time that she would prefer to go home rather than to be here. This is a sickness unto death." At that moment, there was total silence again.

I was not familiar with "sickness unto death." Had I misunderstood? I wanted to be certain. If He loved me enough to make a special visit to comfort and console me, I certainly wanted to understand the message. At times I had wondered why she was not healed. I wasn't mad at God; I just had a curiosity as to what had transpired so that perhaps I could help others.

I immediately checked the concordance for the word "sickness." It referred me to St. John 11:4. In speaking about Lazarus, Jesus said, "This sickness is *not* unto death, but for the glory of God, that the Son of God might be glorified thereby." I am neither a theologian nor a Bible scholar. I can only write what I believe God intended for me. If the sickness that Lazarus had was not unto death, there must be some sicknesses that are unto death. God had plainly spoken to me that "this is a sickness unto death." That explanation was sufficient for me.

Because of His visit, I knew that I was right in preparing for Betty's Homegoing.

On June 17, Mark and the children left for Georgia. It had been wonderful to have them with us. It was always nice to have visitors.

Betty was beginning to have more occasions when she either did not want to eat or was unable to swallow her food. Sleep consumed a large part of her day. I continued to try to fix her favorite foods and puree them.

One night as I was getting her night medications ready I could sense she wanted to talk. I asked if she wanted to talk about going home. She nodded her head affirmatively. We discussed it for awhile. It was getting easier to do.

At one point, very plainly she said, "Louis, help me." It was at times like this it would break my heart because I could not "fix" everything for her. I asked what she needed and she tried to tell me. So we went back to the questions that could be answered by yes or no. She still wanted to go home. I told her that I did not blame her and that she had already won the battle. I explained that she would soon receive her rewards and that I knew God was very proud of her. Because she is so modest and unassuming, she portrayed a look as if to ask, "What did I do?" I told her that when she goes to Heaven, we are going to have a wonderful victory service to celebrate her life. I also told her that we will miss her but we will be with her soon.

As each day passed I was reminded of my conversation with Diane about hospice. Later that evening, I determined to call Austin Hospice the next morning.

I slept fairly well that night and when I awakened my mind was full of thoughts of things that I needed to do before calling the hospice office. I needed to mow and edge the lawn, water the flowerbeds, vacuum, do the laundry and put clean linens on the extra bed. Prior to my leaving the hospital, I had a cleaning service come in once each week and clean the house. Because I was at home all the time now, I took on that responsibility. I had always enjoyed cleaning the house. Many times when I was the CEO of a hospital, I would show the housekeepers how I wanted the floors, etc. cleaned. It was easier to show them than to tell them. I never thought I was too good to do what I would ask someone else to do.

After giving Betty's medications, I ate a light breakfast. I told Betty that Pam would be here soon and that I had several things that I had to accomplish.

I had mowed about two-thirds of our front yard and the mower was really humming since its annual tune up. As I mowed close to a flowerbed, I heard a horribly loud noise. The mower died. Hanging on the mower was the small metal stand that should have been attached to my fertilizer spreader. I had lost it sometime last year and found it in the flowerbed last week. I laid it outside the bed having good intentions of putting it back on the spreader. I had noticed it several times during the week and my thoughts were always the same. However, I thought it was so small that even if I accidentally ran over it with the mower it would not hurt anything. The sensible thing to have done was to have laid it back in the flowerbed. Now the mower had completely severed the metal frame and I knew that quite likely had broken the shaft on the mower. As I was rescuing it from the mower, my first thoughts were, God, you knew that thing was there. Why didn't you remind me of it?

Those were wrong thoughts to have. I didn't stop there however. I even said aloud, "Now I've probably ruined the mower and you know I'm in a hurry."

Have you ever made a smart remark to your Dad or Mom and immediately wished that you could withdraw it? Well it was too late for me. I remembered as a child in grade school when my Dad reprimanded me. I was trying to do homework one night by the light of a kerosene lamp. My Dad happened to walk between the lamp and me. He stood there for a few seconds with his back turned to me. I stared at him very intently with a frown crossing my face. He turned at that time and saw my unpleasant look. He immediately asked, "Am I molesting you in some way?" I knew I was going to be reprimanded.

"Oh, no, sir," was my quick response. He never said another word.

Here is verbatim what my Heavenly Father's response was as he spoke to my spirit. It was so plain that He might as well have spoken verbally to me. I have never forgotten it.

"First of all I showed you last week where the stand was and told you to put it on the spreader. You disobeyed. Then no less than four times I told you to pick it up from the grass or the mower might hit it. Louis, I have given you a fine mind. I expect you to use it. This was not something that you should have needed my intervention on anyway. You are rushing around too fast. Stay away from the mower until I am finished talking to you. I want your attention. Just last night, one of my children who is older and wiser than you are told you at least twice to slow down and get some rest this week. I know what your plans are for today. I want you to change them.

When you are finished with the front lawn—stop. Do the back lawn another day. What will it matter if you don't get it all done today? Why are you in such a rush to vacuum and change the sheets?"

"Well, Lord, someone might come and see that I didn't get it all finished."

"So what? Who are you doing this for? Are you doing it for others or for me? I have not heard you say in a long time that you are mowing the grass for me or making the bed for me." He continued, "You used to say that quite frequently. Louis, you are too concerned about what others will think. That is pride. Pride in the right areas is good. Don't misunderstand me. However, you tire yourself out every day attempting to impress others."

"God, please, that hurts for you to talk to me this way."

"I talk to you like this because I love you. You need to slow down and enjoy having Betty with you. However, you must take care of your body. I give warning signs to you and all my children as well. However, recently you pay no heed to them. Being physically or mentally tired is a warning to you that you must get some rest or you must have a diversion."

"OK, Father. I'll try to do better. I'm not going to mow the back yard today. Who cares if the bed doesn't get made? Who cares if I don't get the laundry done today? We have plenty of clean linens."

Then, like the loving Father He is, He finished with kind words. "Oh, by the way, Louis, the mower is not ruined. The blades are just not as sharp as before."

Chapter 17:

Surfing the Waves

∂∫ρ

O n the morning of June 20 I called Austin Hospice to discuss their services. After a short conversation they suggested that a nurse come out that afternoon and do an assessment on Betty. I reluctantly agreed. I was sure that I would not like the nurse or any of the recommendations.

The nurse came about 3:45 p.m. I liked her immediately. She gently told me about the services they would provide and I told her about Betty. During our conversation she suggested I write a book. I told her I was in the process of doing so. After we visited she asked to visit with Betty. Betty tried to talk with her. I sensed she was asking just what services would be provided. The nurse told her. After asking questions that were not in her field of expertise, she suggested I speak with their financial officer. Before the nurse left, I asked Betty if she had any concerns about hospice services and she shook her head "no."

The next morning I called Austin Hospice and was told I could come early that afternoon to speak with key personnel regarding Betty. I was made to feel welcome and they seemed concerned about the entire family. I met with the Chief Financial Officer, the head nurse and one of the insurance employees. They answered all of my questions to my satisfaction. They told me that Dr. Shallin had already ordered hospice services for Betty. They also explained that hospice would be paid by Medicare Part A with which Betty was insured. One of my questions was about the requirements for hospice.

They explained that a doctor had to order hospice services. This can be done if it is determined the patient is terminally ill and not expected to live past six months. (At this writing, the time has been extended to 12 months.) I asked what happens if the patient lives longer. "The patient will need to be certified again," was the response.

The nurse told me that a nurse would be out the next Tuesday, June 28th to complete the admission papers and her regular nurse would be out the next day. We would have visits by social workers and the chaplain at a later time. Austin Hospice has its own medical director and Dr. Shallin would continue to be Betty's primary doctor.

Even though I felt Betty would live longer than six months, I continued to have an urging from God to start planning a victory service for her. That evening after I had gotten her tucked in for the night, I began to go through some boxes of treasures that we had kept for years. I found a Christmas card that was sent to me by dear friends in 1960. At the time I was a medical technologist and x-ray technician at the hospital in Crosbyton, Texas near Lubbock. I had already resigned from there and was waiting to move to Hobbs, New Mexico where I met Betty.

Almost everyone in Crosbyton knew me and treated me like I was a favorite son. Most were farmers so I fit right in. I had worked there in 1957-59 and then did a stint in the military and was asked to come back to the hospital. I was a faithful member of a local church, taught a young boys' Sunday school class and sang in the choir. After church someone would usually invite me for Sunday lunch. Those ladies knew how to cook. However, there were few single people my age. After I lived there for awhile, my pastor asked me, "Louis, what do you think of our crop of girls?"

My response was, "I believe you've had crop failure."

As I opened the card I read the following note:

Putting all jokes aside, we do wish for you the very best of everything as you leave here and go to Hobbs. If you really are looking for that young lady then here's hoping you find her! Somewhere there must be someone who would want to share the life of one of the finest young men we have ever known. We shall miss you in our Church here, as well

as the hospital, but we know there is a job for you wherever you go. Happiness is found in the work of the Lord, but we don't have to tell you that.

Good Wishes from
J.W., Velma Ruth and Diane Woods

As I read the sweet words, I had to wipe the tears from my eyes knowing that I had found that young lady and now she was going to be taken away from me for awhile. I thought of our wedding vows—"in sickness and in health."

Betty was a brilliant lady and an excellent writer. That evening I also came across an essay that Betty had written in 1954 when she was a senior in Hobbs, New Mexico. Her Dad was so proud of her that he cut it out of the Hobbs Daily Sun, took it to a printer and had it printed on very nice thick paper. He had many printed and gave them away to anyone who would stand still long enough. It is an article that is still prevalent today. It is printed below just as the newspaper printed it along with their comments.

Last Tuesday morning representatives of the Hobbs Woman's Civic Club and the American Legion Auxiliary presented awards to 19 school children for essays on the subject, "What America Means to Me." The papers were written last Armistice Day and each was composed without previous preparation immediately after the announcement was made in schools.

The winning essay was written by Betty Hurst, a senior in Hobbs High School. Here's what she wrote:

A SCHOOL GIRL'S OPINION

"The Liberty Bell—Made of the iron will of every man, woman and child that gave their lives for our freedoms. It rings out the words today of liberty, justice and freedom heard around the world."

"The Statue of Liberty—She stands high and lifted up, not as a ruler, not as a queen, but as a mountain of strength, opening her arms to the poor refugee, to the weary soldier coming home and the many friends and allies of our country."

"Our Flag—Its glorious colors wave heavenward proclaiming the red for blood shed on battlefields, the white for the purity of God, who gave us this country and the blue for the heavens which envelop the whole world."

"To see an open church door, it in itself cries out, There is freedom here."

"Many things have been written, many things are being written and many things will be written on "What America Means to Me," but only by our lives can we really show what America means to each of us.

Betty's essay shows great depth of perception that is rarely found in a high school student. Her words are an inspiration and should be cherished by all who love this country of ours.

Have you ever started something and then had doubts about what you are doing? That is exactly how I began to feel. Had I not told anyone about the conversations that Betty and I had been having, then I would not have to deal with death and hospice. I worried. What if God had intended doing a miracle and now because I've quit believing for one then it was not going to happen? What if the doctors don't believe my letter to them? How am I going to deal with them? Prior to the strokes I would have asked Betty's input for any significant decision. However, now she couldn't speak and it would only frustrate her if I asked her opinion. I knew she trusted me to do what was best for her. During times like this, God would quietly remind me of our conversation when He had told me that "this is a sickness unto death."

I also remembered that both Diane and Dr. Valerian Chyle had suggested hospice before I had thought of it. Dr. Chyle, as a radiation oncologist witnessed death often. I trusted him as much as I trusted Diane. I had great respect for both.

June 22, 2005 came all too soon to suit me. It was the day for Betty's appointment with Dr. Edward Fox, the neurologist in Round Rock that had been treating her long before the strokes. I had not met him until she had been seeing him for several months. She asked me to go with her on one of the appointments so that I could meet him. I knew she trusted him and liked him personally as well. When I met him, I understood her feelings for him. He was a wonderful doctor but most important he was a friend. Later, he rescued us when she was in the Georgetown Hospital from the other neurologist who was so rude. All of these thoughts still did not make me feel comfortable about seeing him again. Even though he had given me his home telephone number, his pager number and insisted that I call him if I just had a question, I was apprehensive. Suppose he asked me, "What is your concern? She appears just like she was six months ago. I don't see any changes." Suppose he suspected that I was just tired of it all and wanted to get out of the situation. These thoughts plagued me for days before the appointment.

When we arrived at his office we checked in as usual. The office employees greeted Betty warmly as they always did. Our wait was too short. Normally Dr. Fox would come to the reception room, greet her and personally wheel her to the exam room. He did not on this day. Even that change made me feel uneasy.

His assistant took us to an exam room. I was very tense and apprehensive. Betty could not hold her head erect. When Dr. Fox entered the room, he greeted us very warmly. He immediately said, "Betty, I can see you have lost more weight. This is not just fat but muscle." (We had not been able to weigh her since the heart attack in July 2004 at which time she weighed 129). He continued, "There are diseases which cause this. Parkinson's and Lou Gehrig Disease are two. However, you don't have those. Therefore, we have to admit it is caused by damage from the strokes. There comes a time when we have to look at a patient and say, wait a minute, this isn't working. We can't just keep adding pills hoping it will help the patient get well."

Then he turned to me and said, "Louis, I got your letter. Thank you for it. Now, let's talk about it." My heart almost stopped, because

I thought he was going to say I was wrong to suggest changes in her treatment.

He continued. "Before we talk about it, I want to give credit to some people. Without them we as doctors would keep doing what we've been doing. I'm talking about you two. Betty, even though you can't speak anymore, you and Louis are still able to communicate. It is simply amazing how you do it. You have excellent communication between yourselves and then Louis keeps all your doctors informed. I have never received a letter like yours. I have never had a family member who says, "Wait a minute, we're tired of this and the medicine isn't working, let's just keep her comfortable."

"Louis, you sent this letter to five doctors. I want you to know there are five doctors who are very impressed that you would do this. None of them have ever experienced this before. We usually deal with families who will not accept the fact that there is no hope of getting well. I want to thank you again for pointing this out to us."

Dr. Fox then began talking about the medicines. He concluded, "It is definitely time for hospice, and they will do an excellent job. Also, if I can help you in any way, you have my numbers." With that, we told him goodbye. I knew this was our last visit with him. I felt a sense of relief and peace. I had more confidence that the decisions we were making were right.

Driving home, I shuddered to think that I had almost cancelled that appointment because Betty was going on hospice. I had forgotten that each time I had visited with Dr. Fox that I always felt so much better. I rejoiced knowing that God had definitely selected all of Betty's doctors even the one that had been so rude. Hopefully he learned a lesson that evening. My confidence in what we were doing had returned. Without any doubts, I knew we were doing what God wanted.

The next day, June 23 I decided to go by the Georgetown Healthcare Home Health Care Agency and let the nurses know that Betty was going on hospice. They had been so wonderful to both of us that I did not wish to just call and tell them. I wanted to tell them personally. The nurse that had been Betty's first home health nurse in 2002 was there. She immediately asked about Betty. I told her that she would be going on hospice the following week. She grabbed me and squeezed me. Her eyes filled with tears. She said, "I am so sorry. I knew the last time that I saw her that she was not doing well."

I went by the hospital to visit Robert Stern, another doctor who was a wonderful friend. I had called and made arrangements to take him to lunch. I wanted to tell him personally about Betty. I had known him since he had worked as an orderly at the hospital in Taylor when I was the administrator. He was a brilliant young man and went on to college and medical school. Then he did a residency in Internal Medicine. He was our primary care physician for several years until he went back to school to specialize in pathology. He is a partner with the Austin Pathology Associates and fortunately for us he was our pathologist in Georgetown. Most of our conversation was about Betty. He, like many of her other doctors had love and respect for her.

We finished lunch just in time for me to keep my grief counseling appointment with Tammy. She listened to me and offered words of encouragement. She also asked about my daily writing. I shared with her that there are times that I would be doing fine and then emotions would flood over me. She said they were taught in school in times like that to "surf the waves." In other words, when anger or emotions come over you, pretend you are surfing and actually see yourself on the wave. Don't try to ignore it. Accept it and determine how it made you feel. It will pass.

That evening Betty wanted enchiladas so I bought a plate from a local Mexican restaurant. As usual I pureed them and she ate all of them with little difficulty. I learned over time that sometimes she could eat with no difficulty and then maybe at the next meal she could not. Strokes are wicked.

The next day I received the following email from Mark. I knew it was difficult for them, living in Georgia.

I just want you to know again how proud I am of you. I have never doubted your actions or your thoughts with regards to Mom. I'm so glad you have such an awesome core of people around you who give you support and encouragement.

I really wish that we were close enough to come over there

regularly. It really hurts Cheryl and me to be so far away at this time. I get kind of angry about it sometimes but I know there must be a reason we're stuck out here right now.

I talked with Lauren yesterday about Mom. We had a little time alone in the car. She did not seem surprised. She is extremely bright so I figured she knew how things were going. I'll have some time with Kristen on Saturday. She has another All-Star tournament in Waycross. It will probably last all day. I'll be glad when this is over. Softball has taken over my summer as well. Her coach practices three times during the week and then either plans a long Saturday practice or schedules a tournament. She really enjoys it and so do I but there is little time for anything else.

Lauren starts guitar lessons on Monday. She will have a half hour lesson once each week. She seems excited about it.

Colton is just Colton. He's enjoying the summer camp although he's loathe to admit it. He and Kristen have been going to Vacation Bible School with their summer camp this week at the Baptist Church. They have a program Sunday afternoon. He is also taking karate twice a week at summer camp. He really likes it. They do push ups and sit ups and run laps around the room. He was talking about getting a uniform the other day. Before summer started he was strenuously objecting to karate. Now he likes it.

We love you both dearly. You are both in our prayers. I'll call you tonight.

Love,
Mark

I replied and attempted to encourage him. I assured him that anger is one of the processes of grief. I shared with him what Tammy had told me about surfing. I also encouraged him to talk with someone about it, such as his pastor or a trusted friend who was not emotionally involved. I told him it would probably be good for Cheryl also. I also cautioned him about assuming that the kids were doing okay. They might need counseling as well.

I remembered getting an email from Jackie McRoberts. Jackie was director of In-Patient Therapy Services at the Georgetown Hospital. She had helped me tremendously after Betty had the strokes. Her grandmother had died about June 1. Jackie shared with me how she explained her grandmother's death to her own children. I knew she would not mind my sending her email to Mark. Parts of the email she sent me are below:

> **I was out of pocket a bit early in the month, but what an amazing way the Lord works. I had not checked my email for a few days and found out that on June 1st my paternal grandmother had passed away that morning. Our family took a quick trip to Muncie, Indiana for the funeral. Before we left for Muncie I went on line and read your very moving email regarding Betty. I was so very touched, but just couldn't really format a coherent response. Please know that both/all have been in my prayers ever since, even more than usual. I waited until after I was back but did forward it to my folks, so there are prayers being sent from Warsaw, Indiana as well. So, then, after I returned from that trip, here you are with an entire mailing on grief. Way to Go Lord.**

> **I have really enjoyed your writings. It is making me a bit impatient for the book, but I know that will come when it is due. I knew you had the gift to share knowledge and experience with others, but I have been even more impressed with your skill in the written word. I look forward to them and whatever type of context you are led to seems to have some meaning/implication for me. I continue to pray for you, Betty, the kids and grandkids. After the experience with my grandmother, I've thought a lot about these issues. I have worked into my conversation with the kids the reminder of**

our beliefs and the excitement and wonder of being able as Christians to count on eternity. At one point, Tommy fluctuated from tears because he knew someday he would lose his mother, as my Dad did, to actually wanting to get on with it and get to this paradise we know will be there. We spent some time brainstorming and dreaming about the possibilities it will include such as: no laundry, lots of chocolate, never cleaning rooms or making beds, plants and animals and nature of all types, (Tommy is counting on seeing some dinosaurs) baseball and maybe some football, etc. It was a special time for us and I treasure that I am able to talk with my kids so openly and confidently.

I'm not promising chocolate, but I know, without any doubts, that you and Betty will be there. I'm counting on hearing from Betty a few good stories and sharing some laughs over some of your escapades that don't make the book. (Or at least hearing her version of events!)

Understand that my heart aches with the pain I feel for your earthly pain. But I celebrate with you the knowledge that truly everything is headed in such the right direction and He works all things for His good. I hope you have some comfort in your journaling on line and know that there are so many of us sending prayers and also able and willing to pitch in with physical assistance as well. Well, I'm sure that was more than you expected, but as you say, there is a delete button and I'll never even know. God Bless,
Jackie.

The next day, June 27, as Director of In-Patient Therapy Services for the Georgetown Healthcare System Jackie came to our house to complete the exam and discharge papers from Home Health for Betty. I asked her to write her thoughts regarding Betty's current condition versus the last time she had seen her. I assured her that I am a "big boy" and to please be very candid about it. She responded:

June 30, 2005

I appreciated being so warmly welcomed into your home Monday afternoon. The amount of paper work is never a joy to complete, especially when recording that not all areas are healed, not all goals are met. However, I felt it was an honor to play a tiny part in that chapter with the two of you.

There have been changes with Betty since the last time I was out. Her hair is thinner overall, obviously her speech and attempts at verbal communication are significantly poorer. I am fairly confident she has lost some weight and some of her joints seemed a bit stiffer.

It is also very obvious that she has been very well cared for. Her skin is really in very good condition. It would be nearly impossible with all that has happened to not have any areas with break down. The first time I saw the area on her lower leg I was amazed at the prominence of the fibular head. The areas on and near her sacrum are incredibly small considering the pressure from the bony areas.

Honestly, the thing I was most struck by Monday, was Betty's eyes. There was a different look in her eyes than I remember. They had an increased light or a glow. She was obviously very alert and aware and even with the apparent discomfort during the spasms, she was receptive. The last time I was out, I was very concerned. She appeared exhausted to me then and the change then seemed more dramatic. I was not sure what the future had in store. I know I didn't know Betty, but in most people, I would describe the look I saw Monday as more peaceful. Again, this week I was overwhelmed with the connection and obvious love and respect the two of you have for each other. I pray that the Lord continues His blessings on both of you, bringing to you those that He has chosen to cross paths with you. You

are in my thoughts and prayers. Please let me know how/ when I can be there for you.

Jackie

Jackie's message to me confirmed some of my thoughts and observations. I had been blessed greatly while at the Georgetown Hospital to have all Christian managers. I knew that I could talk with any of them about the blessings of God and they would not be offended. I realize even now that I could call upon any one of them for whatever I might need and know they would do everything possible to fulfill that need.

The following morning Betty ate very little breakfast. She dozed most of the morning. I felt impressed to give my assessment of her to the children. I shared with them that for the past several days I wanted to write a tribute to Betty to share with her now while she can still understand. It could also be used at her Victory Service. Unfortunately, nothing would come to me and I could not even think how to begin.

Then all at once it began to come to me as I was taking care of her needs. I shared with them that I believed the time was going to be much shorter than I had originally anticipated. I definitely felt it would be a short period. I asked them to share this with the grandchildren also. I would like for them to write a tribute to their G. They could give it at the service or someone could read it for them. I also asked Dawn to sing if she felt she could. She had toured with the Continental Singers the summer after she graduated from Taylor High School in 1984. She is a teacher and single mother of a wonderful son and daughter. She said she wasn't certain but if she were able it would have to be prerecorded. She has a beautiful voice but I did not intend to pressure her about it.

Because God had been encouraging me to start planning a Victory Service for Betty, there was one event that I definitely knew I wanted. Prior to my leaving the hospital in April, Dr. Barbara Brightwell, our beloved friend, chaplain and director of volunteers retired. We had a very nice reception for her that included a dove release. I had never seen a release. Dr. Brightwell had been with the hospital for twenty years. On the day of her reception, we released twenty white doves. It was a beautiful and memorable occasion. Therefore, when I knew that Betty's life on earth would soon be over, I contacted Rebecca Bratton, owner of Lone Star White Dove Release in Cedar Park, Texas. Her response is printed below.

June 28, 2010

Hello Louis,

For a memorial service, I suggest a "Trinity Release." This involves the release of four doves from our white wooden chapel. We will first release a single dove, representing the spirit of the deceased. As it circles, we will release the remaining three, which represents the Holy Trinity (Father, Son, and Holy Spirit). The spirit dove will then join the Holy Trinity and together they will fly home.

The single dove is usually released by hand by a loved one, who will open the doors to the chapel, releasing the remaining three. It is very beautiful, meaningful, and also very healing to the loved ones who are surviving the loss.

I will take care of everything and guide you through the process, so there is nothing for you to prepare for or worry about. Just give me a call and we will discuss the fee.

I am so sorry for what you are facing and I pray that God gives you and your family the strength that you need during this difficult time.
Rebecca

That afternoon about 2:00 p.m., Ginny, the hospice nurse called and told me she was leaving Austin and on her way to Taylor. She sounded very upbeat and energetic. As I had done for the past years when Betty was going to have a new therapist, doctor or nurse, I had already prayed that God would send His specially selected hospice nurses. I had learned months before that whomever God sent might not have been the person that I would have selected. He let me know that He sent some who needed to be ministered to by Betty.

Betty ate very little lunch so we supplemented with the nutrient. She also appeared to be very sleepy. I wondered if she was anxious about the new hospice nurse.

Ginny was the admissions nurse. She spent over an hour with us. Most of that time was spent talking with me. I noticed immediately the compassion she showed towards Betty. It was not an "I'm so sorry" attitude but truly one of compassion. Betty had been having bladder spasms for several months. Even though she was taking a medication for them, they were still painful. Ginny ordered a new medication for her and said the hospice courier would deliver it that afternoon. She also ordered a suction machine. I told her there had been times that I would have used a suction machine if I had one available. A suction machine was not new to me. I had used one both as an orderly many years ago and also when I served in the military. It is used to suction phlegm that might accumulate at the back of the throat so hopefully it will not go into the lungs.

Ginny told us that our regular nurse would be Margaret. She mentioned that Margaret would bring more supplies the next day. Hospice would furnish gloves and linen savers. We had been buying those supplies ourselves. Before Ginny left, she asked if we had any questions or concerns. I did. I was concerned that if something happened to me such as an emergency or I became ill what would I do with Betty? Ginny explained that at that time they would admit Betty to Christopher House, their hospital in Austin. It is not an acute care hospital but strictly for hospice patients. Knowing this made me feel much better.

Later that evening a young lady from Austin Hospice called to make certain that I had their emergency number if I should need it during the night. I was impressed with their concern.

Also, while Ginny was at the house, UPS brought Betty three new Gaither DVDs that I had ordered. After Ginny left, Pam played one of the new DVDs and changed the dressing on the pressure sore. Pam was such a wonderful caregiver. At times she would have to leave the room because of crying. Betty loved Pam and knew she was being well cared for by her. Betty expressed an interest in getting up later in the evening.

Although Margaret was Betty's assigned nurse, on the first day she was to come she had a crisis situation at home so Lisa came. I had learned to be excited when God allowed and orchestrated the changes Himself. I knew either God wanted Lisa to come for Betty or she needed Betty. She was a very vivacious person who was a former ICU nurse. My best description of her was that she was a "live wire." She was very enthusiastic and also very compassionate towards Betty. She treated Betty as a responsible person and spoke directly to her unless she had a question Betty could not answer. I knew that Betty appreciated that. I'm certain it made her feel as if she had some control, which was important to her.

Lisa did not skirt around the issues at hand. Frequently she would start a comment with "As we go on down the road. . . " Betty's eyes continued to be bright and receptive. Lisa dressed the pressure sores and expressed amazement at how well they looked. She had asked me over the telephone if I could stick my finger into them. I replied, "No, they almost look superficial."

"Great!" was her response. She also commented about the excellent skin care that Betty had. As she went over the medication list, she said she would try to get a response as to what hospice would approve. I asked her to press hard for the Lamictal, an anti-seizure drug that Betty's psychiatrist, Dr. Alam, prescribed as an antidepressant. I emphasized that Dr. Alam had worked with Betty for months to get the level just right so that it alleviated part of the depression caused by the chemical imbalance.

When the strokes occurred, the frontal lobe of the brain was greatly affected. This is where the depression originates according to Dr. Fox, Betty's neurologist. I knew that some of the other medications would not be approved because they were not related to her diagnosis. Most were not drugs that would make her comfortable.

After Lisa returned to the office she called to make sure that we had enough medication to last for the next five days. I was appreciative of her concerns and promptness in addressing situations before a crisis.

Lisa also left us some booklets addressing end of life. The author was careful to explain that nothing is concrete and that all of the guidelines are very flexible. Any one of the signs may be present, all may be present or none may be present. Death comes in its own time, in its own way and is as unique as the individual who is experiencing it.

One of the guidelines stated that usually one to three months prior to death "withdrawal" occurs. As I had spoken with our niece, Diane, earlier she had said that it was obvious Betty was experiencing withdrawal. During this process, the individual begins to withdraw from the world around them. They lose interest in current events and then begin to withdraw from people, no longer wanting visits from friends, etc. I was intrigued that some of the symptoms I had put in my letter to Betty's doctors were signs of withdrawal. Now I understood perfectly why the doctors did not object to hospice.

Later that afternoon as I was dressing Betty, the doorbell rang. It was our pastor, Jeff Ripple. He had hardly greeted Betty until she began trying to tell him something. I knew she wanted to tell him about getting ready to go to Heaven. She tried so hard to talk with him and I am sure it was disturbing to him to not be able to understand her. Through yes and no questions I was able to interpret for her. She has seen Heaven and there were times that angels surrounded her bed. She also had seen Jesus. I shared with Jeff that I was hoping and praying that before she went home that she would regain her speech so she could share it all with us.

There were times that she spoke perfectly. I could say, "I love you."

Very plainly she replied, "I love you."

As the three of us were visiting, the doorbell rang again. It was Ann Hagmann, the chaplain from Austin Hospice. She had called earlier and told me she was going to be in Taylor so I invited her to come by. It was great having Ann and Jeff with us. We enjoyed sharing about God and what He had done and what He was continuing to do. We also talked of what He would do for Betty and me in the future.

Betty also tried to talk with Ann. Ann also commented about her eyes. Prior to Jeff and Ann leaving, it was obvious that a bond had formed among us as we sensed the presence of God. They prayed with us before leaving.

Our children kept in close contact each day. About this time I received the following email from our daughter, Dawn:

> I keep meaning to tell you about a dream I have had twice. I actually had the dreams about two weeks prior to your letter telling us about Mom. It is very difficult to write because it seems as if I actually write it, then it is real and I have difficulty with that.
>
> Mom was standing across from me (clothed of course in a stylish outfit). While there was no actual physical barrier between us, there was an understood "line." I commented on how lovely she looked —so vital. My eyes continued to travel across her checking out her clothes and health. Behind her were about six inches of a white robe and sandaled feet of a man (I assume to be Jesus). I had the dream twice. The only difference was Mom's clothes. I woke up both times with a great start—bolt straight up in bed. You would think I would have been very disturbed, but instead felt an amazing peace and I know the Holy Spirit was in the room with me.
>
> Love to you both,
> Dawn

It was such a comfort to know that our children were committed Christians. It would make this final walk for Betty so much easier.

June Prater, our long time friend from Georgetown responded to Dawn's email. Her response is below:

> Hi Louis,
>
> The Lord is certainly faithful to confirm things, isn't He? I believe, too, that Dawn's dream is a confirmation for you. I am reminded of the dream I had of Betty walking up and

down beside her bed in a gorgeous green robe. I will never forget how beautiful it was and her too. Maybe that is what I was seeing also. By that I mean, maybe I was seeing her after she leaves here. I don't know for sure but I thought of that dream when I read about Dawn's dream. Anyway, the Lord is good and if we are sensitive enough, I am sure He shows us things to come. That is what the scripture says the Holy Spirit will do in John 14. I have no doubt that is what He is doing to you and your family now.

May the Lord manifest His presence to you and Betty today as never before.
Love, June

During the next few days God continued to impress me with ideas for the Victory Service. I decided that because we had been members of the First Baptist Church for many years before joining Christ Fellowship that I would like to have her service there. I knew I should contact the pastor of First Baptist, Brother David Johnson and discuss that possibility with him. I knew him from having seen him in the grocery store and other places in town. When I called him he was most gracious and caring. He asked if he could visit in our home rather than in his office. I was delighted because then Betty could visit with him too. We agreed that he would come the afternoon of July 6. Brother David told me when I spoke with him that he and our pastor, Jeff Ripple, were friends. It was good to know that as we planned Betty's service we could all be of one accord. I would have invited Brother Jeff to meet with us but I knew he was out of town.

When Brother David arrived, he gave me a warm hug and expressed his concern about Betty. He also told me that her name had been placed on the First Baptist Church prayer list. We visited for awhile and I shared with him some ideas that I believed God was giving me. Among them was the dove release. He said he was not familiar with a dove release but thought it would be wonderful.

Prior to Brother David leaving he asked to visit with Betty. I took him into her bedroom and introduced him to Betty and Pam. He spoke with Betty in such a loving manner. I noticed that he also had very warm and caring eyes. As I would look from him to Betty their eyes were so striking. After praying with us, Brother David asked if he could visit again. We assured him that he was welcome at any time.

That evening three precious ladies from Christ Fellowship visited us. They had been loyal visitors since Betty had come home after the strokes. Sister Margaret is a precious lady who glows with the love of Jesus. Once while visiting she was having severe allergy problems. She asked me to pray for her. I did and she told me later that God completely healed her of the allergies. I assured her it was not me but her faith in the healing power of Jesus that had made her whole. We have known Sister Meiske for many years. Occasionally she had stayed with Betty's parents when they first moved to Taylor. If we had to be out of town, she would stay with them and assist them. Sister Edna is a petite woman who also radiates the love of Jesus. It was so humbling to have them in our home.

After they left I attempted to feed Betty but she had no interest. I gave her some nourishment in the peg tube. While I was giving her medications, I heard the front door open and a familiar voice called out, "Paper Boy." It was none other than Sam. He and Betty had a special relationship. Her eyes brightened and I could tell she was thrilled to see him. He never failed to give her a big kiss on the cheek. He shared stories about his three children and Betty listened intently. I'm sure she had never forgotten on Halloween evening last year he brought the children in their costumes.

After visiting for a few minutes, he went over close to her and said, "I understand you're getting ready to go on a trip." She attempted to talk while looking at him. It didn't bother him. He visited as if she was speaking perfectly.

Betty and I married July 29, 1961 and on October 11, 1961 Sam was born in South Dakota. After college he moved to Texas. I suspect that God arranged it knowing we would need him during these times. God does supply all our needs according to His riches in Glory. I could not imagine what it would have been like to go through the past three years without Sam.

As Friday came again I decided to go to the mall in Austin. I loved to go "malling" and didn't need an excuse to go. However, this time I was going for a distinct purpose. Since the early 1960's, I made certain that Betty had a fragrance by Estee Lauder named Beautiful. She had stopped wearing the perfume but continued to use the body powder.

I wish I had the words to express my love for Betty. She was indescribable. She radiated the love of Jesus particularly in her eyes.

While in the mall, I also found some shirts that were on sale. I bought three and modeled them for Betty when I arrived home. She was so pleased. I assured her that I knew she would have bought them for me had she been able.

Pam told me that Dr. Freidberg, Betty's urologist, had called around noon and asked that I call him about 2:00 p.m. as he would be in surgery until then. When I called, the receptionist told me he had not returned to the office but would call me as soon as he arrived. I had no idea what he wanted to tell me. Late that afternoon he called and expressed his feelings about Betty. He also gave me some suggestions for the bladder spasms and emphasized to let him know if there was anything he could do for us.

After I had talked with my counselor about my emotions and she had told me to picture myself on a surfboard and ride with the waves, Mark sent me two little surf boards. I kept them on the end table next to my chair and held them when I would become emotional as I spoke with people.

It was at times like this with Dr. Freidberg that I rode those waves. Waves of emotion would surge over me. It did help to "surf the waves." However, at various times I misplaced the little surfboards and then I was out on that wave without a board. I discovered that if I said aloud, "I can't find the surf board," it would usually cause me to laugh and the emotion would pass.

I think back many times about when I asked God to send just the right doctors and other staff members for Betty. Even though many times I did not understand, I knew He had a purpose for that individual to be associated with Betty. As the days went by several more doctors called and expressed their concerns for us. My emotions would overflow. It's something I cannot control. God made me that way. I would rather be compassionate than cold and calculating. I also realized I was going through the most emotional period of my life. I could never imagine what life would be like without Betty. Now I knew that time was very short.

Chapter 18:

Betty's Angels

ঔ

O n July 8, Fay, the Austin Hospice social worker, came for a visit. As each individual came from hospice, they asked many questions about Betty and me. I realized this was necessary so they would know how to better assist us. They asked how we had met, our marriage, children, grandchildren, and numerous other questions. They seemed to be most interested in how Betty and I could communicate when she could not speak.

When the visit with Fay concluded I was emotionally drained as my emotions were on edge. Each hospice representative was very professional, caring, compassionate and understanding. I could not have asked for a better team. Fay was an excellent resource in answering questions about the dying process. She told us signs to watch for and told me to let them know when certain changes occurred. Some of those changes had already occurred.

A perfect example was displayed while Fay was present. Pam came to get me because Betty did not want lunch and she did not want nutrient in the feeding tube either. I quietly talked with her and she agreed to take some nutrient without my actual insistence. I had already determined that as long as she was able to make a decision I would do as she wished. I knew this was her journey and I was only assisting her. Had she told me she did not want the nutrient I would have asked if her mind was clear. She was always able to tell me if she was thinking clearly or not.

Fay remarked about our ability to communicate and also what excellent care Betty was getting. It was always comforting to have a professional comment positively about Betty's care.

Fay is also a grief counselor. I shared with her some of my thoughts and many times she would complete a sentence for me. I asked, "You've heard these concerns before?"

"Yes, many times."

I remembered that my counselor, Tammy also completed thoughts for me. I felt that Fay's visit had definitely helped. She had taken away some of my concerns.

I was looking forward to Jamie coming for the weekend. However, she called and said she was still not feeling well. Thoughts began to come that no one really cared anymore. Then the telephone rang. It was Dawn. She asked if it would be okay if she, Bryan, and Caitlin came for the weekend. All at once the ridiculous thoughts about no one caring left. Dawn was a great help to me, and Bryan and Caitlin helped also. They also loved on their G. I was not ready for them to leave when Sunday afternoon came.

I always looked forward to mail time. Usually we had cards and notes from friends and relatives that were very uplifting for me. On this day we had several notes from folks at First Baptist Church that had been written during or after their prayer meeting. One was from a lady that I could not remember but she certainly remembered Betty and me. Betty had witnessed to many people about God when she owned the Faith Bookstore. Below is printed a note from a friend she had made many years ago:

Dear Louis and Betty:

Just a note to know we are praying for both of you and your family at this time. On a personal note, I wanted to thank you for all your help when I first moved here in 1981 and you had the Christian bookstore. God Bless.

Cathy Koenig

That note was priceless to me. It probably did not take her two minutes to write it but I will never forget it. Because Betty was dozing, I decided to wait until the next morning to read it to her.

When I read it to her, I could tell by the glow in her eyes that she remembered Cathy.

Mark's wife, Cheryl has been special to us since Cheryl first visited us. Betty and I love all three children dearly and Cheryl was another daughter for us to love. I was not surprised to receive the following email from Cheryl on July 9.

Hi Louis,

If you can (or have Pam) read this to Betty for me. I found this online and want her to know how much I love her!

"To His Mother
Thank you for taking such good care of your little boy,
Thank you for filling his heart full of love and joy
For teaching him the ABC's
God's values (right from wrong)
For feeding and helping him
Grow up safe and strong
He is now a wonderful man
You taught him how to live
I'm grateful and I love you
For everything he is!"

Cheryl

Many days Betty had great difficulty swallowing. In those instances, we would supplement with the nutrient in her peg tube. The hospice folks told me it was just another stage in the process.

Betty had so many wonderful friends. Some of her very special ones lived about 30 miles away. We had gone to church with them for several years until Betty could no longer tolerate sitting for long periods. One had called and asked if it would be okay if they came for a short visit. I assured them we would love it. The night before their visit Betty slept well and was wide awake when they arrived.

Prior to Betty having the strokes the ladies would call her frequently and some would call her for counseling. One of her visitors was Sister Ruthie who was 89. She is a saint of God. When the ladies walked quietly into Betty's presence, a holy hush fell over the entire room. Sister Ruthie immediately began praising God. Quietly she began to say, "Oh, I can feel His presence so strong in here. His presence is so strong." Tears came to my eyes and I wished for my surfboards. I knew God was enjoying the praises of His people.

It was a beautiful praise time and, spontaneously, each lady expressed what Betty had meant to her. One said among other things, "Well, I certainly learned one thing from her. Some years ago, there was a bad tornado in Oklahoma City where my son lives. I told Betty about it and she asked if he was injured. I told her no, he was so lucky and not anything was hurt on his property."

Betty replied, "Honey, luck had nothing to do with it; he was blessed."

"I've never said again that someone was lucky or unlucky. She taught me a good lesson and I will never forget it."

It was a precious time and a wonderful blessing for Betty, Pam and me. Although Betty could not speak, she attempted to talk several times. I'm sure she wanted to thank them for coming and tell them that she loved them.

It was obvious that Betty's angel made his appearance every evening as we finished helping her eat dinner. He was always in the same location and Betty watched him intently until he left. My friend Sam suggested I ask her if the angel knew she is ready to go home. On this afternoon I asked her. Betty kept attempting to tell me something but I could never determine an answer. It must have not been a yes or no answer. I asked if it frightened her when he came. She mouthed "no."

Jamie had told us she was coming the next day to stay a few days. I loved it when members of our family came. It was a wonderful relief for me. I received calls from other friends saying they were also coming to visit.

Jamie came on Tuesday after the visit from the sweet ladies. She had been with Betty quite frequently since the strokes and learned to feed her and assist me with other duties as well. The day after Jamie came was very busy. Margaret (the hospice nurse), Ann (the chaplain), and our pastor, Brother Jeff, came. Each came at a different time.

Brother Jeff, Jamie, and I discussed Betty's Victory Service and made some tentative plans for it.

The night before Jamie was to leave to return to Katy, three ladies from a neighboring community came. We had also gone to church with them for several years. Nelda, the daughter of Sister Ruthie who had visited earlier was in the trio. The ladies sing beautifully and their trio's name is Faith, Hope and Charity. They brought a keyboard and set it up in Betty's bedroom. They sang several songs and then Nelda prayed for our family. The presence of the Lord was indescribable. Betty was able to remain awake for most of the evening. I know she was blessed.

Mark let us know that he and the children would be here on July 29, which would be our 44th wedding anniversary. Jamie, Dawn and the children would arrive on the 30th. Mark and the children would need to go home on July 31.

Betty continued to become more disinterested in food. She would only eat a very few bites at an occasional meal. Swallowing was beginning to be very difficult.

During this time I became a little despondent. I tried not to let anyone know. Then, just as I needed Him the most, God showed up. He sent a wonderful rain. It was so refreshing to see the water flowing in the streets and the thirsty vegetation perking up. It was as if He was saying, "I have not forgotten you. I am here with you and I will never leave you nor forsake you."

The coordinator for volunteers from Austin Hospice had called earlier and told me she had a volunteer living in Taylor who would come to see us on the weekends and would give me some relief.

Bryan, our fifteen year-old grandson, always tried to brighten my day in some way. He took a picture of me that had been made many years ago when we visited White Sands, New Mexico, scanned it so it could be emailed, added a surfboard, and made a screen saver for me. Because I was wearing a swimsuit in the picture, I began to receive many comments about it, such as the following, from our dear friend, Dr. Barbara Brightwell:

Louis,

The White Sands picture was priceless!! Sounds like you had a special week with Jamie. I imagine Betty did feel like she was in heaven while the women from Elgin sang for her. Each day has its little bit of heaven for you and Betty. The 44th wedding anniversary will be a celebration of both of your lives together. You are making many memories now for later.

I would like to come by Tuesday or Wednesday afternoon around 2:00 pm for a few minutes if that works for you. If these dates and times do not work for you, let me know about the early part of the week of the 25th. I realize you will be busy getting ready for your family that week, so I will follow your lead.

Our prayers are for comfort for you and Betty.
Barbara

The next day, July 15, started out as any other day. As soon as Pam arrived, I left for the grocery store. I was gone for only a short while. When I returned, Pam told me there was bleeding around Betty's feeding tube. Having given her medications only a couple of hours before, I thought it was probably just some stomach fluids leaking which is not uncommon. However, a 4x4 sponge was soaked with blood and Pam showed me another sponge that was saturated with blood. She said she thought it had finally formed a clot. I examined it closely and agreed.

I immediately called hospice. When I told the operator what it was about, she put me through to Toni who was the nurse supervisor. I spent some time attempting to convince her that the tube had not been pulled and the tube did not get caught between the mattress and the rails. That was impossible because Betty's bed no longer had rails. Toni assured me that she would page Margaret and have her come check it. I also told Toni that Betty was nauseated. I waited for an hour and had no response from anyone. I called Toni again and told her I had not heard from Margaret. "Oh, I just got through talking with her on the phone and I forgot to tell her you had called." She assured me she would call Margaret and have her come check Betty.

I was relieved until Margaret called. I explained everything to her. "Oh, it's not unusual to have the area bleed like that."

I replied, "Maybe not on anyone else, but it is highly unusual for Betty because she has had a peg for over three years and it never occurred before. I also told her that Betty was nauseated and that we had not received the Phenergan suppositories that she had promised over a week ago to have available if Betty became nauseated.

She replied," Well, I ordered those yesterday afternoon so you should be getting them by UPS tonight, so give her one then."

All at once I could hear the voice of the compassionate and caring doctor in Austin when Betty almost died, "Louis, you are her advocate. You must speak for her." She is depending on you." I told Margaret that I would not wait for hours for the suppositories. I asked how she would feel if she was the person who was nauseated.

She replied, "Well, I will call the local pharmacy and you can pick them up there. I will be over later this evening to check the peg." I told her that apparently it had stopped bleeding but that I still wanted her to come check it.

The rest of the day was uneventful except that Diane returned my call and we discussed Betty's condition. She assured me that she was coming over the following Monday evening to see us. She also reminded me again to call her if I needed her.

Very soon after speaking with Diane, UPS arrived with Betty's medications. One was a refill of the medicine we used for bladder spasms. When I checked it, I realized the dosage had been doubled since the last prescription. Just as I started to dial the hospice nurse on call, our electricity went off. We had no power for almost two hours. I did not try to call again until I started giving Betty her night meds. I got an answering machine and left a message to call me about a possible error in medications. Hannah returned my call very soon. I told her my concern and she checked it out. "No, that prescription is wrong. It should not have deviated from the original prescription." I thanked her and asked if she had a minute to talk. I told her neither Margaret nor Toni had called me. Margaret had told me she would come check Betty. Hannah took my complaints and assured me that management would receive the complaints Monday morning. I told her that I had thought of calling the Executive Director and ask what was going on in nursing service. She did not discourage me from doing that but assured me they would be calling.

I wondered what other families did who did not know to check medications and did not know to speak up for their loved one or did not know to ask questions. I sat on the big chair next to Betty's bed and cried. I was not feeling sorry for myself. I was angry and I knew this was also a part of the grief process. I was distressed because I was ignored all day and also because Betty did not get attention from hospice the entire day. She also slept most of the day. I knew it was not going to be long until she went to her eternal home. Was I ready for that or just trying to fake it?

I sent an email to all my friends and relatives telling them what had transpired.

The next morning I had many emails expressing concern yet encouraging as well. June Prater called very early to make sure I was OK. I suppose I didn't do too well in convincing her that I was OK because very soon Gene called and told me they were coming over. June would stay with Betty and he was taking me to lunch. I didn't argue with him. We had a wonderful lunch and visit.

When we came home, June told me that Valerian Chyle had called. I returned his call and he asked if he and Mary could come over. What a treat!! Valerian is a radiation oncologist and a wonderful friend as well. He had been a tremendous support for us when our son, Mark, had bladder cancer in 2001. His precious wife, Mary is a great friend and attorney. She is also a marvelous chef.

When they arrived, Betty made every effort to stay awake. They visited for about two hours. I wanted Betty to be able to talk with them too. It was a very refreshing visit and we told many dog and cat stories. Pepper, our Sheltie, immediately went to them and showed her love. As they left, they assured me that they were available if I needed them.

Once again, Betty did not eat anything except maybe three bites of food.

The next day was Sunday, July 17. Our volunteer, Crystal, arrived about 10:00 a.m. She was a young woman and worked as a pharmacy technician in Austin. She was also attending college and studying to become a pharmacist.

I asked how she became involved with hospice as a volunteer. She told me that her Dad had been in hospice and she became familiar with the volunteer services at that time.

The first time I spoke with her was by telephone. I shared with her that Betty would love for someone to read to her. So she asked immediately what she should read to Betty. I gave her Betty's devotional books and also told her that Betty loved to have the Bible read to her.

Even while Betty was still able to speak the Bible was always on her mind. A young woman who attended our church would come on occasion and read to her. She really enjoyed reading from Betty's Bible. One day as Betty and I were talking about Frances, Betty instructed me to buy Frances a Bible just like hers. I obeyed. When Frances came the next week, Betty gave her the Bible. Frances was so touched she almost cried.

As I would go back into the room to check on Betty, I noticed that the devotional books had been put aside and Crystal was reading the Bible to her. She was so intent that it reminded me of a very thirsty person who can't stop drinking a cool glass of water until it is completely gone.

She continued reading until noon. I went into the room with my lunch and when she took a breath, I told her I was not rushing her but she could go anytime. She said, "I want to finish this chapter." When she was finished, she told Betty that she hoped she had enjoyed her reading the Bible to her. I assured her that Betty had loved it.

Smiling she said, "I've never read the Bible aloud before. In fact I started reading it for the first time about a month ago. A friend of mine talked to me and gave me my very first Bible."

I asked if she was a new Christian and she said, "Yes, I am and I am totally changed inside. My husband is a Christian but he doesn't know the answer to many of my questions. My friend has been helping me and I'm asking God to send me to a good church."

After Crystal left, I had to sit awhile and just reflect on the goodness of God. Even though Betty could not verbally communicate, God sent a thirsty new Christian who would read the Bible to her. It had been a blessing for both of them.

The next day I had another counseling appointment with Tammy. Because of road construction I was almost late. This made me nervous and anxious. My appointment was scheduled for 10:00 a.m. and I drove into the parking lot about two minutes until 10:00. I rushed in and signed my name on the register. I was the only person in the waiting room. Tammy came out immediately and invited me back to her office.

The entire session centered on what had happened with hospice last Friday. I shared with her that I had been told many times that they were there to support me. I did not feel that support. The best way I could describe my feelings was I felt like a person with varicose veins who has to wear support hose. The hose works fine until they are stretched too far and then they begin to sag. I admitted that I was sagging. She did not sympathize but encouraged me to continue to confront those who were responsible. I assured her I would.

After the session I went by Sam's office and we went to Wendy's for a sandwich. God has a way of using Sam to calm me. He had used him many times. I tried to think of other topics to discuss with him. He is a good listener. Sometimes I just didn't like what he said after he listened to me. He has a way of expressing empathy, which makes me feel better. Rarely does he sympathize.

When I arrived at home, Pam told me that Margaret, the hospice nurse, would be arriving soon. When she arrived, Pam invited her in. I walked into the hallway and she began to profusely apologize for letting me down the past Friday. She said I had every reason to be upset and she wanted to tell me that we could have another nurse.

I invited her into the family room and told her that I had several issues to discuss with her. We talked for at least an hour and a half. She assured me that the entire issue was being investigated and they would put procedures into place so that it would never happen to another family. I assured her I could accept that and I would accept her apology. I also told her that when I accept an apology, I never want the subject brought up again. It's in the past and forgotten as far as I am concerned. She said she would never forget it and would be a better nurse because of it.

I asked Margaret a sobering question. I said, "You've been in nursing a long time and you've been a hospice nurse for a long time. I want to ask a question. You know what it is, don't you?"

"Yes, I do," she responded. She told me that based upon her observations and what I had told her was happening, that it could be from a month to six weeks. She hastened to say that she was not God but just strictly observing Betty. This was actually longer than what I had thought.

Late that afternoon Diane arrived. She is like a healing balm, so encouraging and loving. However, she can still be candid which is what I needed.

Betty was so glad to see her. She tried to talk and cry but was unable to do either. Diane loved on her which I am sure helped both of them. Diane had lost her mom several years ago from breast cancer. Her dad was now suffering from Parkinson's disease and Alzheimer's disease. Her older sister had a malignant brain tumor that is inoperable. Her husband had lost two fingers in an accident. Yet through all of these tragedies she radiated the love of Jesus and made time to visit with her Aunt Betty and Uncle Louis.

I took this opportunity to ask Diane questions that I had never asked. What are the statistics of patients who had bilateral strokes as Betty had suffered? She said she knew of no statistics but that she could not remember having seen what Betty experienced before. She also shared again what other doctors had told me. It was a miracle that Betty had lived and had also improved so much. As other doctors had said, she said again that Betty was so courageous.

Before leaving for home she also shared with us that she would be the incoming Texas State President for the American Heart Association. She is the first neurologist to have that position. As she was leaving, she spoke lovingly to Betty and told her goodbye. As she left the room she said, "I have a very personal interest in ending strokes."

Margaret told me on one occasion when we were discussing Betty that from her observation of Betty and me that I would have reversed the roles if it had been possible. I said, "Absolutely." I would have taken it all upon me had there been a choice. However, I know that God had nothing to do with bringing those diseases, strokes and heart attack upon Betty. He has been most faithful in bringing us through it all. I'm reminded of the song, "Through it all, I've learned to trust in Jesus, I've learned to trust in God'. I've learned to depend upon God's word more in the past three years than all the previous years added together.

The next morning, Tuesday, July 19, 2005, I sensed a change in Betty. I wondered if she was starting another phase of her journey. She did not attempt to eat any breakfast or lunch. She slept almost all morning.

In the afternoon Dr. Barbara Brightwell visited. She is a long-time friend. She is a member of the Board of Directors for the Georgetown Hospital where I worked for several years. She was also director of a large group of volunteers at the hospital and also director of the chaplains' ministry. Prior to that, she had been Dean of Students at Southwestern University in Georgetown, Texas. Dr. Brightwell also coordinated the healing service for Betty at the hospital soon after the strokes. We had a wonderful time with her, and she prayed for us prior to leaving.

Margaret came later in the afternoon. She discussed with me the processes that had been put into place to keep other patients and caregivers from having the terrible experience that we had.

Later that evening as I was getting Betty ready for the night, her skin felt extremely warm. I immediately checked her temperature and it was 104. I checked her blood pressure and it was very low. I immediately called hospice.

The nurse on call asked if I had medications for an emergency. I told her "no." She said she would have to bring some. It was already after 9:00 p.m. She explained that she was at home in south Austin and would need to go to a pharmacy to pick up the medications. I did not ask, but wondered what she meant by "emergency?"

I started a record of Betty's temperature and blood pressure readings for the nurse to see. Sometime after 10:00 p.m. she called and said she had been stuck in traffic as there had been an accident on I-35 but would be here as soon as possible. She arrived close to 11:00 p.m. I appreciated her letting me know where she was and when she thought she would arrive. Obviously, the plans that had been put into place a few days ago by hospice were being followed. I was pleased.

The nurse started preparing the medications and stated that one of the meds would also lower her blood pressure. That puzzled me. Her pressure was already low so why would she give her a medicine that would make it even lower? I asked her about it. She quietly said, "Louis, when I'm through giving the medicine, I need to talk with you in the kitchen."

In a few minutes she said the meds should start working soon and Betty's temp would go down. She then motioned for me to follow her. I was not sure I wanted to hear what she was going to say. I knew in my heart that it was not good. The time was getting shorter and shorter.

The nurse quietly said, "Louis, Betty has entered a new phase of her journey tonight. The medicine will not hurt her but it will help her to be more comfortable. It doesn't matter about her blood pressure now. You are going to wear yourself out if you keep checking it."

I said quietly, "I understand."

By now Betty was quietly sleeping. Her skin felt cooler. The nurse left and told me to call if I needed her. I sat down on the big chair by Betty's bed, raised the footrest and put a blanket over me and tried to sleep. I slept very little. Thoughts kept coming to me about what I had to do when morning came. Again, my favorite song, or probably one of many, *Joy Comes in the Morning*, reminded me that "weeping only lasts for awhile." I wondered if I had any tears left.

Chapter 19:

Almost Home

♪♫

As soon as it was light I called the children. Mark was on the way to his home in Georgia after a business trip in Florida. He said as soon as he got home that he, Kristen, and Colton would leave for Taylor. Lauren was at a church camp. She and Cheryl would fly to Austin as soon as she got back from the camp. Jamie and Dawn said they would come immediately. When Pam arrived I shared the changes in Betty with her.

I received the following email from Dr. Brightwell:

Louis,

It was a blessing to be with you and Betty yesterday. Yours and Betty's strong belief in God is strengthening to every person who knows you. It is heart breaking to know she won't be on this earth much longer, however, we all look toward the day when we will go "home." We will continue to pray for comfort and strength for you and your children.

Shalom...Barbara

About mid-morning, hospice called to check on Betty. I told them that she was sleeping and we had not attempted to awaken her. Also, it appeared that her kidneys were shutting down. Hospice told me they would be sending a nurse later and that she would also stay all night. The changes were so difficult for me to accept.

I wanted her alive and healthy. It was difficult to accept these changes signifying that death was imminent.

Soon after that call a dear friend came. Teresa Glenn had been a valuable member of our team with Betty. She was director of the Cardiopulmonary and Radiology Departments at the Georgetown Hospital. She brought a stethoscope to listen to Betty's lungs. She gave me a refresher course in what to listen for. She said there was fluid in Betty's lungs and that was normal in this stage of the process. I had suctioned Betty earlier that morning. We tried to keep her turned on her side most of the time. Teresa reminded me that she and her family were going on a mission trip to the Czech Republic the latter part of the next week. I was happy she was going but sad that she probably would miss Betty's Victory Service. Again, I thanked God for such loving and compassionate friends from the medical profession. I realized this journey had been much less stressful because I had a complete cadre of professional friends that I could call for help. I'm not certain I would have survived without them and our many other friends.

Jamie, Dawn, Bryan, and Caitlin arrived just before lunch. I felt so much better having them with me. All of us stayed close to Betty's room. Most of our time was spent sitting close by her.

The hospice nurse came soon after lunch. I liked her instantly. She was an LVN and obviously well-trained. She was very caring and helpful. I felt so much relief knowing that I would not be making decisions alone for Betty,

That evening I sent the following email to our friends and family:

Subject: Almost Home

The time that Betty has been living for apparently is almost here. We are told that from all the signs she will be going home within the next 24 hours. I know the angels are waiting to usher her to Heaven and God has her mansion ready. We will let you know when she goes and also the arrangements for her Victory Service. Please pray for Mark as he is on his way home. The girls came today. We love you. Louis

That night as we prepared for sleep, the nurse asked where I would be in case she needed me. I told her that I would sleep on the sofa in the family room. Jamie chose to stay in Betty's room for awhile and later cuddled up in one of the big recliners in the family room.

I awakened frequently during the night. I would quietly walk to the door of Betty's room to see her. Sometimes the nurse would be dozing with her head on Betty's mattress. She always sensed my presence and would raise her head. I would usually ask if there were any changes and she would reply, "No." After working the 11 p.m. to 7 a.m. shift one summer during college, I can certainly empathize with all health professionals who work the night shift. Betty did not need any medications as apparently she was in a coma. I would bend over her bed and kiss her gently. At times I would hold her hand. Most of the time, Jamie would be in Betty's room also. Dawn, Bryan, and Caitlin attempted to sleep. Dawn and the kids had lived with us for awhile when the children were much younger, and I knew it was very hard for them to see their Mom and G in this condition. However, they were so brave with it all.

I knew Mark, Kristen, and Colton were on their way home. I insisted that they get a motel for the night. I wondered how they were doing. This was not a fun trip to Texas. I told Betty they were on their way. I knew if she could, she would wait until all of us were with her before she went "Home." I knew it was hard on Cheryl and Lauren not to come with Mark.

I also felt sorry for Pam. One night the previous October I received a telephone call from the Veterans Hospital in San Antonio. Pam's husband, Don, had been a patient there for several weeks but was doing better. The person calling told me she had called Pam's home number but there was no answer. I asked if she could tell me anything. "No, because of confidentiality issues I am unable to tell you. This is an emergency and I must speak with her." I told her I would contact Pam's daughter who is a registered nurse. I called Christy and told her about the call. I warned her that I had a suspicion it was the worst. She said she would talk with her mom. In a little while she called me back and told me her dad had died.

I felt so sad for Pam and the family. It was also upsetting to Betty. We had prayed many times for him. Prior to Betty having the strokes, the White family had been involved in a single vehicle accident when a tire blew out while on their way to Alabama for the wedding of Pam's Dad. Don's legs were paralyzed as a result of the accident. He also had other injuries as well.

I paid Pam for the hours she had worked plus several additional days. They had a service in Taylor and then took the ashes to Alabama, their home state. Now Pam had been going through all of this with Betty. I was amazed at how strong Pam was. She said God was her strength. She had cared for Betty for almost three years. I assured her that when Betty died that if she did not find another job right away that she could draw unemployment.

Early Thursday morning, I received the following email in response to the email I had sent. It was from our dear friends Sonny and Jane Terrel from Oklahoma:

Good Morning Louis,

Our prayers and thoughts are with you and all your family during these times. We pray that the kids and other family and friends will have safe travel to Taylor. We know Betty is ready and just waiting for the time to be at home with our Lord. We are glad that she will not be in a stroke-ridden body anymore. Our hearts are saddened as this time approaches.

Again, we are sorry that we have not been there for you, but our family situations seemed to keep us tied here.

To most people that I would be writing this type of memo, I would encourage them to lean on God to help them through the valley. But what can I say to the two people who have set the mark so high in their level of faith and trust in our Lord, except THANK YOU for your example of how to live as a trusting Christian when times get really tough. The examples that you and Betty have set throughout your life and especially over the last few years will live forever. THANK YOU again.

We love you and pray for you and your family.
Sonny and Jane

The nurse left about 9:00 a.m. Prior to leaving she instructed us not to give Betty any liquids, including water, as they could cause her to choke. Even giving Betty liquids through her peg tube could cause her to choke. The nurse assured us she would return later in the evening if she was needed. I was very thankful we would not be alone at night. Jamie, Dawn, and the children loved on Betty frequently and all of us assured her that if she was ready to go it was okay. She made no response but we knew there was a possibility that she could hear us. We stayed close to Betty the rest of the morning knowing the next breath could be her last.

Outside Betty's bedroom, I asked the girls who would be able to make the necessary calls after Betty went home. I knew that I could not even if I had the surfboards close. Jamie said she did not think she could call. Dawn said she thought she could if I would make her a list of people with their numbers. Dawn has always been good in emergency situations so we gave her that responsibility. I made the list for her.

We had talked previously with Brother David Johnson about having the service at the First Baptist Church. He had said there were no events scheduled at the church for the next week. Therefore, we agreed that if Betty went home within the week, we would have the service on Saturday, July 30, at 2:00 p.m.

Because Betty had donated her body to the Texas A&M School of Medicine, there would be no rush to have the service.

At approximately 4:00 p.m., Mark, Kristen and Colton arrived. They loved on Betty and talked to her. I was thankful that everyone was present that would be coming at this time. It was also comforting to have them with us.

The hospice nurse arrived about 5:00 p.m. She checked Betty and said she did not appear to have changed. She was about the same as she had been that morning.

Thursday night was about the same as the previous night. However, the nurse told us that she believed the time was close. She waited until after 9:00 a.m. to leave. Pam had arrived about

8:00 a.m. Because we were not giving Betty any nourishment there was no reason for Pam to stay. I would be able to turn Betty by myself or the kids could help me if needed. I assured Pam we would call her when Betty went Home. She told Betty goodbye and left.

I realized that now I had the responsibility of notifying hospice if Betty died. We continued to love on Betty and let her know it was okay to go "Home" if she chose. There was little response. Around noon Betty's breathing pattern changed. She would take a few breaths and then it would be some time before she breathed again. I knew the time was much closer. I had seen patients in the hospital who developed this breathing pattern.

About mid afternoon I suggested Dawn call June and Gene Prater and tell them the time was short. They came very quickly and told Betty goodbye.

In the early evening, Jamie, Mark, Bryan, and Colton went to the grocery store. Kristen, Caitlin, Dawn, and I were in Betty's room. I suggested to Caitlin and Kristen that they go into the TV room for awhile. I looked out the bedroom window and realized that the Holman's trash container was still at the curb. Their son, Brent, always took my trash container to the curb and I always tried to remember to bring both containers back to their proper location behind one of the large shrubs.

I walked into the kitchen to do something before going out to move the Holman's container. Dawn cried, "Daddy!" I ran back into the bedroom and it appeared Betty had completely stopped breathing. Kristen and Caitlin came running too. I listened to Betty's chest and her heart was still faintly beating. She took another breath. Then, just as Mark, Colton, Jamie, and Bryan returned from the store, Betty took her last breath. Dawn reassured me later that I was holding Betty in my arms. I had no idea what I was doing. I knew that the one I had loved and would have given my life for was now with her Heavenly Father. The labor of dying had ended.

Chapter 20:

Betty Wins

♪

W ithin a few minutes, I remembered that I needed to call hospice. The nurse was probably already on her way to Taylor. Without crying, I listened to Betty's heart with the stethoscope that Teresa Glenn had left for me. I could not detect any sounds. I called hospice and told them Betty West had just died. About that time one of the kids told me the nurse had just arrived. The nurse was an LVN; I knew an RN would have to pronounce Betty dead. The person on the telephone told me they would send an RN immediately. The LVN was the same nurse who had been with us the previous nights. I was glad to see her. She was not only efficient but very caring and loving. She agreed that Betty did not have a heartbeat. The time was 7:39 p.m.

Dawn began making calls. Brother David Johnson was first on the list. I knew our pastor, Jeff Ripple, was out of town.

Before anyone I arrived, I brushed Betty's hair and put lipstick on her just as if we were going outside for a stroll in the neighborhood. I did not realize that the past Sunday evening when I took her for a stroll would be the last one. I was glad I could not see into the future several times in the past three years. There were times I thought I would like to know what the future might be. Because God is loving, He would only reveal those things to me that I could stand at that moment in time. As the song *I Can Only Imagine* says, there were many times my imagination would run wild. Then God would gently say, "Peace, Be Still."

The peace that came upon all of us was indescribable. I had known for years that God had given me the gift of administration. For me to be able to listen to Betty's chest and notify hospice was a miracle in itself.

Within a few minutes, the doorbell rang. One of the children went to the door. Soon Brother David Johnson entered Betty's room. He gave me a warm hug and as I looked into his eyes, I saw the eyes of Jesus. I cried uncontrollably. Even now when I think about that moment, I become emotional. I saw compassion and love in Brother David's eyes. He then greeted everyone else. Soon our friends Sonny and Ann Brueckner arrived. We had been friends since moving to Taylor in 1969. Other friends arrived and expressed love and concern.

Time passed quickly, and about 8:30 p.m. the registered nurse from hospice arrived. She greeted us warmly and listened to Betty's chest. The official time of Betty's death on the death certificate is 8:30 p.m. on July 22, 2005.

The nurse completed the paperwork and told me she would need to contact the Taylor police department because Betty had died at home. I explained the procedure she would need to follow to donate Betty's body to the Texas A&M School of Medicine. She was not familiar with those procedures.

Soon the doorbell rang again and a young female police officer entered. She introduced herself and explained that she would need to check Betty because she had died at home. I told her I was aware of the requirement and to feel free to check her. She lifted the sheet quickly and lowered it. She asked the nurse if Betty had any marks on her body. The nurse described the superficial pressure sores. The policewoman completed her paperwork. The nurse who had been with us the last two nights told her, "Everyone should have the privilege of being with this family for two days. They are amazing." The policewoman hugged each of us and expressed her sympathy.

The registered nurse with hospice called the funeral home in Bryan, Texas that would be picking up the body. They asked various questions about Betty and then asked the nurse to please call a local funeral home. They told her to tell the home to call them and they would explain the procedure. I knew they would do a partial embalming procedure and the funeral home in Bryan would then come to Taylor and pick up the body.

The nurse called a local funeral home. While the family waited for them to come, we sat in Betty's room with her body. The grandkids were curious and some wanted to touch or kiss her. We brought

Pepper in for a short while. About 9:45 p.m. the funeral home per-sonnel arrived. They asked if I wanted to stay with Betty for a longer period of time. I thanked them but declined. I knew Betty was now with Jesus. What I was looking at now was merely her worn-out body. She now had a new body in Heaven. She had made all those arrange-ments as a little girl.

I gave her another hug and kiss. I walked from the bedroom to the family room and sat in my recliner. The hospital employees in Cameron had given it to me as a Christmas gift. That big chair had been a comfort to me on many occasions but especially for the past few years. It had supported me the first night of the strokes and now it was supporting me during Betty's death. I did not cry. Dawn told me about the folks she had called.

In about fifteen minutes, the nurse and the funeral home employees came down the hall with Betty on the stretcher, made a turn to the left and down the hall to the front door. I noticed Betty was covered with an emerald green velvet cloth. It was the same color that June Prater had seen in her dream. It was difficult for me to believe what I had dreaded for so long had come. I sincerely do not believe I could have continued to live had it not been for God's peace and love that completely saturated my entire being. I realized for the first time that evening that Betty's fight was over.

In James 1:2-6 is a good description of the life of Betty West...." Consider it all joy, Betty, when you encounter various trials, knowing that the testing of your faith produces endurance. And let endurance have its perfect result that you may be perfect and complete, lacking in nothing." She had won the Crown of Life which is described in James 1:12, "Blessed is Betty West who persevered under trial; for once she has been approved, she will receive the crown of life, which the Lord has promised to those who love Him." She had run the race and she never quit until she won.

After talking with the family for awhile, I sent the following email:

Subject: She is Home

Betty went home this evening at 7:30. All the children and grandchildren were here all day with her except Cheryl and

Lauren who could not be here. I cannot believe the peace I had when she left. Please don't think I'm callous because I believe all of you know by now that I'm not. My medical and administrative skills came forth and I handled everything without crying until Brother David, the pastor from First Baptist Church arrived. I had a good cry and then I was fine. I was able to talk with hospice people and when the nurses got here they had to notify the police. Since Betty has willed her body to the Texas A&M School of Medicine, we also had to notify their contacts. The local funeral home picked up her body at about 10. All of us are doing quite well and friends and relatives have been calling which is great consolation.

The service will be Saturday, July 30, 2005 at the First Baptist Church in Taylor. Believe me, it will not be a funeral service but a true Victory Service that we have been planning for weeks. It is my tribute to Betty, my wonderful and very special loving wife of almost 44 years. Please do not send flowers but if you wish to make a memorial gift, make it to the charity of your choice or I will send you the ones we have chosen in another email.

All of you are invited to attend the service. If you think you will be able to come, please let me know asap. We will have lunch for those who are out of town. We will also send out a list of motels if you should need to stay overnight. I know it is because of prayers and love that we are able to go through this. Betty went very peacefully when she finally got everything settled. She worked on it for at least three days. That's her. She would never have unfinished business. I miss her already but I know she is having a wonderful time in Heaven. I told the kids this afternoon that I am sure she has a red Volkswagen with a stick shift. We had one for several years and she loved to drive it as she would always say, "by the seat of my pants." Jamie says she also has on a beautiful emerald green robe flying in the heavenly breezes as she drives all around Heaven.

We could almost hear the angels and all of her friends and loved ones who are already there, shouting "Here she comes. It's Betty. Here she comes."

The night passed quickly. Saturday had come. Dawn, Bryan, and Caitlin left for Katy. They would return to Taylor early the following week. Mark, Kristen, and Colton left for Cheryl's parents' home in Lockhart about fifty miles away. They planned to return to our home Sunday morning. They would pick up Cheryl and Lauren at the airport the early part of the week. Jamie stayed with me.

By 9:30 a.m., neighbors and friends began arriving bringing food and offering sympathy. We are one of the few families living in Taylor that do not have other family members living here. However, many of our friends are as close as relatives to us.

Jamie had written most of the obituary and just needed to add the date of death and the Victory Service information. I contacted the Austin paper and was assured they could get the obituary in the Sunday paper. Jamie emailed the obituary and Betty's engagement picture. She also sent the same to the Taylor paper. I was relieved when that had been accomplished.

Jamie and I made a list of what needed to be done the following week. I contacted a local restaurant and made arrangements for the family meal to be catered prior to the service. I did not want friends to have to provide the meal, although both churches offered. I wanted this to be a celebration of Betty's life.

Jeff Ripple, our pastor at Christ Fellowship, had been on a mission trip to Mexico when Betty died. Early Saturday afternoon he rang the doorbell. We were delighted to see him. He apologized because he had been gone but I assured him that Betty would have wanted him to be on the mission trip. He and the family gathered in a circle and he prayed for us and for the planning of the Victory Service.

We attempted to continue to do those things that needed to be done. However, there were times we just did something to get our minds off the situation. Jamie and I decided to go shopping at the mall late Saturday evening. Considering the sad feelings we had, we had a wonderful time. We even laughed at times. We knew that Betty would want us to have a good time. Hopefully, anyone who saw us would not suspect that we had just lost a precious love of our lives.

Sunday morning Mark, Kristen and Colton came back to Taylor. About mid-morning we had a most welcome visitor. Juanita Roose skipped Sunday school to be with us. Her husband, Fred had come by Saturday afternoon and we had a good visit with him. We had been friends with Fred and Juanita since moving to Taylor in 1969 and Fred installed our back yard fence. We had shared happy and sad times with them. Prior to the strokes when Betty had a doctor's appointment, Juanita would often drive her. Juanita would drive the van and would help Betty into the wheelchair and assist her into the doctor's office. Betty told me many times how much she loved Juanita and what a sweet person she was. Juanita had lost her mom and dad in an auto accident just prior to our moving to Taylor. She was familiar with grief.

Juanita asked about the service and we told her some of the plans. She was thrilled to know that Anita Volek and Carol Laurence were going to play the organ and piano. She said she and Fred would get to the service early because Anita and Carol always played beautiful music for at least thirty minutes before the service.

Dawn, Bryan, and Caitlin returned on Monday. Dawn began selecting pictures that would be used during the service. Unlike many services I had attended where pictures were shown prior to the service, I had requested they be shown continually, starting thirty minutes before the service and continuing throughout the service. Jamie, Bryan, and Mark began scanning pictures they believed I would want into the computers. The other children also helped to select pictures. Occasionally, Mark, Bryan, and Jamie would take a break and select pictures also. Periodically, they would show me the selections. I loved all of them. I was so proud of my kids and grand-kids and I knew Betty would have been proud also. Throughout all the preparation we were showing our love for Betty and each other. Kristen, Caitlin, and Colton also arranged pictures of their beloved G and poems they had written about her on poster board to be displayed in the fellowship hall of the church during the luncheon. The picture boards would then be moved into the foyer of the church.

Throughout the week, Jamie and I met at various times with the two pastors. They were very helpful in preparing for the service.

I could tell they were as enthusiastic about a Victory Service for Betty as our family was. There was never a cross word but there was laughter at times. Both pastors have such warm personalities and it was a joy being with them.

At one point when I suggested that I wanted the children from Christ Fellowship Church to participate, I was rather hesitant. I did not know exactly how to word my request to Brother David. He immediately picked up on my hesitancy and asked, "Do y'all plan to dance in the aisles?" Then he laughed.

I replied, "Well sorta." All four of us had a good laugh. Finally I told him we would like to have the little children dance to the music of *I Can Only Imagine*.

"Permission granted," he replied. I knew Betty would be pleased that the four of us were excited and enjoying planning her Victory Service. After the hurdle about the dance had passed, we planned the rest of the service. I knew I would not have a problem with the dove release. My desire was to have a service that would honor both God and Betty. It definitely would not be a "show" but a service that would draw all of us closer to God.

It was wonderful to see the two pastors work so harmoniously together. We also discussed the plans with Mark, Cheryl and Dawn. We would definitely have an American flag at the front of the Church. We also asked Stephen Sorensen, son of our wonderful friends Steve and Trish Sorensen, to play a trumpet solo of *The Star Spangled Banner.* Betty was the most patriotic person I have ever known. The Victory Service was a family project that would always be in our memory. I welcomed any ideas from the kids and grandkids because I wanted them to feel they had a part in the planning of this very special memorial service.

During the week I made an appointment with our attorney, Pat Quinn. I wanted to proceed with any legal affairs and get them behind me. Pat is an excellent attorney and a friend as well. We visited about Betty and he told me what I needed to do to prepare for the probate. It would probably be at least a month before we were ready. I discovered that it was good to have time between Betty's death and the time for the actual service. Neither my family nor I felt rushed or overwhelmed because we had plenty of time to plan the service.

Jamie prepared the program for the service and took it to the printer. We chose to have Betty's engagement picture on the front of the program along with her name, date of the service, and location. Many times I had searched through pictures of loved ones who had died and there was very little information included. We included the Order of Service and the essay Betty had written as a high school senior, "What America Means to Me." On the back of the program was printed "Gone from My Sight" by Henry Van Dyke.

Prior to Betty's death I asked a few close friends and family, as well as Bill Robinson and Lisa Jeffery, who had been her therapists, to give a short talk at her Victory Service about their relationship with Betty. I also asked the grandchildren to do the same. I wanted to write a tribute to her. Mark, Dawn and Jamie said they had expressed their love to her before she died. As the day of her service came closer I continued to have difficulty writing a tribute. What could I say in a few minutes about my love and respect for her? I knew I would have to record it. The little surfboards would not keep me from crying during such an emotional time.

Throughout the week we received many cards and letters from friends and relatives. Because several of her doctors had called me to express their sympathy, I was surprised to get cards and letters from them also. A few are included below:

Dear Louis,

Although I was saddened to hear of Betty's passing, I was comforted by the knowledge of the comfort and care she received in her final months. All my comments to you at the last appointment were heartfelt ….she was very fortunate to have such a loving husband.

Good luck to you—take care.

Sincerely,
Edward Fox, MD

Dear Louis,

We were very sorry to hear that Betty had died.

I always enjoyed visiting with her. She had quite a fighting spirit. Even in very ill health, she had a good sense of humor. We will miss her.
If there is anything we can do, please let us know.

Tony Shallin, MD

I also received a letter from Dr. Robert Stern. He was our internist for several years before becoming a pathologist at the Georgetown Hospital where I was working when Betty had the strokes.

Louis,

Many times over the past few weeks, I've thought about your picture in the Taylor Daily Press when you were a young administrator in a brand new hospital building in a small central Texas town. The twinkle in your eye was clear even in the old, yellow, faded newspaper. Your life was changing and it looked like you were so eager for the challenge.

How many times in the years since have you had to face life-changing events and new challenges? I know the answer—a bunch. And, as best I can tell, you took on those challenges with the same vigor that you approached that new hospital in Taylor. In your care of Betty following her stroke, you took this vigor to a new level. Your care for her was truly extraordinary and blanketed with love.

So now I look on with interest to see how you respond to this new challenge. This one is the toughest, I guess. But, I can see how your already deep and loving character has been expanded by the last few years. I see how much you have to offer to those going through grieving and stress. I see how

effective you could be with the American Heart Association or the American Stroke Association or so many other causes.

But for now, even the Louis Wests of the world need to rest. I hope you can find sleep these days. I hope you can spend time with and hug and love the important people in your life. I hope these difficult days can also be days of reestablishing old relationships and strengthening ongoing friendships, and living in God's love and peace.

I wish I could have known Betty when you were that bright-eyed young administrator. My guess is that her eyes were burning even more intensely than yours. Even after I got to know her, after she started having challenges with sister and parents and after she started to have physical problems, her eyes were always so bright and piercing. Honestly, I felt she could look right into my heart and, thankfully, those piercing eyes were always accompanied by a smile—even as I expressed my exasperation in not helping her get better. But the thing about Betty that I will carry with me the rest of my life was her wonderful resonating voice and how she would laugh, particularly when she talked about you. We did talk about you behind your back. We didn't think you would mind.

So happily Betty lives on for me, and so many others. Her eyes, her voice, and perhaps most of all, her courage, are part of her legacy. These things have deepened my existence in the Holy Spirit, and for that, I love her.

So I will call in the next few weeks and I will buy lunch, and I will hear what the bright-eyed administrator is up to now.

Bob

Betty touched many lives prior to the strokes. Many never forgot that touch. Only eternity will tell how many she touched after the strokes. Also included are excerpts from a few messages that I received prior to the Victory Service:

Mr. West

My prayers are with you and your family. The time I spent at your home with Jamie is always fond memories. Mrs. West once told us as girls that it is as easy to fall out of love as it is to fall in love and that a marriage has to be nurtured. I have carried this with me the past eleven years of my marriage. I am very grateful for her wisdom and guidance.

I pray that God will give you peace at this time of loss.

Susan

Dear Louis and Family,

Our family is eternally grateful to you and we would not be where we are today had it not been for your prayers back in 1974. We loved Betty; she was a dear friend. We know we will see her again one day.

Our love and prayers,
Pat and family

Louis, Mark, Dawn, and Jamie,

Words can never express our sadness with the loss of your precious Betty.

Betty left such a Big Footprint in this world. Through all her illness and before, she still praised God for all things.

She was a loving friend who was always there. I don't think I have ever known a Mother or wife who loved her family

as deeply and unconditionally as Betty. Those precious grandchildren were the light of her life.

I loved her dearly and I know she loved me. I am so much richer because of that love and her deep and abiding faith in God.

You all are in our hearts and prayers.

We love you.
Shirley and Jack

Dear Mr. West,

I rejoice with you and your family that Betty is in the arms of our Father now, and will remain safely and gloriously there for eternity. I will <u>always</u> have a place in my heart for her because she helped to show me the way during that agonizing time of my life. Her bookstore and the peace I found there are memories I cherish.

My prayer is that God continues to bless you with His peace and comfort and the assurance of Betty's presence with Him now and always. May He provide in every way for you and guide and protect you and your loved ones.

Very Sincerely,
Pam

Throughout our marriage we expressed our love for each other in various ways. Betty enjoyed giving me cards on special occasions and then often she would give me as she would say a "just because" card. A copy of the verse from one of the many "just because cards" is printed below.

**Too often, I haven't told you
how very much I need you.
I do, you know.**

**Perhaps I don't want to box you in
by saying the words too often.
Perhaps I'm really afraid to admit
how much I have
come to depend on you.**

But I do need you so very much...

**I need you when I'm laughing—
just as much as when I'm crying.
I need you when I succeed—
just as much as when I fail.**

**And what's so wonderful about it all
Is that you're always there!**

**My love,
Betty**

I can also say that she was always there for me. She was my most ardent cheerleader and best friend.

On Wednesday night before the Victory Service on Saturday, several visitors came to the house. It was not planned but just happened. It was so relaxing and a wonderful time of fellowship. Two of my very dear friends, Sam Schultz and Teresa Glenn came. Teresa was leaving on the mission trip the following day but wanted to come show her support. Sam is like family. Several weeks before, he and his family made arrangements to go to the coast on the weekend that we later selected for Betty's service. He offered to cancel their plans. I said, "No, you have been here for us since 2002 when Betty had the strokes. She would be the first to tell you to keep your reservation. Go and have fun with the family." I thought that would be the end of discussion. I should have known better.

Thursday night, Bryan, Jamie, and I stayed at the Best Western Motel in Taylor. The next morning when we arrived at home Mark and Dawn told us that Sam and Julie and their children had come by earlier hoping to see me. They brought cards and gifts for me. It was Betty's and my 44th anniversary.

The smaller card had a little note attached which read "Funny Betty." A little note was also attached to the larger card that read "Serious Betty." I opened that card first. It was beautiful. On the front of the card written in gold was "**For the One I Love on Our Anniversary.**" Inside the card was written words very similar to the card she had given me years before:

> **I hope there is never**
> **a need for you to wonder**
> **how strong and deep**
> **my feelings are for you.**
> **We may have changed a little,**
> **grown a lot,**
> **but what's been constant**
> **is how much I need you**
> **in my life...**
> **If my words sometime fail me,**
> **always remember what's in my heart—**
> **You touch my soul...**
> **and always will.**

Sam printed the following message:

"This card is not signed by Betty, but contains the thoughts she had these past 44 years. You'll know that she was with Julie when it was selected to give to you."

Happy 44th Anniversary Louis

(Go grocery shopping today).

Included with the anniversary card was a gift card for groceries. Sam had discovered that the symbol for the 44th anniversary was "groceries."

Neighbors and friends from First Baptist Church and Christ Fellowship church kept our refrigerator stocked with delicious food all week. Valerian and Mary Chyle had told me soon after Betty died they wanted to bring dinner for Friday night before the service on Saturday. All they needed was the number to prepare for. I estimated there would be at least twenty friends and relatives from out of town.

Friday morning was spent making last minute preparations for the service. I knew that some of my family would be arriving in the early afternoon. However, I still had not written my tribute to Betty. After a light lunch I went into her bedroom and closed the door. I had already given her hospital bed to Pam for a friend who could use it, and replaced it with a full-size bed. I had also given Betty's standing frame and other equipment to the Johns Community Hospital Rehab Department. Her bedroom did not look as it had for the past years. However, I could still sense her presence.

I brought my tape recorder and a pad and pen into her room. I sat in the large chair that I had used so many times in the past years. I tried to visualize Betty lying in the new bed that I had bought. I prayed. Words started coming and my hand moved the pen to the pad and I started writing. It reminded me of the time when as a college student I worked in the medical clinic and transcribed notes as the doctors dictated. The words continued pouring forth and formed effortlessly on the pad. God was giving me the words that He wanted. I meditated and wrote for approximately thirty minutes. It was finished.

I turned the recorder on and began reading from the pad. Occasionally I would have to stop the recorder, get my emotions under control and hit rewind for a few seconds. In about fifteen minutes I had recorded it to my satisfaction. I was pleased. I also felt that God was pleased.

Just as I finished, my sister Laverne and her husband, Dorris, arrived. They had driven from Denton. After we visited for a few minutes, Jamie asked if I had finished the tribute. I nodded my head affirmatively. "Do you mind if I listen to it?" I did not object and hoped that she would let me know if she had any suggestions. In about ten minutes she returned. "You knocked it out of the park, Dad. You hit a home run."

In addition to Laverne, I had another older living sister, Lucille. She and her husband were in an auto accident a few years prior to Betty having the strokes. Her husband was killed instantly. Lucille had severe injuries. Although it was not their fault, she had never recovered emotionally from the accident and her husband's sudden death. She was now living in a nursing home in Gainesville, Texas. She also seemed to be having problems with dementia or Alzheimer's disease. I knew she would not be able to come to the service. I did not have the slightest thought that within two weeks she would also be going to join Betty in Heaven. However, her daughter Wanda and her husband would be present at Betty's service.

My brother, Weldon, and his sweet wife, Emma Jo, would not be able to come. Both are elderly and in poor health. I knew their prayers had sustained us for years. Although I would have loved to see them, I understood why they could not be present.

During the afternoon, other relatives and friends arrived. My brother Leslie and his wife Evelyn came from Gainesville. It was good to visit with everyone. Sonny and Jane Terrell from Oklahoma arrived. Our dear friends Mildred Fulfer and Tony Haley came from Harlingen. Betty and Mildred were friends before Betty and I married. She was like a sister to us and had been a great encouragement in our spiritual walk. Our kids loved her dearly.

About 6:00 p.m., the Chyles' arrived. They had ice chests full of delicious food. It was obvious that Mary had been baking all day. I knew Valerian had been at his office throughout the day treating cancer patients, yet he and Mary took time to minister to us. Valerian had been such a support for me when Mark had bladder cancer in 2001. Both had supported and encouraged me throughout Betty's lengthy illness.

Despite the sad occasion, we had a good time visiting and eating the delicious food. Betty's Aunt Adina and her daughter, Phyllis, arrived later and there was still plenty of food available for them. I appreciated so much those who had taken time out of their busy schedules to be with our family at this time. Other family members and friends would arrive Saturday morning prior to the afternoon service.

Chapter 21:

Joy Comes in the Mourning

ℐℙ

S aturday morning I awakened early. I was not dreading this day but excited about it. I sensed His presence in every room of my home. How thankful I was that He never left me throughout this journey. He had been present in every situation. Never once after the first day did I ever ask, "God, where are you?" I also knew that my dad and mom had prepared me for this day. They had instilled in me the love of God and taught me His ways. Betty and I had also done the same for our children. There was no reason not to trust God to care for us on this special day of our lives. I had given this day to Him to use for His glory. I only wanted to be His instrument to share His love with others at the service. I was amazed at how calm and relaxed I was. Without Him I could do nothing. I knew as long as He held my hand, I could do anything He asked of me.

By 10:00 a.m. many out of town family members arrived. It was comforting to see them. Some I had not seen in over a year.

I also asked the Taylor Police Department to please patrol the neighborhood frequently. Thieves often take advantage of the situation when they know everyone has gone to the service for a deceased family member.

Lunch was to be served at 11:30 a.m. As we arrived at the church, three young boys came sprinting across the parking lot to greet me. I recognized them as Diane and Dale's sons. I was pleased they were glad to see me. I soon knew the reason. They began talking at the same time and it was not difficult to understand their question. "Uncle Louis, do we **have** to wear a tie?" I burst out laughing and in my mind, I caught a glimpse of Betty laughing like no one else could.

I asked, "What did your Mom and Dad tell you?"

"They said we do."

"Then I suppose you should do what they say. However, as far as I'm concerned, it isn't necessary."

As I entered the fellowship hall, the young woman who was catering the meal was getting everything organized. There was also a beautiful floral arrangement given by friends of Jamie on the serving table. I made my way to the sanctuary. Someone had already reserved the pews for the family. The florist had also delivered floral arrangements and greenery. I had ordered a large floral arrangement and thought that would be sufficient. We had asked that memorial contributions be made to various charities. However, the arrangements looked beautiful.

As I returned to the fellowship hall, both pastors and many of the out of town folks had arrived. One of the pastors asked the blessing. Everyone was enjoying visiting with each other. It was comforting to have so many family members present. Although I wasn't hungry I managed to eat. After visiting for awhile, I headed back to the sanctuary. I had written cards of appreciation and included an honorarium for the pastors, musicians and those who were to provide the special music and operate the sound system.

As I entered the sanctuary, people were already coming in. My eyes caught a pretty, petite lady. It was Eva Aldridge. Eva was working at the hospital in Taylor when we moved here in 1969. As I started towards her, she arose and put out her arms. She gave me a big hug and said, "You came for two members of my family; this time I wanted to come for you."

I was amazed that I was able to greet the people with a smile instead of crying. Some were present that I had not seen in years. As the time drew closer to 2:00 p.m., the sanctuary was full of people who had come to show their love and support and express their love for Betty. Additional chairs were brought into the sanctuary. I had not anticipated the large number of people. I should not have been surprised because Betty was loved by so many.

The display of pictures and poems that had been made by Caitlin, Kristen, and Colton was brought from the fellowship hall into the church foyer. The slideshow of pictures that Mark, Dawn, Jamie, and Bryan had put together played continuously on a large screen over the pulpit.

Rebecca had brought the four white doves in a beautiful chapel made of wood and wire and placed it in the foyer next to the guest book.

Soon it was 2:00 p.m. It was time for the Victory Celebration for Betty West. The family and very close friends had seated themselves rather than march in as a group. Carol Laurence and Anita Volek had been providing beautiful music for the last forty-five minutes. It was time to celebrate.

The service began with what was supposed to have been a trumpet solo by Stephen Sorensen playing the *Star Spangled Banner*. He had hardly begun to play until the congregation stood and joined him by singing. Betty loved America so much and I knew it would have thrilled her that the congregation could not remain silent. It was a wonderful way to begin a Victory Celebration.

Pastor David Johnson from the First Baptist Church welcomed everyone and prayed that God would be honored throughout the service. Because we wanted the congregation to participate in this celebration, he then led two lively hymns, *I'll Fly Away* and *I Stand Amazed*.

We also had asked the trio, Faith, Hope, and Charity to sing at various times throughout the service. They had visited in our home just two weeks before Betty's death. Betty loved to hear them and they loved Betty.

The five grandchildren and Cheryl also presented individual tributes, printed below:

BEDTIME WITH G
By: Caitlin Buegeler Age 12

When I was a lot younger, and I was at this stage where I was really scared of shadows, I started sleeping on a cot in G and G'Pa's bedroom when I visited. G'Pa would be doing things around the

house, like laundry and telling my brother goodnight. But in those few moments, I was in a different world. I'd better explain...

My G and I would lie down on G and G'Pa's waterbed and listen to G tell wonderful stories about how G and G'Pa had met. She would tell me a part of it each night. It went from them seeing each other in church for the first time, to their wedding, to their honeymoon. I always LOVED those stories, and each night now, I try to remember a piece, a night, of her stories. Sometimes I think, "How can they have met?" But I always know that God put them together, not Cupid (even though it seems...).

Like I had mentioned, G would tell me the story of how they met. I would like to share what I remember of it to you.

G always said that they were at church. She sat down and a nice gentleman sat (or was sitting) beside her. He looked WAY too young for her, but he was so handsome. She was in church and so she had to fill out one of those cards that had a name, address, and phone number space on it. So she put it in the box at the service. But what G didn't know was that the gentleman was looking over and memorizing her phone number before she put it in the box. But as I said, G didn't know and the service continued on, as did their lives. G told me that she wished she could see him again. And later on, they did. The gentleman, who is my G'Pa now, called her on the memorized number, asked her out, and guess what? She said,"YEESSS!!!!"

And that is how it began.

And it was like magic.

"My Grandma"
By Kristen West Age 10

My Grandma is so wonderful and so very thoughtful. I remember when I was little, I would go over to their house and G would ask,

"Kristen, will you come read with me"? I was so excited and I would run to the TV room and pick out the books I would always read to her.

Then we moved to Georgia and that's when G had the strokes. We were all devastated. But if you knew G, she never lost her spirit and G-Pa showed the world that he loved G better than you can imagine.

One of the precious things G got to do after the stroke was she would sit in her wheelchair and she and G-Pa or she and Pam, her caregiver, would go on walks with precious dog, Pepper. G looked so beautiful when she went on those walks. She wore bright colored clothes and a beautiful straw hat.

She had a heart attack in 2004. Bless her heart, she had to go through so many devastating things but she never lost her spirit.

When I was little, my Dad, her oldest child, told me stories about her cooking and how she loved to mow the lawn or play ping pong or tennis.

We were all blessed to have G. We should all be thankful that the Lord has made her and other people like her. Can you imagine what the world would be like to have all people like her? Good thought, right?

Everyone has a time to go be with their friends and family and be at the right hand of Jesus. This is her time. We will miss her dearly but just remember that she is in a better place.

Love, Kristen.

Tribute to Betty West
By Cheryl West

I remember being so scared meeting Mark's parents the first time; my stomach was in knots as we walked up the sidewalk to their home in Taylor.

Would they like me? Would they accept me? Will they think I'm good enough for their son?

The moment I met Betty, I knew everything would be fine. She hugged me and smiled that beautiful smile.

The years have gone by so quickly with our living away. I regret that our children did not have the chance to get to know their wonderful G the way I did. The level of faith she exhibited and the knowledge she had to share will last forever.

Our children have a wonderful sense of humor and I credit their Daddy's side of the family for that. Betty never criticized but when it was needed, she always had advice to share.

She was an inspiration to me and to those who were blessed to have met her. A poem, "Work of Art," expresses my feelings for Betty.

Sometime God is quite remarkable;
You can see His artistic talent all around.
You can see the majesty of His work in every being,
Every happening and every sound and
At times He excels Himself and makes a
Dolphin or a Bird of Paradise or
He creates someone with so much love and kindness
That you would never meet anyone
Who is even half as nice.

So now Betty is back in her Father's arms. Please take care of her; you've got a special one there. We are just thankful for the times we've had with her. We had many magic moments in which to share and know that God is proud of His work. He too did not want to spend any more time apart because beauty is always in the eye of the beholder. Betty was truly beautiful—His Work of Art.

Our G
By Colton West, Age 7

Our G was always special to me because she read books to me until she had the strokes. I always looked forward to her reading to me.

Now I know she is in a better place so I have to read books to myself.

I love her still even if she is gone. I will love her no matter what and I will never forget her. I know G still loves me.

My Tribute to G
By Lauren West, Age 13

I'm Mark's oldest. My Grandma or "G" as we called her had a stroke the first week after we moved to Georgia. At the time, I was going into fifth grade and didn't really understand what was going on. I do remember when we got the call about her having a stroke; my Mom was headed to a movie. She started crying so hard that she cancelled her plans and stayed home with us.

A lot of things happened and we got to come about once or twice each year because we lived so far away.

When we would visit, I remember it was hard for me to be in the room with her because I couldn't understand what she was saying. I knew she wanted to talk to me but could not speak well. However, this summer when we came back, I tried to stay in the room as long as possible because I knew it wouldn't be long. One night while we were sitting with her, just my Dad and me, she had her head tilted to the side so we could see her. She really couldn't talk then so it was a miracle that she said this as she said it just like she would have before the stroke. She turned to my Dad and said, "I love you honey." Dad didn't hear her though, so I told him. He said, "I love you too."

I remember after she said it, I felt a strange presence in the room. As I was writing this, I realized it was the Holy Spirit who had entered the room and given her the strength to speak.

"G" always had the Lord Jesus Christ with her and I know that some day, I will see her again in Heaven. She wants to see you there too.

My Tribute to G
By Bryan Buegeler, Age 15

I'm the oldest grandchild and I'm Dawn's son.

Betty West was a very special person in my life. From the time I was born until she passed away, she was always there for me.

When I was little, I used to visit her at least twice a month. When I would visit, G would always have things for me to do. It varied from playing board games to taking trips around town. One time for instance, she took me to Sonic on the way to the bank. At Sonic, she bought each of us a vanilla milk shake. I was sitting behind her in the back seat of the van. All of a sudden, my straw poked through the bottom of my cup spilling stuff everywhere. Luckily G had the towel that she always kept in the van and was able to easily clean it up.

One of the most special things about her was that nothing upset her and she always put other people first.

Another thing we would do together was go to basketball games. G, G-Pa and I would take trips into Austin to see the Lady Longhorns play basketball. I remember the long walk up the ramp to the stadium. Sometime when we would go, I would be allowed to push G in her wheelchair. For some reason, pushing the wheelchair seemed like a special treat for me. Whenever G would go some-where with her chair, she always had a mauve color pillow that she sat on. One time on the ramp at the game, she stood up for some reason and the pillow fell out of her chair. I noticed the pillow on the ground and picked it up for her. Every time I see that pillow, I think of going to the basketball games with G and G-Pa.

When I was little, both G and G-Pa came up with games to occupy me. G-Pa would pay me money to count cars and semi-trucks during road trips. He quickly gave that up.

G took a slightly different approach. She paid me to read. Every time I would sit in her lap and read a book with her, she would give me a dime or a nickel. I would then put that money into a plastic cup from 7-11 and use that money to buy a new book. G is the reason why I read so much today and also why I have so many books.

My most memorable experience with G was playing Battleship. When I would visit, G would always have the game ready. She would always be the red color and I would be the blue color. When we would play, she would sit in her chair and I would sit across from her in G-Pa's chair. She always won until I realized that she put her ships in the exact same place every time we played. After that, she could never figure out how I always won.

Even though G is in Heaven now, I will always remember the fun times that we had when she was here.

The children have a way of expressing their love and admiration for their G like no adult could ever do. Knowing that my recorded tribute of Betty was following their tributes almost intimidated me. My tribute to Betty is printed below:

MY TRIBUTE

Many years ago, God created a baby girl in Monument, New Mexico. Fifteen days later, a little boy was born near Plains, Texas.

The two were separated by only 30 miles.

Twenty- four years later, the boy was a man. After having moved from the area for several years and after having become a man, he moved to Hobbs, New Mexico to work in the hospital in January 1961. The little girl had become a beautiful young lady and was still living in Monument that was only 10 miles from Hobbs. She was now working for an oil company.

And God said, "It is not good that Louis should be alone; I will give him Betty." He arranged for the two young people to meet in the First Baptist Church in Hobbs. The two sat together in Church one morning in March 1961. The young man was no dummy. Although not a fisherman, he knew a good catch when he saw it. So there-fore, when eyeing the beautiful brunette from across the church, he got up out of his seat and made his way to her. Not a word was spoken between them. The young woman finally pulled the glove from her left hand and he observed no rings. She raised her hand as a visitor and completed the typical visitor's card. The young man having learned to read many years before almost popped his right eye from its socket in order to read the information on the card. The most important statistics were committed to his memory. Betty Hurst, Monument, New Mexico, telephone 7-1240.

Before having the opportunity to call her, the young man became very seriously ill and was admitted to the Lea General Hospital for 8 days. As his strength returned, he began to think more of Betty Hurst. He summoned the courage to call her in May 1961 for a date to the Hobbs Rodeo. Amazingly she accepted.

On our first date, I saw Betty's strength and something more. Stronger than strength, I saw a softness. A loneliness to match my own. For both of us, it was as if we had known each other for 24 years. A strong love fell upon us almost immediately and therefore we married for better or worse, in sickness and health, for richer or poorer on July 29, 1961.

Betty was kind and sweet and deliciously humorous and witty. Yet she was something more. She was an athlete. I was not. She gently started to try to transform me. She loved to play golf so on our second date we went to the golf course. She never lost patience with me, and for my birthday in October, she gave me a set of clubs. I sincerely believe it was at that time that her patience began to develop to its highest potential.

I was not interested in golf. I only played to please Betty. Three years later, I chose golf as a PE class when I went back to school at Texas Tech. For our final grade, we had to demonstrate for the instructor. His comments to me were, "you might play around in your back yard before considering being a serious golfer." I got a C and that was humiliating because I was not happy with any grade lower than a B. Betty consoled me and told me how proud she was of me.

Betty would give me special gifts that I would have never bought for myself. For our first Christmas she gave me a rifle. Firing a rifle was one thing I was very good at doing. I had been awarded medals for my shooting ability while in the military. I was excited to show Betty this talent. We went out in the country to her parents' home and shot tin cans. Despite the fact that I shot very well, she still beat me.

For our first anniversary she gave me a piano that we still have. At last I could do something she could not. However, she sang beautifully. I would play for her and as her beautiful soprano voice wafted through the house or church, Heaven would seem to come to earth.

Throughout all of our years together, we never had a serious argument. When the kids would later ask us if we ever had a fight like some of their friends' parents, Betty's answer was always, "I have tried but your Daddy wouldn't fight." I was no dummy. I knew she would probably win at that sport too.

Perhaps I sound as if I lived in Betty's shadow. Not true. She always built me up and encouraged me in all endeavors. She was my lover, my confidante, and most of all my best friend. I have no talent or ability to repair the car, do electrical or plumbing work or repair a roof. For years I felt inferior to my friends who could do all of those things. However, through her positive perseverance with me and reminding me of the talents that I have, I am almost relieved of those inferiorities. She would always remind me of the fact that I could do an excellent job with the vacuum cleaner, dust cloth and mop. I even eventually learned to cook. Seriously though, she saw in me things that I took for granted. Yet to her they were real blessings. As she experienced the many illnesses and tragedies in her life and because God had prepared me many years before, I was able to keep her in our home for almost three years instead of a nursing facility. I never looked at caring for her as a job or responsibility but a privilege that God had given me. We were blessed also with having an angel as a caregiver for as long as Betty lived. Pamela White was invaluable to both of us. Betty loved her and Pam certainly showed her love for Betty.

Betty and I often talked of her loving doctors. I suggested that all of them had been hand-picked by God. In Austin she had Dr. Pham as her internist. In the hospital in Taylor she was treated by Dr. Scott Farquarson who was so positive and loving to both of us. She was also blessed by her primary care physician, Dr. Tony Shallin, her neurologist, Dr. Edward Fox, Dr. Anisa Godinez, her rehab doctor or physiatrist, Dr. Steven Garland her cardiologist, her urologist, Dr. David Freidberg, Dr. Alam, her psychiatrist who worked so faithfully in helping with the depression caused by the strokes, many wonderful therapists and nurses who poured their love into her along with their skills. One who was so faithful and listened to me when I was up and when I was down and offered encouragement and hope was her niece, Diane Solomon, a neurologist in San Antonio.

Throughout her sicknesses Betty never complained but would cling to her unwavering faith in God. Many years ago she became aware of the power that is in the Name of Jesus. She developed such a strong love and faith that she had absolutely no fear of anything. She also taught our children about the love of Jesus.

Jesus was so real to her that when she had the strokes, visitors and hospital personnel could tell that she was different from most patients. Because of her wit and humor, she brought laughter to all who entered her room. After the strokes in June 2002, which affected both sides of her brain, God completely healed her of polymyositis which is incurable. He also healed her of neuropathy, high blood pressure and irritable bowel Syndrome. Consequently she never experienced the excruciating pain that she had for years. Doctors told her they could not scientifically explain what had happened. She would immediately lift her right arm and say, "I can; it was God." She continued to amaze all who saw her with her patience, love and faith.

Just before her death, I was able to tell her that because of her faith in Jesus Christ she has won the fight she so valiantly fought and we would celebrate her victory complete with a dove release. She has now received her reward of eternal life in a place prepared for her that has no diseases, sicknesses, paralysis or tears.

Through using yes-no questions, she had told me days before her death that she had seen glimpses of Heaven and that angels were in her room. She said she was not afraid. She showed our children, grandchildren, and many others that death is not to be feared if your faith and trust is in Jesus Christ.

While in Johns Community Hospital in 2002, the therapists worked with her eye hand coordination by batting balloons with her better arm and hand. She challenged anyone who came into the room to play balloon with her. She always warned them ahead of time that she would win. Some would try to be very gentle with her at the beginning of the challenge. They soon discovered that they were no match for her. I will always remember on one occasion when I accidentally hit the balloon too far to her right for her to be able to reach. At least I thought I had. She stretched as far as she could and sent it sailing back to me so fast that I missed it. Rather disgusted with myself, I said, "Betty you just won't quit, will you? You never quit until you win." With her mischievous grin, she said, "That's a good one Louis. Put it on the wall." We made a banner for her room that stayed with her for months, "Never Quit Until You Win." She never did give up until she won the battle. If this tribute sounds as if I am very proud of her, then it has accomplished its purpose. This has been only a small summary of Betty's life. The rest is written in Heaven.

Betty loved everyone. It did not matter if they were old or young, male or female, rich or poor. However, she especially loved little children. Because of her love for the little ones, we included the little children from the Christ Fellowship Church. So as the popular Christian song *I Can Only Imagine* played, the little children danced.

Because June and Gene Prater are so much a part of our family, we asked them to share their thoughts. They shared special memories of how Betty always prayed for them when they were on mission trips and how God answered her prayers. They were especially thankful for her praying about their going to Russia. They are convinced that had she not been persistent they would have never gone. Consequently God used them in a mighty way in witnessing while they were there and they saw many Russians come to Jesus. June stated that she knew that when Betty got to Heaven, she probably saw some of those for whom she had prayed.

We also wanted to include Lisa Jeffery who was one of Betty's Physical Therapists. Lisa said that Betty had made such an impact on her spiritual life that she would never be the same. She said she was the only person she had ever known who could win someone to Jesus Christ without speaking a word. Betty made such an impact on Lisa that she ran a marathon for the American Stroke Association in Betty's honor and raised over $5,000.

Sonny and Jane Terrel had been friends since 1966 when we moved from Lubbock to Luling, Texas. They shared what an impact she had made on their family. Jane shared about Betty's beautiful soprano voice and how she believed that Betty sang like an angel might sound.

Bill Robinson was Betty's Occupational Therapist when she was in the hospital in Taylor for a hundred days. He shared how he was blessed to see miracles happening right before his eyes.

The last tribute was by our precious niece, Diane Solomon. Betty was Diane's godmother.

When Uncle Louis asked me to speak, I asked God to give me a scripture for this time. Last Thursday morning He gave me the scripture I Corinthians 13:13. "For now abide faith, hope, love, these three; but the greatest of these is love."

To be with my Aunt Betty was to feel loved and special. When I spoke with my brothers and sisters, we each felt that we were the special one to Aunt Betty. It takes a special person to do that.

She inspired us by her faith before she became ill and later she just blew us away by her faith.

Betty allowed God to use even the tragic events of her illness to His glory. She kept her eyes focused on Jesus through it all.

She was an active, athletic woman who had to face great physical loss and pain. Through her faith she maintained hope even when we doctors felt like there was none.

It was a miracle. Not only did Betty maintain her hope, she had hope with her great sense of humor and with her courageous perseverance.

Most of all, Betty's life was a beautiful love story. She loved Jesus who has taken her hand and led her home. She loved Louis with a love for all eternity. He returned that love with tender, devoted caring...a love so deep and so pure that it truly is Christlike. He would have readily reversed the roles and taken on Betty's ill-nesses if he could have.

Betty loved and doted on her children and her precious grandchildren. She loved each of us in this room and we all felt cherished.

There's a line on an article that Uncle Louis sent me about grief. It's just like him to be sending me something but it says, "The loss of a loved one does not mean the loss of love for love is stronger than separation."

I give thanks for Aunt Betty's life and for her continued blessing of love.

Pastor Jeff Ripple stated how difficult it was to speak about Betty because there was so much to tell. His question was "What would you leave out about Betty West?" He spoke of her great faith and courage and how she "lived in a River of God's Peace" and that she reached the summit of God's mountain. He shared that he knew that she would want him to tell about Jesus and make certain that everyone understood how important it is to put their faith in Him. His closing question was "Just think if you left earth today, where would you go?"

After Brother Jeff spoke, Jenna Williams performed the song *Dancing with the Angels* in American Sign Language. As she signed, I could visualize Betty with a totally new body dancing with the angels in Heaven. She no longer had a body that could not function and she had that beautiful soprano voice again with which to worship God.

Pastor David Johnson read Psalm 55:5-6 "Fear and trembling come upon me; and horror has overwhelmed me. And I said, Oh, that I had wings like a dove! I would fly away and be at rest."

Pastor Johnson announced that after the congregation sang *Because He Lives* there would be a dove release on the front lawn.

Immediately after the hymn, the family began to exit the auditorium as Carol Laurence played the *Hallelujah Chorus*.

The four white doves were beautiful in their little chapel. It took several minutes for everyone to exit the auditorium and the doves were the center of attraction. An explanation was given about the release because most people had never seen one at a Victory Service. The owner explained that one of the doves represented the spirit of Betty and the others represented the Father, Son, and Holy Spirit.

I took the dove from the little chapel that represented Betty and held it as members of the family and close friends gathered around and touched her if they chose to do so. It was a time for healing.

I had been told in advance that I would know when the time to release her came. Secretly I thought to myself, "What if I never have that feeling?"

The owner must have read my thoughts. She said, "Don't worry. You will know when the time comes."

She was right. I knew exactly when it was time. I let her go and she circled very high in the sky. I opened the little chapel door and the other doves followed the lead. It was beautiful. They circled for a short time and then disappeared into the sky on their way back to their home. Betty was free and was being surrounded by the Father, Son, and Holy Spirit.

A few days after the service, we received the following message written in a beautiful handmade card. It is a wonderful interpretation of the dove release.

Dear Louis and Family,

When you released the doves following Betty's Victory Service, the imagery was so beautiful as a reminder that she had been released from every earthly bond that had held her down for so long. What a joy to know that our precious friend, wife and mother is truly

Free at Last!

Her life story and your love story is such an inspiration...for all who saw first hand her valiant fight, her victories, God's grace and mighty works and your faithfulness...we have seen Jesus Christ glorified and will never forget!

Love always,
Jo Lynne, Charley and Jenna Williams

GONE FROM MY SIGHT
By Henry Van Dyke

I am standing by the seashore. A ship at my side spreads her white sails to the morning breeze and starts for the blue ocean. She is an object of beauty and strength. I stand and watch her until at length she hangs like a speck of white cloud just where the sea and sky come to mingle with each other.

Then someone at my side says: "There, she is gone!"

"Gone where?"

Gone from my sight. That is all. She is just as large in mast and hull and spar as she was when she left my side and she is just as able to bear her load of living freight to her destined port. Her diminished size is in me, not in her. And just at the moment when someone at my side says: "There, she is gone!" there are other eyes watching her coming, and other voices ready to take up the glad shout:
"Here she comes!"

Further Reading

Stroke Warning Signs from the American Stroke Association

SPOT A STROKE F.A.S.T.

F.A.S.T. is an easy way to remember the sudden signs of a stroke. When you can spot the signs, you'll know quickly that you need to call 9-1-1 for help. This is important because the sooner a stroke victim gets to the hospital, the sooner they'll get treatment. And that can make a remarkable difference in their recovery.

F.A.S.T. is:

- **Face Drooping** Does one side of the face droop or is it numb? Ask the person to smile.

- **Arm Weakness** Is one arm weak or numb? Ask the person to raise both arms. Does one arm drift downward?

- **Speech Difficulty** Is speech slurred, are they unable to speak, or are they hard to understand? Ask the person to repeat a simple sentence, like "the sky is blue." Is the sentence repeated correctly?

- **Time to call 911** If the person shows any of these symptoms, even if the symptoms go away, call 9-1-1 and get them to the hospital immediately.

What to do if you think someone is having a stroke

Immediately call 9-1-1 or the Emergency Medical Services (EMS) number so an ambulance can be sent. Also, check the time so you'll know when the first symptoms appeared. A clot-busting drug called tissue plasminogen activator (tPA) may improve the chances of getting better but only if you get them help right away.

A TIA or transient ischemic attack is a "warning stroke" or "mini-stroke" that produces stroke-like symptoms. TIA symptoms usually only last a few minutes but, if left untreated, people who have TIAs have a high risk of stroke. Recognizing and treating TIAs can reduce the risk of a major stroke.

Beyond F.A.S.T.—Other Symptoms you should know

- Sudden numbness or weakness of the leg
- Sudden confusion or trouble understanding
- Sudden trouble seeing in one or both eyes
- Sudden trouble walking, dizziness, loss of balance or coordination
- Sudden severe headache with no known cause

For more information about stroke, call the American Stroke Association at 1-888-4STROKE or visit their Web site at http://www.strokeassociation.org/STROKEORG/.

Heart Attack Warning Signs from the American Heart Association (AHA)

Heart Attack Warning Signs

- **Chest discomfort** Most heart attacks involve discomfort in the center of the chest that lasts more than a few minutes, or that goes away and comes back. It can feel like uncomfortable pressure, squeezing, fullness or pain.
- **Discomfort in other areas of the upper body** Symptoms can include pain or discomfort in one or both arms, the back, neck, jaw or stomach.

- **Shortness of breath** with or without chest discomfort.
- **Other signs** may include breaking out in a cold sweat, nausea or lightheadedness.

If you are concerned that you or someone else may be experiencing a heart attack, call 9-1-1 immediately.

For more information about heart attack, call the American Heart Association at 1-800-AHA-USA-1 or visit their Web site at http://www.heart.org/HEARTORG/.

Poems and songs dedicated to Betty West

♪♪

The "G" I Loved
By Kristen West, (Age 10)

Thoughtful and caring
Loving and nurturing too,
We all really love her
Yes we truly do!

Like a rose
Always in full bloom
Her smile
Lit up the room.

Her jokes were quick
And always on time,
And every so often
She'd spout out a rhyme.

Salsa, enchiladas, guacamole too,
She liked Rosie's, Matt's and Serranos as well,
She liked Mexican food,
Can't you tell?

Her spirit soars up above
Like an eagle or a dove,
Above the clouds and sky of blue
You all loved her
I did too!

Our G

So kind, so sweet, so gentle she was
Her spirit so great, it soars up above.

Plays games, plenty or few
Fed us lunch, we love your stew.

Our G, so perfect
A worshipper,
A mother and grandma.

G, we might cry from sadness,
Sometimes we cry from happiness.
We'll do both, But not all the time.

We are happy for you, out of your misery
Don't suffer anymore, Re-unite with Christ.
We know you'll love us forever.
We will love you forever too.

G, we really, really love you.

G, you rock our socks Off

G, You're in heaven, Precious as can be,
I see a raven, But a dove it will be.

All my love, Caitlin (Age12)

The Mission Field

Words and music by Les Thomas
Used with permission by Les Thomas
To hear this song, go to http://soundclick.com/share.
cfm?id=4706687

Betty was a wife, a mother of three
She had a love for Jesus all could see
She rose above the crowd on bended knee
With all her life she sang a song
By word and deed it was loud and strong
She only asked that we sing along
And she called...she called it a mission field
And she called...she called it a mission field

Struck with an illness, no one could say
Betty would be wrong to give God blame
Still her song remained the same
Slowed but not stilled, she soldiered on
Stubborn as ever to share her song
Making her music last a whole life long
She was called...to the mission field
She was called...to the mission field

Can't you hear the music of how her hymn
has healed?
The resurrection heart song that has been
revealed?
The melody of mercies?
The lullaby of love?
The chorus of creation in her mission field?

Thought some would say the end was soon
No words to speak, Betty sang her tune
A mission field the size of a hospital room
Now choirs of angels loud and strong

Lift up their voices that same song
And those she touched now sing along
All because...because of her mission field
All because...because of her mission field

Though some would say the end was soon
No words to speak, Betty sang her tune
A mission field the size of a hospital room
But no less of a mission field
No less of a mission field

CPSIA information can be obtained at www.ICGtesting.com
Printed in the USA
LVOW130101130313

323939LV00002B/4/P